The Art of Civil Action
Political Space and Cultural Dissent

Philipp Dietachmair &
Pascal Gielen (eds.)

Antennae-Arts in Society
Valiz, Amsterdam

To Mark Fisher (1968–2017)

The Art of Civil Action

Political Space and Cultural Dissent

Philipp Dietachmair & Pascal Gielen (eds.)

With contributions by
Andrew Barnett
Llorenç Bonet
Ilya Budraitskis
Giuliana Ciancio
Philipp Dietachmair
Milena Dragićević Šešić
Pascal Gielen
Max Haiven
Yudhishthir Raj Isar
Stefan Kaegi
Ivan Krastev
Thijs Lijster
Tomislav Medak
Borka Pavićević
Dan Perjovschi
Igor Stokfiszewski
Hakan Topal

Contents

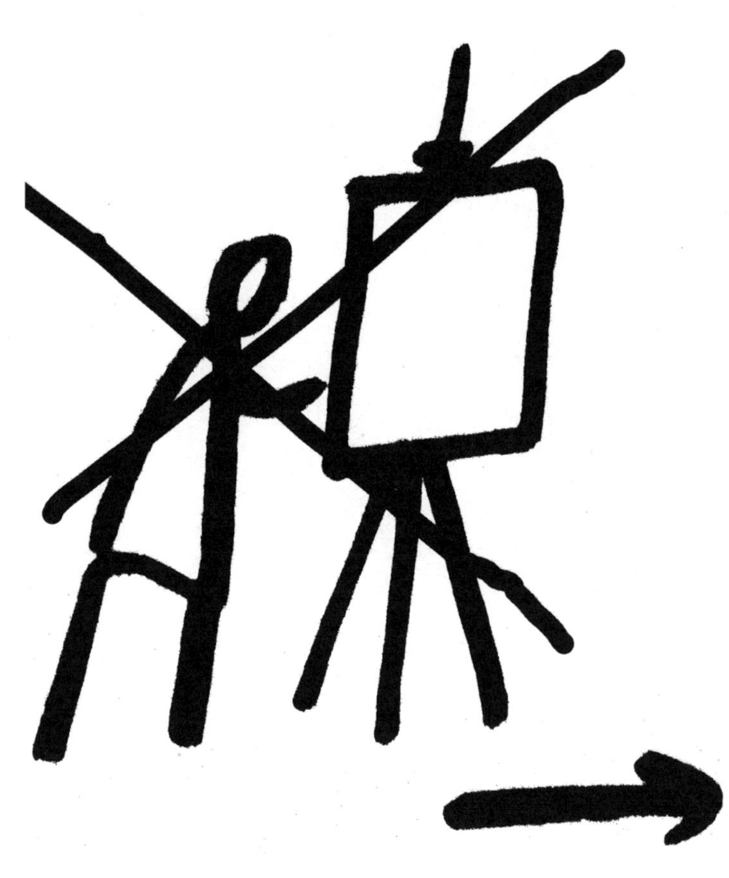

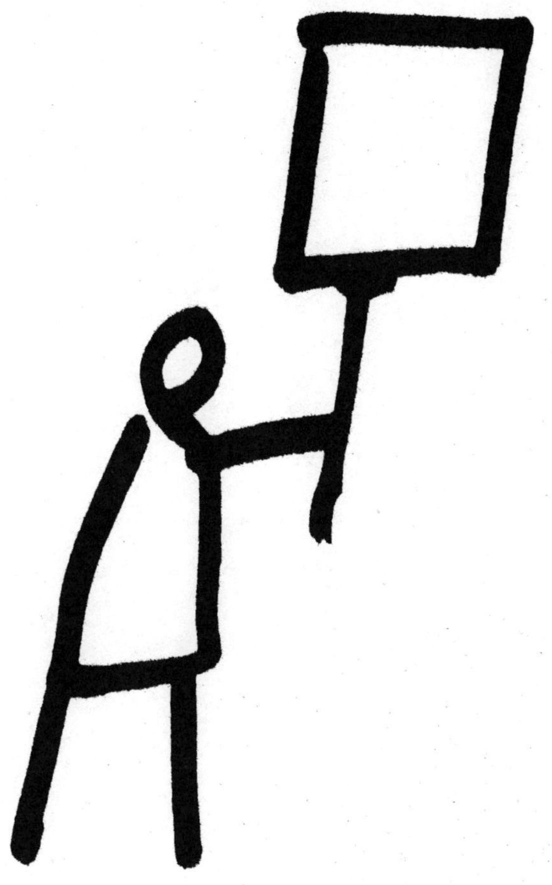

Dan Perjovschi

Introduction
Public, Civil and Civic Spaces

Pascal Gielen &
Philipp Dietachmair

During the past decade and its multiple crises the notion of civil space as a dynamic terrain between governments and the markets has become more relevant and recognized again. This new vitality of the civil sphere around the globe has perhaps most prominently been highlighted by social movements such as the Indignados in Spain or Occupy Wall Street. Today, entire processions of activists and citizen initiatives seem to uphold a nonstop parade of political dissent and civil action. In many cases, activist initiatives operate merely locally, as the contributions to this volume confirm. However, it seems that new ideas for civil action have started to spread and initiatives that have started in particular places are beginning to show mirror effects all over the world. As Ivan Krastev for instance argues in our interview with him for this publication, the new discourses about social equality in Europe and the US have a lot to do with what has been put on the agenda by Occupy Wall Street. Virtual networks and social media help to instantly disseminate the public demands and aesthetic codes of new social movements globally. Their tactics and organizational forms thus often resonate on much more transnational levels. Anyone who browses the web today quickly realizes that the Internet serves as a highly instructive manual for any type of citizen initiatives, be it for a subversive or revolutionary practice, simply for mocking politics, or for a truly committed reformist initiative. The new digital technologies and their global reach provide civil action groups with immediate and widespread resonance. This global public forum naturally also works for groups that promote much more conservative and regressive ideas. The digital space is indeed also the global market square for radical cultural agendas and contributes to the rapid growth of an 'uncivil' society, as some authors argue in this book. What has nevertheless inspired our search for the *Art of Civil Action* are the various new forms of cultural activism we discovered in the many progressive movements and politically engaged art initiatives around the world.

From the Zapatistas in Latin America to Pussy Riot in Russia, from Recetas Urbanas and Sanidad Universal in Spain, from the Umbrella Movement in Hong Kong to Anonymous in Canada, from to the occupation of the Maagdenhuis in Amsterdam to Teatro Valle Occupato in Rome, from Culture 2 Commons in Croatia to the Šarena revolucija in Macedonia, from Hart boven Hard in Belgium, to the KOD Komitet Obrony

Demokracji in Poland or the many Refugees Welcome initiatives all over Europe, however diverse the background of all these initiatives may be, they all define a new global landscape of civil society. It has to be acknowledged that their actions often disappear as fast as they have popped up. But perhaps the ongoing sequence of civil actions that mobilize, stop, transform, repeat and continue, often in an entirely different shape, is what really matters most to them for showing dissent, for disrupting prevailing hegemonies. Moreover, there is a growing cross-referencing and interconnecting happening on a global scale, which might eventually allow these diverse movements to mutually reinforce in significance and strength. Without any claim of being complete, this book shall map a few key areas in this new civil society landscape by exploring some of the social and political contexts that shape civil undertakings today. Our specific focus for this publication is the relevance of arts and culture in the civil sphere. All our inquiries represent an effort to understand what role culture can play in the instigation, functioning and perception of a meaningful civil action today.

As editors, we comprehend culture as a wider process of signification that gives meaning to ourselves as human beings and determines our environment as well as all the social, economic, ecological and political factors that shape it. Artistic expressions provide us with the abilities and tools to innovate processes of signification. Time and again they allow us to assign new codes, symbols, and meanings to questions of larger relevance. To make sense of a particular situation, or a particular context and all the factors that might form it, is a crucial precondition for civil action. In other words, the signification of the conditions of human life as such is a vital process in the determination of the civil sphere. Means of artistic expression, whether they are skilfully mastered by trained professionals or serve 'citizen artists' as inspirational tools to speak, to visualize, to show, to engage and, most importantly, to express an opinion, are effective tools for developing an emotional and deeper understanding of civil concerns. As many of the accounts in this volume show, broader questions of cultural identity, cultural dissent and controversy frequently release constructive energies of irritation that drive social engagement. Cultural imagination can also encourage us to define new and broader horizons to strive for in our communities and societies. For all these reasons, culture may become an even more powerful factor for civil action in the future.

Before this introduction provides you with a sneak preview of the colourful world of arts and culture in civil action, we nevertheless need to clarify our assumptions and our understanding of 'the civil'. What do we mean exactly when we refer to 'civil space'? How does it differ from other common notions such as the 'public' space and 'civic' initiative? Also, where precisely can we locate the space where civil processes take place and where do all its different forms of organization take shape in our societies? How is the space of the 'civil', its procedures, structures and actors related to the state and the market?

At the Doorstep of Legality

It is perhaps right in the gaping gulf between legality and illegality, between creativity and criminality that the civil space sees the light of day. In the grey area between what is allowed and not, or not yet allowed, civilians initiate that which a government or state has not yet thought of (or does not want to think of) and for which there are no interested markets. For the record: civil action does not coincide with criminal behaviour. Civil actions simply concern non-regulated domains, areas not yet covered by law. For instance, a civil action may denounce the fact that something is not, or not sufficiently, regulated by law; or it may develop a practice for which there simply is no regulation, or at least not a good one. Whether the actions involved are lawful or not remains to be seen. It is then up to public opinion to judge the claim or action on its legal, but also its moral and ethical merits. However, within a democracy, at the end of the day it is the legislative and judicial powers that decide whether to categorize the issue at hand as legal or illegal. At the moment of the actual civil action itself this is still undecided: will this practice be tolerated, embraced, or even passed into law, or rather not? Or is it more likely to be criminalized? Civilians who take a stand, who invoke their civil rights, are in other words still uncertain about where they will end up, how they will be judged. They simply do not know if these rights will be assigned to them. This is why a civil action is always a risky undertaking in which one sticks one's neck out and risks one's own social position. The articles about the situation in Russia and Turkey in this volume make clear that the border between legality and illegality often shifts all too easily. Civil undertakings that at one point in time are legal or tolerated tend to be quickly criminalized when democracies start to shake to their foundations.

But also for the allegedly more 'democratic' regimes civil action often represents provocations that result in being declared illegal. 'Know your laws and know your constitution', is what the architects of the Spanish Recetas Urbanas studio strongly suggested during a research seminar in Antwerp. As their contribution to our book shows, artists and cultural initiatives who reclaim the civil domain had best not be naïve when it comes to challenging the democratic state and its enforcement of the law in 'civic space'.

'Civil' and 'Civic' Space

Because of this undecided nature of the space in which the civil action takes place, it seems wise to distinguish between the terms 'civil' and 'civic'. Although both concepts are often used interchangeably in everyday usage and in the media, this books reserves the term 'civic' for tasks that are essentially determined by state authorities. For us editors, 'civic' describes a set of objectives that are defined by governments of states and carried out by their authorities and public institutions. These objectives cover a precisely pre-defined framework of 'civic tasks' that the state provides for its citizens through particular services, initiatives and places it controls. In other words, these 'civic places' are already regulated, by law or otherwise. The civil space, on the other hand, lies still open. To paraphrase Michel de Certeau's analytical distinction between place and space: the civic place is a place that is established or has taken root in policies, education programmes, regulations or laws. By contrast, the civil space, in the Certeausian logic, is a space that remains fluid, a place where positions still have to be taken up or created (Certeau 1984). The inquiry on the 'civic roles' of arts organizations in England, which features among the many case studies in this book, illustrates our distinction of the 'civic' versus the 'civil' domain quite well. In contrast to this study from England, most of the activist practices discussed by our other authors follow our editorial focus on the 'civil' as a dynamic space of dissent and unregulated action. Government interventions often turn initially unstructured and free civil places into spaces whose civic functions they ultimately regulate and control with their directives. As the Recetas Urbanas text in our book shows, taking up civil action can shed much light on the possibilities and freedom of manoeuvre in a particular area. Moving into such places of absent or undefined regulations therefore often calls authorities into action to turn them into controlled civic spaces of their own.

Another example of regulated civic space are the school curricula that nation states define. Schools and other state institutions convey an official cultural canon and thereby constitute an essential civic mechanism that tries to make sure that citizens follow a set of predefined notions marking the space of the nation state. Governmental efforts to generate 'cultural citizenship' have also been implemented through founding and subsidizing state museums, opera houses, theatres, et cetera. Many of the national art institutions we know today nevertheless initially played a decisive role in the constitutive processes of establishing our civil societies, at least those in the northern hemisphere. From the late eighteenth century onwards many of todays 'public institutions' were important machines for the construction of a cultural hierarchy in the emerging nation states. Well-known processes of socialization and canonization made culture a highly effective tool for the building of nations and the social education of its state citizens. Around the world, this civic role of culture has remained a common tool for governments in the construction of national identities. Especially younger states, for example Singapore, or more recently Macedonia, still spend large amounts of public funds on cultural nation-building processes. The controversy around the new World War II Museum in Gdansk, in Poland – whose curatorial concept was dismantled by a nationalist government as part of their efforts to frame a new national identity that imposes their own interpretation of history – is another example of such cultural construction processes in civic space. In Poland, Macedonia, Russia, and many other nation states the civic space of culture has therefore also become a contested area of civil action again, as some of the contributions in this volume clearly indicate.

All over Europe, discourses in civil society have started to question, criticize, and attack the traditional role of the state in culture and its established civic institutions. For a number of reasons serious doubts about the role of the state and its cultural institutions have also emerged in the more 'established' nation states of Western Europe, where over the past few decades cultural democratization processes and the emerging post-colonial critique have started to reject this top-down 'civilizing' process in culture. Reasonable criticism has confronted notions of a Western elite that promotes its own forms of 'high culture' as the only valuable form of arts, wherein the uneducated masses and people immigrating from other cultures still require proper initiation and education. At the same time, globalization – the combined process of a diversification of culture through migration and the homogenization and internationalization of culture through mass consumption – puts enormous pressure on what has been traditionally considered to be part of the established national cultural canon. These historical evolutions cause a crisis in the legitimization of the traditional civic space that public art institutions used to occupy, just at a time when the nation state increasingly loses its 'monopoly of creating common narratives', as Ivan Krastev argues in his contribution.

Civil and Public Space

In addition to the above advocated differentiation between the 'civic' and the 'civil', there is another distinction that should be made clear. This concerns terms that are best kept apart rather than have them coincide, as so often happens in everyday usage in this case also. Here too, a distinction, or at least a strong nuance, may prove productive. The civil space often requires collective actions, initiatives and organizations. People have to make an effort, organize something or simply 'do' something in order to shape a civil space. By contrast, public space is the space we can enter freely, that is or should be accessible to anyone. Or, following Jürgen Habermas, the space of public opinion where people can make their more or less idiosyncratic voice be heard, freely, and preferably with good arguments, like in the media, in public debate or in the time-honoured salon conversations (Habermas 1989). We can articulate the relationship between these concepts as follows: whereas the public space is a space for the free exchange of thoughts, opinions, ideas, and people, the civil domain provides the framework for organizing these thoughts, opinions, ideas, and people. Within the latter space, a thought, opinion or idea is expressed in a public action or in the form of an organization. In other words, civil space needs the public domain. After all, the latter constitutes the utterly vital source of inspiration for the former. Public space provides, as it were, both new ideas and new people (new citizens) but they can only claim and obtain their place in society through self-organization in the civil domain. Vice versa this also implies that public space is reliant on civil space, as the latter makes the public domain possible by organizing it or claiming a place for it; for example by enforcing the freedom of speech by legal means, but also by founding organizations and institutions such as newspapers, blogs or other platforms, for that purpose. Simply put, and without wishing to minimalize the performative character of free speech or of deliberative democratic processes, the public space is all about the free word and the free circulation of people, while in the civil domain the action takes centre stage. The interaction between both constitutes the famous *praxis*, where the action is suited to the word but also where actions can and may be put into words. It is precisely at this intersection of actions and words that both culture and art play a significant role.

Art and Politics

Those who have been scouring biennales and arts festivals over the past decade have been treated to a veritable feast of political discussions and critical debates. Sometimes art is hardly the topic anymore, but rather globalism, neoliberalism, precarity, 'commonism', or ecology, to name but a few. However, those activities of articulation are mostly limited to the discursive space, which in addition hardly moves beyond the borders of the parish of the already converted. The debate is limited to the level of the, often quite restricted, public domain, as described above. Words and actions are often still very far apart here, which means that true civil initiatives do not materialize. However, this takes nothing away from the fact that the professional art world and cultural field are increasingly taking the role of civil 'education' upon themselves. The time-space that is skimped on in universities and schools seems to be shifting to biennales, museums, and theatres. If we add to that the thinning of the (democratic) debate, the cutbacks on research journalism and the commodification of the writing and speaking space in mainstream media, we may perhaps conclude that cultural institutions are among the few remaining places for articulating new political ideas and civil strategies.

And there is more than just lessons, or room for debate. The space itself is being experimented with. For example, discussions may take place in a setting that looks like the British Parliament, and we only need to think of the artistic projects of the Dutch artist Jonas Staal to see how more and more thought goes into the shape or architecture for civil actions. The artistic domain offers the opportunity to experiment with the form of public debate. Admittedly, sometimes it is just about building aesthetic façades or backdrops, but more and more artists are also deliberately experimenting with the composition of real social settings and the organization of their own labour.

In this book we try to look beyond the so-called professional art world. Or, as Igor Stokfiszewski states in his text, we look at undertakings that go beyond cultural institutions and artistic scenes. What we mean by this, is that we look at cultural organizations and artists that take the risk of civil action (or are forced to do so). We see it as a risk, because by doing so, those cultural organizations and artists not only risk becoming criminalized, as stated before. They also put their classic defined position and identity as a professional cultural actor in jeopardy. Just as the well-known example of the Paris Situationists, they risk losing their artistic identity and radicalizing in pure political activism. Or, if you like, they step out of fiction, outside the walls of the black box theatre and white wall museum, to act in real life, to claim public and civil space (again).

For about forty years now, all over Europe autonomous art spaces and independent cultural organizations that took this risk have formed an autonomous cultural scene operating outside the public art institutions of the state. These developments happened in parallel to the weakening legitimation for the role that national cultural institutions have traditionally played in creating civic space, as we argued above. Take the example of the many abandoned industrial buildings that started to be turned into venues for subcultural production and activity since the 1970s and early 1980s. Initially often occupied illegally, many of these venues became more structured endeavours and self-organized arts initiatives over time. Their independent forms of civil organization often marked the beginnings of many of by now well-established 'alternative' cultural centres. Today, there is even a transnational civil society network named Trans Europe Halles connecting many of these 'cultural factories' across Europe and it counts almost 100 members in 32 countries.

In the 1990s, the establishment of such cultural structures that were independent from the state but were not operating commercially also began to spread across Central and Eastern Europe. In some of the formerly socialist countries there had also been pockets of freedom for dissident artistic expression and even self-managed cultural venues, as the conversation with Serbian theatre maker Borka Pavićević in this book shows. Nevertheless, the liberation from the compulsory cultural system of Socialist

Realism, which dominated the arts of the socialist states in Eastern Europe, resulted in a strong desire for another cultural offer that was more in line with contemporary developments around the world. This cultural void could not be filled by the outdated socialist state institutions that remained in place and was further deepened by the privatization and commercialization of the cultural landscape. At the same time, the import of artistic productions from Western Europe did not satisfy the desire for cultural processes that would genuinely reflect the turbulent experiences of post-socialist transition in these societies. Everywhere in the countries of the former Soviet Union, Central and Eastern Europe, and the former Yugoslavia new centres of contemporary art and alternative culture started to emerge whose founders (and also their mostly Western donors) rather identified with being part of a contemporary form of civil society than of the institutionalized arts world. As for instance the Clubture platform that we studied for this book shows, in Croatia 'independent culture' was coined as a new value proposition and activist discourse for initiating a progressive social movement. The political claims of Croatia's civil society initiatives in the field of independent cultural production also resonate with the term 'social culture' that Igor Stokfiszewski's text proposes based on his review of socially-engaged arts initiatives and autonomous cultural spaces in Poland.

The extension of cultural strategies towards the civil realm frequently occurs in the context of political turbulence and socio-economic instability. Many examples of cultural activism that we reviewed for this book therefore can be found in Southern Europe, where the financial crisis still has a deep impact on societies, and also in EU Neighbourhood countries like Russia, Ukraine, Turkey and the Arab region, where political calamities and violent conflicts shake people's lives to the core. During the post-socialist transition in Central and Eastern Europe many activist initiatives of cultural workers also aimed at improving labour conditions for independent cultural production, or campaigned for a structural modernization of their cultural policies. And of course a lot of these independent cultural undertakings and activists are themselves trying to get legalized, recognized and maybe even subsidized by their own governments. In that case, civil movements that demand a better legal framework for a certain issue, are sometimes paradoxically promoting the elimination of their own reason for existence. It is not a coincidence that they often evaporate once their goal has been reached. The movement comes to a standstill as it becomes rooted in a civic law or a civic rule. Nevertheless, all over Europe civil society initiatives continue to advocate a broader recognition of their interests and a larger role for culture in state policies. At the same time, much wider social or political issues that reach beyond just inspiring contemporary artistic production have entered the agendas of many cultural organizations. As a new inquiry presented in this book shows, many cultural organizations in the UK have even left behind their classic task of producing artistic content and assume new 'civic roles' instead. As social service providers for the state they tender for public commissions and offer their artistic skills and cultural expertise for youth work, community projects, arts therapy, social education and many more civic initiatives they deliver on behalf of the public institutions.

In times of fundamental political shifts and new global challenges, cultural workers and artists as well as political activists and civil society campaigners seem to have discovered new synergies for collaborating on different questions of democracy, citizen participation, social justice or inclusion. For a growing variety of players issues of 'glocal' relevance such as urban development, global economy, ecological challenges, and sustainable development seem to further fire up this civil-cultural alliance in many political contexts around the world. During the Gezi Park demonstrations in Istanbul, for example, a civil action that addressed a seemingly very local ecological question of protecting a small downtown park and merely challenged the urban development policies of the city at first, turned into a great symbol of cultural dissent against the general politics of the state. As artist Hakan Topal introduces in his text, these events even resonated globally when he established the Gezi Platform NYC and organized solidarity demonstrations in several parks of New York. Our interview with Tomislav Medak, a cultural worker and activist from Zagreb, also demonstrates how a local issue, in this case the unavailability of working spaces for alternative culture, first caused a stand-off with the mayor over the artistic occupation of a city-owned factory, then moved on to issues of privatizing public space in the city and ultimately turned to much broader political questions of social and economic development in Croatia.

Why both the true civil action and the civil space find themselves in between illegality and legality is perhaps better understood by looking at the problem of – modern or (post)revolutionary – politics. As Hannah Arendt states in *On Revolution*:

> ...those who get together to constitute a new government are themselves unconstitutional, that is, they have no authority to do what they have set out to achieve. The vicious circle in legislating is present not in ordinary law making, but in laying down the fundamental law, the law of the land or the constitution which, from then on, is supposed to incarnate the 'higher law' from which all laws ultimately derive their authority (Arendt 1990, pp. 183–184).

So, the constitutive power and the constitutive body are always outside of the constitution, since they precede it. They are therefore neither legal nor illegal, which immediately presents the problem of authority within modern democracies: of whom is it accepted that they place themselves outside, or rather above the law, precisely in order to establish that law? Civil space relates to civic place in a similar ambivalent manner. The former precedes the latter, running the risk of never, ever being (lawfully) recognized or legalized and thus of remaining permanently in the sphere of illegality.

Soviets of Democracy

This curious position of the civil space also has a historical reason, as again Arendt demonstrates. In the last chapter of the same book, she writes of 'a treasure' that was lost in both the American, French and Russian revolutions she discussed. She is referring to the rural communities in the new continent, but even more to the Paris Commune and the spontaneous self-organization of, for example, Russian workers in *soviets*. Remarkably, 'the men of the revolution', as Arendt calls them, didn't really know what to do with the murmuring of this all too colourful multitude. Nevertheless it was perhaps the same multitude that took the revolutionary idea most to heart. As we know, the troupes of Versailles rather brutally swept the communes aside, while Vladimir Lenin, although paying lip service to the *soviets* in founding the Soviet Union, did in fact opt for the secure path of the one-party system. Arendt's analysis therefore shows that revolutions could in fact have followed two diverging historical routes. One, that of party politics (sometimes via a stop-over at enlightened despotism) which for various modern forms of administration ended up in liberal representative democracy; or, two, that of a local, bottom-up initiative of many varied forms of self-governance. Although on that latter path the way was also paved for democracy – perhaps a more radical democracy then we mostly know today – (revolutionary) history has mainly ignored this option. That is why Arendt speaks of 'a lost treasure'. However, following her insights further, we could say that most of the independent cultural initiatives and civil movements described in this book are filling this void. Some of the new municipalist practices that grew out of activist movements discussed here have met with reasonable success among voters in Madrid, Barcelona, Athens, and Zagreb. These 'fearless' initiatives, to quote the dictum of the inaugural world summit of municipalist cities in Barcelona this year, move in the other direction that political history might have taken during and after revolutions, by picking up where the Paris Commune and the *soviets* left off. And, as mentioned earlier, they sometimes take the same risks as their predecessors. They are still in danger of being shoved aside or being criminalized, violently or otherwise.

The Art of Civil Action

Visually framed by the ironic sketches of artist and activist Dan Perjovschi, *The Art of Civil Action* presents a heterogenous selection of essays and conversations in two parts. Section 1, 'Understanding Civil Cultures', introduces our conceptual tool box for this volume. Without striving to provide a complete picture the contributions in this first part will clarify some of the characteristics and questions of contemporary civil action and their political potential in relation to how they build on cultural strategies and artistic practices.

For a start, and based on a pilot research as well as some exploratory field studies carried out in 2016, Dutch philosopher Thijs Lijster and Belgian sociologist Pascal Gielen have analysed the different stages in the development of civil action and the role of art and culture in such undertakings. For describing the evolutionary sequence of emerging civil action their text proposes a model they call the 'civil chain'. Their analysis builds on preliminary case study results of the community arts and urban activist association Les Têtes de l'Art from Marseille and the cultural civil society cluster Culture 2 Commons in Zagreb. Gielen and Lijster not only try to clarify the role of art and culture in the civil actions of these organizations but also assess their potential to scale up to transnational levels. Can these civil initiatives, driven by their cultural agendas and artistic methods, really help to build a transnational civil space beyond the nation state? According to the authors, the answer to this question needs to be dealt with with quite some modesty. Many cultural activists and their civil campaigns foremost seem to focus on local issues and to be concerned with their immediate environment. In the two contexts Lijster and Gielen have studied, aspirations towards achieving something in a transnational civil domain only played a very subordinate role, if they were of any concern at all. However, all players interviewed for these case studies underlined the high strategic relevance international collaboration processes have for their work. Exchanging information, knowledge, practical tools beyond national borders, even providing logistical support to likeminded initiatives from abroad is very important to them. The authors conclude that even the emotional energy of singular artistic initiatives or successful activist campaigns on a local level can provide sufficient encouragement and enthusiasm on a transnational scale to inspire new initiatives of civil action elsewhere.

Intrigued by his book *Democracy Disrupted: The Politics of Global Protest*, we engaged in a conversation with political scientist Ivan Krastev from Bulgaria and asked him about his unconventional analysis of social movements as the new 'antipolitics of the street'. Our questions focused on recent trends in activist campaigning and how Krastev sees the role of aesthetics and cultural questions in different forms of civil engagement, especially in the global public space of the Internet. Social media for him however are an instrument that hampers the development of meaningful collective action rather than one that helps to activate civil space. The reason is that instantaneous connectivity gives digital public space a superficial easiness, as he observes, which does not lead to more collective civil action but only stimulates the development of gated information communities. Krastev also remains quite sceptical about the potential of cultural activism to achieve political change as long as the 'social poetry' in many of the campaigns does not get translated into 'tangible political prose', as he formulates it. Nevertheless, Krastev sees cultural questions and the mobilizing power of artistic articulations as important elements in future forms of political activism. According to him, cultural activism will however take place in an increasingly polarized landscape of political agitation where different cultural views on the world will lead to more confrontations between conservative, regressive groups from outside the big cities on the one side and progressive political movements in the urban, cosmopolitan contexts on the other.

The effects of globalization on cultures, cultural diplomacy beyond national borders and questions of global cultural citizenship are key subjects in Yudhishthir Raj Isar's academic work. His frequent consultancy assignments for cultural organizations, international organizations and foundations often focus on very practical issues of civil society processes in the cultural field. Raj Isar's contribution to our book therefore begins with a tangible reality check of the potential of civil cultural action on transnational levels. 'Do artists and their organizations everywhere deal routinely with global questions?' he asks, and 'are they significant players in the transnational forms of organization that certain sectors of civil society are indeed forging?' Rightfully he concludes that 'the arts sector has provided no leaders in terms of transnational civil society mobilization in general'. Based on his previous work with many regional and global civil society networks in culture and the new EU cultural diplomacy initiative 'Culture in External Relations' Raj Isar then revisits some of the recommendations he has made earlier and concludes with suggesting some concrete measures that he considers 'tantamount for acting in a spirit of *global cultural citizenship* and participation for *all* in a framework of cosmopolitan solidarity'.

This first section on understanding civil cultures ends with a critical analysis of the European civilization concepts during the colonization of Canada and the moral liabilities that the alien cultural perceptions of the 'civil' and 'civilizing' imposed during this process have left among the communities of the First Nations. Max Haiven, writer, movement organizer and researcher in the fields of culture, media and social justice helps us to dismantle all innocent notions and heroic romanticism surrounding our concepts of civil action for this book and looks at them from a sharp post-colonial perspective. Haiven very precisely analyses how historic processes of colonial European signification have destroyed indigenous notions of civilization among Canada's First Nations. This violent civilization process, he argues, has also eliminated entirely different cultural notions of the 'civil' that have defined native communities before the colonialization of the 'new world' by Europeans began. Until today, Haiven argues, these historic European concepts of civilization dominate the political discourse when it comes to issues of social integration in the proudly multi-cultural Canadian society. The artistic interventions of multimedia artist and activist Raven Davis introduced in this text shed much light on some of the discrepancies in Canada's explicitly multi-cultural identity and illustrate how artistic performatives in public space can effectively contest social injustice and exclusion in political space. Haiven's review of the art of Raven Davis work bridges the first with the second part of this publication where we will bring readers 'on the ground' of concrete artistic practices and civil cultural undertakings in specific political contexts.

Section 2, 'Getting on the Ground', thus opens with an interview that Giuliana Ciancio and Pascal Gielen had with director Stefan Kaegi, a member of the Berlin-based theatre collective Rimini Protokoll. In their highly unconventional theatre projects Rimini Protokoll often engage citizens and spectators to perform as themselves and in various roles. They create artistic spaces of civil action. In a radical democratic way the audience of their shows engage with concrete social or political issues in their local communities and around the world. Or, as Kaegi articulates: 'We try to give a voice to the people that are not the most prominent or canonical voices to be heard.' In this interview Ciancio and Gielen highlight the concrete artistic strategies the theatre collective pursues to achieve this ambition.

Recetas Urbanas, a studio of socially engaged architects in Spain, run by Santiago Cirugeda and Alice Attout, takes the translation of citizens' voices in public space even a step further. Many of their architectural projects and interventions are in direct response to the social needs a community or specific group of people has identified in a particular location. In these spaces Recetas Urbanas then starts to build concrete structures such as playgrounds, pop-up apartments, temporary social housing, lecturing rooms, schools and art venues. The studio does not build or deliver projects for the real estate market. It also does not work on behalf of the public institutions or for government agencies but rather offers citizens open source recipes for building whatever they need by themselves. Their concepts often work in undefined spaces that they discover in the loopholes of official planning regulations. Their architectural interventions and communal structures provide real, purposeful, and functioning places that aim to hand the city back to its citizens. They help local communities to discover unexpected opportunities for civil action, for constructive occupation and for the concrete re-appropriation of public space. Their radical build-it-yourself techniques of civil space naturally often challenge the borders of legality, as editor and publisher Llorenç Bonet highlights in his case-by-case review of some of the key projects of Recetas Urbanas in Spain. Many of their approaches and techniques provide new solutions for a sustainable urban architecture and empower its users as active political agents. This specific type of knowledge has meanwhile become inspirational for initiatives in many other places and has started to contribute to a growing transnational exchange network in this field.

At this point of the 'Getting on the Ground' section our book shifts perspective. We move from artistic practices and collectives in the first part of this chapter to political activists and cultural civil society organizations in particular regional contexts. This also brings us to civil actions in rather challenging political circumstances and to countries where the space for free artistic expressions is rapidly shrinking.

We begin this part with the situation in Russia after the conflict with Ukraine and the annexation of Crimea. Ilya Budraitskis, a historian and cultural activist from Moscow, reviews some of the contradictions that have emerged around the Kremlin's propaganda politics in the field of culture and its regressive patriotic agendas. He challenges commonly accepted perceptions of European journalists and experts that tend to juxtapose Russia's focus on traditional values and patriotic collectivism with Western individualism and market orientation. Budraitskis shows that especially the cultural sector is a policy domain were conservative rhetoric and neoliberal practices in Russia coexist as an ideological hybrid. The contemporary Russian state is a 'rational client' he says: 'The logic is simple: if the works do not meet the needs of the state – patriotism, moral values and unity in the face of enemies – then it will decline to pay for them.' Patriotic cultural agendas meet wide approval among a silent majority in Russian society, Budraitskis explains, whereas confronting conditions of civil un-freedom stays in the limited sphere of cultural activism. Critical culture represents a social minority position that does not enter into serious conflict with the official cultural policies. 'The rights of the critical artist are defended only by those who are interested in their existence', Budraitskis analyses rather pessimistically.

For our next contribution we return to Croatia and the independent cultural scene in Zagreb whose activist practices have informed the 'civil chain' model that Gielen and Lijster propose in their text in section 1. For field research on the Culture 2 Commons case study of 2016, Philipp Dietachmair interviewed Tomislav Medak of the Multimedia Institute/MaMa which has played a pivotal role in the evolution of many cultural civil society initiatives in the country. A second conversation in summer 2017 complemented insights collected the year before with new developments around the recent local elections in Zagreb. In Dietachmair's synopsis of both talks Medak reviews how improving the context for independent culture since the post-war 1990s prepared the ground for activist confrontations around Right to the City Zagreb and over time contributed to the emergence of a new political project that has meanwhile succeeded to enter the City of Zagreb's local assemblies. Whether members of this civil movement who were recently elected into these representative bodies can transform into genuine political actors and how they will approach their new 'civic role' in relation to their 'civil' origins remains an open question at this moment.

After this rather encouraging account of cultural dissent and civil action in a very harsh and nationalist environment we turn north to another contested political space of post-socialist Central Europe. Igor Stokfiszewski is a literary critic, dramaturg and member of the activist network Krytyka Polityczna which supports an alternative media platform and various socially-engaged art spaces in a number of communities in Poland and Ukraine. Stokfiszewski's text builds on his practical encounters with initiating social theatre and community art projects in Poland and is based on his review of a substantial number of autonomous cultural practices, places, and organizations that have emerged all over the country. Based on a mapping of the conditions and particularities of socially engaged cultural projects, both in autonomous and institutional contexts, his text proposes a new concept he calls 'social culture'. This terms describes practices that go beyond artistic production or works, and, as Stokfiszewski explains, it embraces 'any independent movements, organizations and institutions oriented towards democratic, pro-subject, pro-community and pro-development social impact by means of cultural instruments'. 'Social culture' seems to be very much complementary with the concept of 'independent culture' that we encountered in Croatia. It is perhaps not surprising that both these concepts of cultural civil action have emerged in the context of societies that have been strongly determined by the highly disruptive transition processes from state socialism to neoliberal market economies. Also, in both countries proponents of a progressive cultural scene are repeatedly challenged by the predominance of conservative and nationalist forces in politics. 'Social culture' and 'independent culture' therefore also reflect deep conceptual dissent with the prevailing social development models and power structures in Poland, Croatia, and the whole region of Central and Eastern Europe.

A number of European foundations and universities have supported the pilot research of Gielen and Lijster mentioned earlier. This has inspired the UK branch of the Calouste Gulbenkian Foundation to launch their own inquiries into the civic (!) role of arts organizations, at first with a specific focus on England. Andrew Barnett introduces the main theoretical findings of their study and the five place-making metaphors their researchers have chosen for describing the different 'civic' functions of the arts in the cases they have analysed. In the light of our strict distinction of the 'civil' and the 'civic' for this volume, Andrew Barnett's contribution represents a veritable expression of provocative 'dissent' with our own conceptual notions of the 'civil' roles of culture in this book.

From the northwest of Europe we move to the southeast for the remaining contributions in our volume. First we return to the region of the former Yugoslavia, and literally to socialist Yugoslavia and the conditions for political and cultural dissent in its capital Belgrade. This is where Borka Pavićević has started her work as a provocative theatre maker and where she became involved in the dissident movements of that time. In conversation with Milena Dragićević Šešić, whose research and teaching has influenced many critically engaged cultural workers in the region, Borka Pavićević reviews her history of political and cultural dissent from the beginnings in the 1960s to her anti-war campaigns during the breakup of Yugoslavia and the establishment of her pivotal Centre for Cultural Decontamination. As historically very aware female cultural activists, both discuss the connections between a distorted culture of memory and a lack of transnational engagement in the region and conclude with what civil society in Europe might learn from the collapse of the Yugoslav idea of a cosmopolitan, modernist, and multi-cultural political space.

The 'Getting on the Ground' section is concluded even a little further to the southeast in Turkey, where the New York-based curator and sociologist Hakan Topal explores conditions for engaged artistic work in a quite dramatic and depressing political situation. Since the failed coup of July 2016, journalists, intellectuals, writers, and artists experience severe repression and have repeatedly ended up in state prisons. Nevertheless, even in such difficult circumstances Topal believes that the inspirational light of fearless civil action can shine strongly when artists, academics, and activists dare to speak freely and from their heart. Topal's analysis focuses on the events around the Gezi Park protests in 2013. He underlines the power of artistic activities in public space and shows how these have forged new bonds between seemingly incompatible social actors. For him, this is one of the most powerful functions for culture in civil space and a strong reason to take the role of culture in civil actions seriously again. Incidentally, Ivan Krastev's analysis of the Gezi Park events for our conversation in section 1 drew the same conclusion. For both of them and many other contributors to this volume, cultural dissent can thus indeed be a quite performative tool in making political space more socially interconnected, civilian and human again.

Despite our international ambitions for this book and an impressive diversity of civil action we have discovered around the world, *The Art of Civil Action* has limitations in scope, and we are quite aware of them. Our modest book cannot provide more than a first fragmented glimpse of cultural undertakings in civil space. It has been compiled by two editors who have looked at the indeed vast landscape of global civil action through the eyes of two white male North-Europeans of the same generation. So not only practical obstacles and budgetary restraints limited our scope, but certainly our own cultural background as well determined our selection in many unconscious ways. Only when finalizing our project we discovered with some embarrassment that there were for instance hardly any female voices among our contributors. We certainly do not want to leave readers with the impression that civil space is not the place of action for women – on the contrary.

To point out the conversation between Borka Pavićević and Milena Dragićević Šešić or to highlight that Rimini Protokoll, Recetas Urbanas and Culture 2 Commons are by no means exclusively male collectives, is perhaps only a poor excuse. All we have left is to wholeheartedly subscribe to the Canadian Max Haiven's view and the key message of his text that European civilization, culture, and civil society are indeed quite limited in scope. It may seem we both have become victims of our own civilization in that sense. The least we can say is there remains a lot to be done on the civil terrain. Nevertheless, we hope that despite its limitations and shortcoming this volume will provide you with an inspiring and insightful journey through the very diverse and colourful world of civil initiatives in the cultural field.

Both of us found our cultural expeditions through the global civil sphere exciting, to say the least. We would like to thank the European Cultural Foundation and the UK branch of the Calouste Gulbenkian Foundation for making this quest possible. We are also very grateful to our publisher Valiz and thank their editors for their flexibility and strong conceptual support. We both started out on this journey from the same privileged part of the world, where we grew up in a time and social environment in which the securities of the welfare state guaranteed the well-being of all. It is probably against this background that we have come up with the subtitle for this book: Political Space and Cultural Dissent. Amazed by the elections of Donald Trump in the United States and the global re-emergence of 'nations-first'; astonished by the statement of Recep Tayyip Erdoğan that 'democracy is like a tram to ride: when you reach your stop, you get off'; embarrassed by the refusal of so many states in the EU to show empathy towards refugees and embrace global solidarity; perplexed by the transnational European alliances of anti-European nationalists; and astonished by the inhuman and cold rationalism of troikas dealing with the financial crisis; we can only conclude that all our encounters with the many cultural activists who act in growing dissent with this political hegemony have also deepened our own convictions that we can no longer just build on complacent acceptance and 'pragmatic consensus' with the predominant politics of our time. The hard-headed 'consensual attitudes' of academics, (community) artists, social workers, active citizens, philanthropy and many NGOs during the last decade have very obviously proven to be inadequate for arriving at real and desirable changes in our societies. What prevails is a strong belief in 'no-alternative' compromises and a surprising confidence that the only conceivable solutions will always simply be meeting everybody's interests 'midway'. The way out of this dilemma leads through finding new inspiration and radically different answers in the art of civil action, is what we became more and more convinced of. For all the infectious enthusiasm, artistic power, human energy, social idealism, personal trust, and global empathy we discovered we are therefore truly grateful. The risky undertakings between creativity and criminality of all the deeply engaged artists, critical thinkers, cultural organizations and civil movements we met among our authors, their rejection of fainthearted concessions, their radical denial of mediocre thinking and their refusal of lukewarm consensus when acting in civil space restored our faith in the possibilities of a more vibrant, open and warmer time in our societies.

Bibliography

- Achterhuis, Hans. 2010. *De utopie van de vrije markt.* Rotterdam: Lemniscaat.
- Arendt, Hannah. 1963. *On Revolution.* New York: Penguin, 1990.
- De Certeau, Michel. 1984. *The Practice of Everyday Life.* Trans. by S. Randall. Berkeley, CA, etc.: University of California Press. Originally published as *L'Invention du quotidien* (Paris: Union Générale d'Éditions, 1980).
- Habermas, Jürgen. 1989. *The Structural Transformation of the Public Sphere: An Inquiry into a Category of Bourgeois Society.* London: Polity Press. Originally published as *Strukturwandel der Öffentlichkeit* (Frankfurt: Suhrkamp, 1962).
- Krastev, Ivan. 2014. *Democracy Disrupted: The Politics of Global Protest.* Philadelphia: University of Pennsylvania Press.

Part 1

Understanding Civil Cultures

intra NA

ION TRANS AL

The Civil Potency of a Singular Experience

On the Role of Cultural Organizations in Transnational Civil Undertakings

Pascal Gielen
& Thijs Lijster

The Civil Chain and the Origin of Civil Action

Civil action is born from emotion, says the Spanish sociologist Manuel Castells (2015). Although such actions always imply the hopeful expectation that something in society can be improved, this initial emotion is often of a negative nature, fed by fear, discomfort or at least irritation. The reasons for this can be manifold. An individual may feel threatened by beggars or by drug dealers hanging around in the neighbourhood. But they can also feel ill at ease because there are too many policemen, soldiers or security cameras in the streets. Employees may feel intimidated by their boss or colleagues and may also experience stress because of a too heavy workload. Others may be utterly frustrated because their printer is malfunctioning, again. In short, feelings of annoyance, irritations, frustration or injustice can have many causes. And, as may be evident from this broad range of examples, certainly not every negative emotional experience leads to civil action. People who experience stress at work can speak to their employer or can seek professional help or therapy to learn how to cope with that stress.

Discomfort can be channelled in many ways. Those who choose therapy or decide to hire a lawyer opt for a private and individual solution to their problem. Such an initial step undoubtedly requires courage. Discussing our sometimes highly personal and therefore subjective perceptions always assumes the will and courage to communicate. Once that obstacle is overcome we are still not dealing with a civil action yet. Indeed, communication with our therapist or lawyer has little to do with citizenship or public spirit. In order to 'enter' civil society we need to specifically address a collective and generate public support. The initial emotion must be recognized as a shared emotion, as a shared fear, frustration or irritation. Civil action is only possible if we take our personal discomfort out of the private sphere, when we 'de-privatize' the subject matter. However, such a step towards civil space requires an important skill: the ability of (self-)rationalization. This is required to articulate an initial intuition or basic emotion. It is the cognitive competence of analyzing one's own feelings and perhaps point out possible causes. Rationalization, and especially self-rationalization, therefore precedes communication, although the causes of certain emotions might be further clarified in dialogue with others.

And, finally, after the processes of rationalization, communication and de-privatization, the skill of organization is required in order to set the civil action in motion and, if necessary, keep it going in the long run. For instance, one must organize oneself in order to write an opinion piece, but also encourage others to do the same. Protesting in the streets or rolling up our sleeves to clean the neighbourhood requires at least a modicum of (self)-organization. What is important here is that those processes of self-rationalization and of self-organization can temper the initial emotion that triggered them in the first place. For instance, having to find one's way through a maze of legal rules, being obliged to study political procedures, or having to follow the long and winding road through bureaucratic institutions in order to arrive at the right form of (self-)organization can make one lose the energy to go on. Both processes therefore require that we literally rationalize that initial emotion, to distance ourselves from it and in a sense 'bureaucratize' it (all forms of organization presuppose setting up a minimum number of rules and procedures and sticking to them). In themselves such processes are not dramatic and even necessary to initiate civil action. However, this points to the fact that the basic emotion as mentioned determines the 'drive' or the energy of the civil undertaking. Or, in an analogy by Castells: it is an initial fear converted into anger that defines the engine of civil action. It is the steam that powers civil organization or an initiative with a civil mission. This also means that civil action derives its basic energy from very direct, mundane and mostly local human experience. The chances of success and continuance of every civil initiative therefore depend on finding the right balance between rationalizing and organizing on the one hand and keeping up the energy that is obtained from a basic emotion on the other hand. This balance is all the more urgent the more cultural organizations 'scale up' their activities, for instance from a local to a regional or from the national to the transnational level. Each step up the ladder demands more rationalization and organization, and thereby one risks evaporating the initial drive and emotion, as well as losing track of the local problems that started it all.

From the above we may conclude that a cultural organization that adopts a civil role situates itself at the end of a chain of successive, distinctive operations. And that such an organization will continuously have to take into account all the previous stages

in the chain in order not to alienate itself from its own source of energy. Analytically, this succession of processes – which we call the civil chain – looks like this: (1) emotion – (2) (self-)rationalization – (3) communication – (4) de-privatization (or going public) and, finally, (5) (self-)organization.

A cultural organization that adopts a civil role finds itself at the end of this chain. It is indeed an organization. It only plays a civil role because it de-privatizes or makes public a specific social issue. It can only do so through communication, which it not only needs in order to bring its civil mission in the public eye, but also to extend the organization itself, for which it needs communication through its founders, members and other involved parties. This communication assumes an ability to articulate and thereby rationalize a basic feeling. At the same time, however, it is important to maintain that initial emotion. Necessary processes of rationalization and organization can after all take away the drive and energy from the organization.

Looking at the chain analytically, we can see that the civil ambition can only be fulfilled through three transitions. The first one takes place at the emotional level. An initially negative feeling (of discomfort, injustice, etc.) must be converted into a sense of positive energy, of simple enthusiasm to 'get cracking' or at least of not resigning oneself to the situation. Castells gives the example of fear that must be 'positively' converted into outrage and hope (2015, pp. 247-248). By 'positively' we mean that outrage and hope lead to action. However negative the results of bursts of outrage may be, they always indicate an accumulation of energy. Through outrage, the paralyzing effect of fear changes from passive to active. Feelings of discomfort, irritation, insecurity, injustice and the like often result in defeatism or resignation. Especially when people feel they are alone in their efforts, they tend to resign themselves to the situation. Only when a sometimes hard to pinpoint 'spark' turns negative energy into positive energy does civil action become an option. It is from this same emotional transition that a civil organization derives its energy.

A second necessary transition is to be found on the level of communication, as only through communication can a transformation take place from the individual to the collective level. We can, for example, test whether we really feel what we feel by consulting a therapist, in the sense that we can check whether such a professional recognizes our feelings as also occurring in others or is familiar with them from the scientific literature. It is only in that confirmation that an individual problem can become a collective one, in the sense that others share our supposedly individual feeling. In the same sense city dwellers can have a chat with their neighbours about street litter. This is also communication in which a basic experience is shared and tested. Only if a neighbour confirms that: 'Yes, you're right, there is a lot of litter here these days', the feeling of discomfort is collectivized and the possibility of civil action emerges. Organizations that adopt a civil role often originate in such shared sentiments. So, without collectivization there is no civil action and no organization. Both examples of collectivization also illustrate, however, that de-individualization in itself is not enough to speak of civil action.

To do so requires yet another transition, from the private to the public sphere. As indicated earlier, feelings and issues can be shared and therefore collectivized in both the private and the public sphere. For example, as long as the employee suffering from stress only discusses the problem with a therapist or only collectivizes it in a self-help group, we cannot speak of a civil action. Only when this worker, perhaps together with the therapist, articulates the initial feeling or syndrome in social terms does it acquire civil value. This means that, say, stress is no longer only explained as a mental condition but is recognized as a structural problem too. Stress is then not only about the irritated nerves of individual employees or about the annoying personal character of their boss, but also about, for instance, high work pressure, about increasingly precarious working conditions such as flexible and mobile project labour, or about the decrease in long-term employment contracts and job security. In other words, in the transition from the private to the public sphere a personal issue (being a stress-sensitive person) is not only translated into a collective problem (a stressful environment, stressful working conditions), but the cause of the problem or feeling of discomfort is then also located in broader social phenomena. This is why the transformation from the private to the public sphere implies the politicization of the initial feeling. If 'the political' stands for openly shaping our living together, this translation is an appeal to the political to articulate and address the issue. Note: we deliberately speak of 'the political' and not 'politics', as the latter may suggest that the politicization of an emotion would only mean addressing politicians or authorities, while 'the political' is much broader.

To paraphrase the French philosopher Jacques Rancière (who is more extensively discussed below): the political is defined by taking part in living together and in actions that (may) rearrange the relations within a society. The political therefore does not simply coincide with a fixed position within political institutions (parliament, government or political party), but is all about questioning and moving such positions (Rancière 2015, pp. 35–52).

This notion has a bearing on our study object, since it means that any civil action or any civil role adopted by a cultural organization is potentially political in nature. And perhaps here also lies the rarely made distinction between the public sphere as understood by Jürgen Habermas (1989), and the civil domain. As mentioned in the introduction to this book, whereas the former is a space for expressing opinions or views, the latter goes one step further. An opinion piece in a newspaper or a debate among intellectuals remains, after all, too easily confined to the discursive domain of verbal dispute and rhetorical musings. In the civil domain this 'non-commitment' vanishes. There, opinions are linked to political demands and administrative responsibility and will at least stir up or irritate the political, for example by referring to civil and other rights and obligations related to an expressed opinion. Besides, in the civil domain those responsible can be addressed. Who, for example, should enforce these rights and who should fulfil these obligations? The very moment that answers to these questions are demanded, civil action occurs or transforms the public sphere into a full-fledged civil domain. We may suspect therefore that the cultural organizations with a civil role studied here are specifically intermediating between the public sphere and the civil domain. In that case they also contribute to the process of politicization.

What About Culture?

Before we begin our quest with specific cultural organizations, let us pause to look at another crucial matter, i.e. culture. For this we will make use of a definition we have given in previous work (Gielen and Lijster 2015) which was built on a description by Belgian sociologist Rudi Laermans (2002). He defined culture in a broad anthropological sense as 'a socially shared reservoir or repertoire of signs'. Culture is in the first place all about the semiotic process of signs and assigning meaning (signification) and being able to do so. To Laermans' definition we added that culture is not only about a formal semiotic play but also about signification in the sense of giving 'meaning' to life. The use of signs to give meaning to oneself and one's environment is very much an affect-charged process. Stated rather solemnly: culture always also concerns questions about the meaning of life and just as much about the meaning of one's family, friends, and colleagues, one's city, region or nation. From this extended definition we were able to argue that culture is in fact the basis or foundation of all societies. All human practices depend on assigning meaning, after all. How we trade, but also how we make laws or define rights and civil rights, has everything to do with the way in which we assign meaning. Likewise, everything about how we see an abstract European or transnational space, is the result of processes of assigning meaning and 'sense'.

To observe organizations from a cultural point of view also means paying particular attention to these processes of assigning meaning. We assume that especially cultural organizations play a crucial role, as they have all the means to 'signify' civil interests at their disposal. They can even play an important role in a battle to define what is civil and what is not. Our focus will be on how culture is used in said strategies of rationalization, communication, de-privatization and organization.

Also, in line with our definition of culture, we will not limit ourselves to a semantic analysis. It is precisely the affects that are expressed in morality, values and ethics that play a crucial role in these processes of assigning meaning. As we already noted in relation to Castells, a basic emotion is the engine for civil action. The question therefore is how this affect acquires such meaning in processes of rationalization and organization that the energy of the organization is maintained.

Finally, the above definition of culture demonstrates that we do not reduce culture to art or Culture with a capital C. That does not alter the fact that we will give attention to the functioning of art and aesthetic design in adopting a civil role. This is because we suspect that especially artistic expression has a special quality of expressing feelings that are at the roots of civil action. As a specific form of assigning meaning, art may therefore play a vital part in the conversion from a negative to a positive energy. Besides, artistic forms of expression provide the chance for alternative forms of rationalization, communication and organization. After all, as the cliché has it, art expresses exactly that of which one cannot speak. This popular notion aside, we know only too well how easily images and music can reach out to a wide audience and bring masses into action. Perhaps, more than words and most certainly more than scientific reports, they have the mobilizing potential to make an idea catch on, to make people engage in civil action. But art can be more than just a mobilizing force. It is first and foremost imagination and as we know, quite a few artists have used that capacity of the imagination for much more than expressing their most private fantasies. Quite often they also create a possibly different world, for example by showing that social interaction can take place in a completely different way than was thought of before. Or they make it heard, seen and felt how a dominant political regime would work out if we would radically think through certain positive or negative aspects of it. Works of art often do create both utopia and dystopia. When we read such books or watch such performances or movies we understand only too well that we are in a world of fiction. However, it is precisely this transference to an imaginary world that provides us with the possibility to look at the non-fictional world or simply everyday reality from a completely different perspective. We may suspect that this fresh but sometimes strange perspective will at times feed political and civil ambitions. In that sense, culture and cultural organizations also provide the signs and the imagination to think of and shape a transnational civil space.

Culture in Transnational Public Spheres

In the new transnational context it is no longer obvious where to locate the public sphere, who belong to it or feel it concerns them or how far its influence reaches. The 'public' is no longer identical to the civil population of a certain nation state, also because through migration (either voluntary or forced) the inhabitants of a certain place are increasingly not citizens of that nation state (but are, for example, expats, labour migrants or people without documents). According to Fraser we should therefore disengage the notion of 'the public' from the traditional notion of citizenship (as in being born in a certain nation state) and see it as all those who are 'affected' by certain political issues: '[T]he all-affected principle holds that what turns a collection of people into fellow members of a public is not shared citizenship, but their co-imbrication in a common set of structures and/or institutions that affect their lives' (Fraser 2014, p. 30).

The critical power of a transnational public sphere depends on two questions: that of legitimacy and that of efficacy. We could also say: the first question is to the 'who' of the public sphere (who is being represented, who feels it concerns them?) and the second question is to the 'how' (how are public opinion and emotion transformed into action and policy?). Below we will further discuss these questions and also outline each time how specifically art and culture can play a meaningful part.

When it comes to the 'who' of the public sphere, a weakness in the classic theory of Habermas of that sphere presents itself. It is the assumption that in principle anyone can participate in rational deliberation and communication, which, according to him, should lead to the consensus that forms the foundation of democracy. (Admittedly, he himself calls this a 'contrafactual ideal', but he does not seem to provide any concrete indication of how this may transcend the elitist affair of intellectuals, which this deliberation traditionally is.) By contrast, the already mentioned French philosopher Jacques Rancière rejects thinking in terms of foundational elements and states that democracy is created time and again through dissensus. Besides, and here we return to the importance of art and culture, according to him politics is not a matter of looking for the right arguments, but a matter of aesthetics. Or: in his view, politics is the way in which our shared space is divided.[1]

He means this in a very literal sense as well: so, for example, how the communal space of the city is divided between public and private (just think of the political struggle surrounding Gezi Park in Istanbul, a public park that was to make place for a shopping mall), how visible various social, cultural and political groups are in the media, or in parliament. But also in how far people are seen and heard figuratively speaking or in a political sense: in how far people are represented or see their interests expressed in policy, legislation, et cetera. The 'sans papiers' are often not only invisible because they are in hiding or kept out of sight in refugee centres, they are also invisible politically because hardly anyone speaks on their behalf and because their interests are hardly looked after in national parliaments. According to Rancière, every political act is aimed at a rearrangement of that communal visible space. In relation to this he speaks of the common basis of art and politics as 'the sharing and (re)distribution of what can be perceived with the senses' ('partage du sensible').

This is the aesthetic moment of politics, but also precisely the 'political of art', in that it is capable of showing what had been neglected until then. As stated earlier, art and culture can make us aware of voices that we did not hear before, of political emotions and interests that suddenly acquire a public face. A striking example of this is the project *Ausländer Raus* (Foreigners Out) by the Austrian artist Christoph Schlingensief. In 2000, he had twelve asylum seekers stay in a shipping container in the centre of Vienna and had the public decide who was to be extradited through Big Brother-like voting rounds. Naturally, this performance led to much controversy but it also catapulted an interest group into the public space. It shows that art and culture can play an important part in making the invisible visible and in creating a communal space in which similarities and differences can be 'fought' over (in a playful sense).

Since the 1990s, the notion of 'cultural citizenship' has emerged in political philosophy. The term was introduced to do justice to the fact that nowadays the notion of citizenship is very much interwoven with culture (through processes of globalization, migration and mediatization, as mentioned before) and also to counterbalance the idea that having a passport or civil rights is all that is required to be a full member of a society (see Stevenson 2003 and Vega and Boele van Hensbroek 2012). Citizens do after all also need to feel that their culture is recognized and respected and that they can manifest their presence in the public sphere. Especially art and cultural organizations have a task and responsibility here. However, do note: cultural citizenship is a two-edged sword, as culture not infrequently is a reason to make people who have had civil rights for a long time already, feel they are still not full members of the community (see the official use of the word 'allochtone' in the Netherlands, which refers to someone who themselves, or one of their parents, was born abroad).

As to the second question, that of efficacy or 'how', it is harder to tell how art and cultural organizations may play a part or even if we can expect them to. One of the problems of the crisis in the contemporary public sphere is that local or national authorities are less and less able to autonomously address the interests and concerns of their citizens because they neither have the power nor the policy instruments to solve transnational problems. As Fraser says, the challenge nowadays can be summarized thus: 'on the one hand, to create new, transnational public powers; on the other, to make them accountable to new, transnational public spheres' (Fraser 2014, p. 33).

This quote from Fraser does however provide a hint for one way in which art and culture may contribute to a transnational public sphere, i.e. the representation, mapping and identification of contemporary power structures. In describing the 'civil chain' we already mentioned the step of de-privatization or making public of emotions, by which we can transform these emotions into a political force. Precisely in that step the power of imagination is crucial and imaginative power definitely belongs to the domain of culture and art. We see this imaginative power at work in, for example, the projects by Renzo Martens, who, in his controversial film *Enjoy Poverty*, encourages inhabitants of Congo to turn their misery into profit by selling photographs of war victims and undernourished children to international press agencies. The film basically works as a *J'accuse* at a transnational level and has triggered many a debate about the role of Western businesses and NGOs in Africa. But also a more gruesome example like the worldwide popular fury among Muslims about the Danish Muhammad cartoons demonstrates how art and culture can be a power that can either bind or split communities and do so in a way that transgresses national borders.

However, the next step in the civil chain, that of making the self-organization public, is perhaps the most challenging one. Manuel Castells lists a number of characteristics of contemporary networked social movements, including their ability to connect the local to the global, their tendency to go 'viral' – to jump from one place to the next – and their self-reflexive nature (Castells 2015, pp. 246–271). For each of these characteristics, cultural organizations can be a platform. Because of their embeddedness in a local, often urban context they are usually quite well-informed about what political, cultural and social issues are at stake in a city, and they also know how to link these to transnational themes such as globalization, commodification and multiculturalism. In addition, the international network that is often at their disposal anyway may serve as an infrastructure of (self-)organization for social movements and as a place for experimenting with forms of protest and community building. The Württembergischer Kunstverein in Stuttgart is an example of this: here's an art institute that opened its doors for the protests against Stuttgart 21, a large-scale renovation plan for the inner city in which cultural heritage would be sacrificed for the sake of gentrification and streamlining traffic and large parts of the public domain (public parks and squares) would end up in private ownership. The Kunstverein not only literally offered its rooms for meetings and events of the protest movements, but also organized exhibitions around themes such as critique, the commons and public space (see Christ and Dressler 2015).

These are of course only a few examples. The formation of a transnational public sphere is a political challenge that by far transcends the interests and responsibilities of art and cultural organizations. Nevertheless, this challenge allows us to say something about the role of these organizations in the public space, namely that they not only and not mainly try to connect to an existing public sphere, but rather that through their activities they contribute to shape and transform this public sphere time and again and in doing so they also may shape society anew, every time. Perhaps this is where their most important task lies, in the fact that by their participation in and transformation of the public sphere they can provide a new and alternative interpretation of what a transnational civil society might mean. To understand better how this works concretely, we will have a closer look at two cultural organizations.

The Art of Mirroring

Les Têtes de l'Art, established in 1996 in Marseille by three actors, in the first place wanted to have a legal structure for their professional concerns. Although current director Sam Khebizi and his two colleagues Laurent and Lavigne were quite successful as a comic trio, they soon found the theatre scene too confined and self-absorbed. With Les Têtes de l'Art they wanted to build a bridge between the artistic and the social world, or, as they put it, make the connection with 'the real world'. The latter is regarded as more diverse and therefore more challenging than the traditional art world and its audiences.

When our field researcher Philipp Dietachmair probed a question about an 'initial irritation' or 'emotion' in an in-depth interview with the current director of Les Têtes de l'Art Khebizi, the latter did vaguely refer to a 'shock' that he experienced as a young resident of Marseille, when he found out that there were still *bidonvilles* (slums) in the city. Perhaps this is just an indicator that informs the social sensibility and fuels Khebizi's and

Les Têtes de l'Art's drive. This almost natural link between an individual sensibility like Khebizi's and the organization seems a relevant element. Castells also notes that the basic emotion and drive for civil action often reside with individuals, and that organizations are frequently the result of initiatives by one individual or a handful of charismatic persons (2015, pp. 12–13). More or less durable forms of organization stand on the shoulders of a single individual, which immediately also reveals the potential weakness of such initiatives, as quite a few of them are totally dependent on the person who started them. This figure also embodies a definite but sometimes hard to determine drive.

Khebizi is definitely aware of this 'fragility'. Several times during the interview he states, for example, that Les Têtes should be a structure that could also continue without him. It is one of the reasons why, after ten years in place, the board of Les Têtes was reshuffled. Khebizi's wife and close friends have been replaced by an assembly of artists, which not only makes the organization more professional, but also means that Khebizi must give account of his functioning within a more critical framework. At the same time we see how the organization rationalizes an initially mostly intuitive way of operating by putting it into words and by formulating a vision in 2008. Khebizi even took a course in management and no longer calls himself, as he did in the beginning, an 'artist' or 'artistic director' but 'managing director'. This also illustrates a tendency towards rationalization and especially professionalization. From then on the people of Les Têtes work more according to plans and more tasks are being delegated within the organization.

Returning to our 'civil chain', we see on the one hand a confirmation of the logic and chronology we have outlined. An admittedly vague basic emotion and personal drive are gradually framed by a solid and professional organizational structure. On the other hand, an important qualification of this chain, which is a result of these first observations, is that the organization itself is also transformed and becomes more rational. The stages or phases in the chain that we described do not seem to 'hook up' in reality, but rather 'slide' into each other in an almost organic sequence. This observation means that from here on, we will no longer speak of a civil chain but of a civil sequence. The various stages remain recognizable, nevertheless. For instance, in the case of Les Têtes de l'Art we can discern clearly defined periods of rationalization during which not only initial intuition and intuitive acts are taking shape in an articulated view, but the organization itself also becomes more rational. In addition, from the interview with Khebizi we can deduce that this process of rationalization is not only initiated in part but most certainly also enhanced by that other element in the civil sequence, communication. The head of Les Têtes de l'Art specifically stated that the municipal authorities of Marseille approached him in 2003. They were interested in his activities and even had ideas for specific 'assignments' for Les Têtes. At the time, however, Khebizi felt slightly 'embarrassed' as he could not precisely explain to them what the organization was actually doing. After all, neither vision nor methods had been written down or rationalized yet. It was this very invitation to communicate that more or less forced the artistic leader to further specify certain self-rationalizations – such as 'bringing art closer to social reality' – and make them more explicit. In that sense, communication enhances the rationalization process.

Although all these endeavours support better communication with governments and potential partners and also make both the approach and the methods of the organization itself more effective, it is not these rationalization processes that sustain the drive within the organization. The initial emotion as well as the personal drive remains relatively vague, even after this process of rationalization. And perhaps making explicit these words, concepts and methods is not what catches on with people (both within and outside Les Têtes de l'Art) and keeps the drive and energy in the organization. But then, what is?

Answering the question as to how they keep the fire burning, Khebizi talks about wanting to work *with* people and thus bridge the gap between art and society. It is precisely this simple act of making art together with others or 'doing things' that plays an important part. Drive is not so much communicated in words, and energy rarely comes from a well-articulated view. Rather, they emerge from the activities that are organized, the artistic interventions that are staged and the actions that are undertaken. Just like the transference of emotions can take place subconsciously and non-verbally through mirror neurons, the drive and energy are primarily communicated through the actions themselves. It is therefore not surprising that at some point in the interview Khebizi speaks of 'mirroring' when he mentions other actors and organizations that imitate or partly take over the methods of Les Têtes. Seeing others act makes us act as well, actions generate actions and energy generates energy. In this we also see the power of culture-specific artistic interventions. They generate a 'mimetic effect', which spurs others into action. Artistic interventions and performances in public space, or an educational project with children often indirectly and in an especially positive manner point out the social issues within a group, neighbourhood or square. Cultural civil actions not only bring to light what is not visible, but also make manifest how the surroundings, a space or a neighbourhood may be experienced differently.

In this respect, artistic activities differ from other civil actions such as protests, opinion pieces or petitions. Whereas such civil actions are generally limited to social criticism, the artistic civil action has an extra element: an alternative experience. For a little while the artists provide an often quite modest, but possibly different world, which in most cases generates positive energy. Les Têtes de l'Art illustrated this quite literally with their initiatives named Place à l'Art, a sort of 'fair' where people in the neighbourhood can together engage in all sorts of creative and artistic activities, producing a very positive social dynamics in places where before drug dealers and other petty criminals created an unsafe social environment. The outrage over an unsafe environment is immediately 'compensated' for with a positive alternative. Or, referring again to the transformations in our civil sequence: at the emotional level, especially artistic interventions provide opportunities for converting negative feelings or irritations into a positive experience and energy. Conversely, for some it might be precisely this alternative experience that makes them understand that their living conditions or precarious social environment are far from ideal. Crucial in this is that it is 'through' the artistic process or the work of art itself that participants are given an experience of alternative possibilities. Our other field researcher, Maité Juan, provides the following example of Bel Horizon (a degraded building in the centre of Marseille):

> After the request of an inhabitant of the high-rise flat, the participatory television of Les Têtes de l'Art organized a collective work of several months in 2013-2014. A group of adults and children from the tower block worked together on a script and collectively produced a fictional video about a problematic situation that affected all inhabitants. The fiction involved children and adults of the tower block

as actors. It told the funny story of an investigation carried out by the inhabitants to find out who threw waste out of the windows of the building. The artistic vector allowed for alternative representations to the negative image attached to the place and encouraged the meeting of inhabitants in the tower. After this fiction, a second project, in 2015, consisted in realizing five short films about the wishes of inhabitants about the rehabilitation of the tower.

The Bel Horizon case is just one of many actions by Les Têtes de l'Art that demonstrate how an artistic experience works within civil action. As noted earlier, (negative) criticism of a certain situation goes hand in hand with theatrical action that generates a rather positive experience of an alternative situation. This positive experience in turn evokes new criticism and civil action. Or, as we said: the artistic activity of Les Têtes is what is keeping the energy alive. If such a positive experience does no longer or not yet exist in the social reality, this actually provides a cultural organization with an interesting tool to create this experience all the same, especially in a fictional setting. A play or film creates a distance from the world we actually live in and precisely thereby generates the context for an alternative world. It is this experience that can make participants reflect on their real social reality. For them art generates – in the words of the sociologist Niklas Luhmann (1997) – a 'second order observation': from the artistic, imaginary or fictional 'second order' experience they can better observe how they live and experience their own everyday 'first order' reality. In the cases of Place à l'Art and Bel Horizon we see how this experience then encourages people to intervene in real life or at least long for and demand a different reality.

From our modest observations of Les Têtes de l'Art's activities we also learn something interesting about the difference between civil actions and artistic civil actions. In the first place, artistic processes provide the possibility to transform an initially negative emotion or an irritation into a positive (aesthetic) experience. In the second place, especially the artistic aspect provides a chance to experience something that is lacking in reality within a different context, albeit an imaginary one. This experience of a fictive 'reality' may – and indeed this is only a potential – bring people to start questioning the reality they are living every day. Finally, whereas many civil actions (such as protests or petitions) derive their energy but also their legitimacy and efficacy from representativeness, cultural actions do so from their theatrical character or, literary, their 'performance'. A rally or a petition is as convincing as the number of people showing up or signing: the greater the number, the more convincing. In other words, public support in quantitative terms determines the value of the civil action to a high degree. But in cultural civil action there is at least one other element. In those actions the experience itself of, for example, working together in preparing and presenting a performance, production or music recital, co-determines the efficacy of the civil endeavour. Here it is the quality of the experience rather than the quantity in terms of the number of participants that determines the civil potential. What we are trying to say is: with cultural civil action it is precisely this unique sensation that is sometimes experienced by a very small group which charges them with energy and makes it convincing. It is this singular experience that makes the civil engine run and keeps it running.

It is for good reason that the sociologist Luc Boltanski and the economist Laurent Thévenot (1991) have described representation or representativeness as a crucial quality of what they call the 'civic world'. A union leader can only be effective if he is able to convince the members (sometimes by opening the strike fund); a politician only derives his mandate from his electorate; and special interest groups can only look after their interests if indeed there is a group behind them. What we have discussed above is that cultural civil action introduces a new element into this classic civil value regime of quantitative representation. The persuasive power of an artistic intervention or cultural manifestation does not depend on the size of the group involved or the wider consensus on a criticism or new idea. It can just as well base itself on precisely the unique, idiosyncratic, even most deviating and 'crazy' sensation. In other words, civil power and power of persuasion are thus based on the quality of a singular experience.

Our initial observations of the civil activities at Les Têtes de l'Art teach us something about the specific role of the arts. As we said, deploying art 1) makes it possible to transform a negative emotion into positive energy, 2) has a mirroring or 'mimetic' effect and keeps the energy alive, 3) offers the chance to look at lived reality in a different way and perhaps criticize it, and 4) increases the possibility to bring a unique, deviating or uncompromising idea or view of society into the civil arena. How persuasive such an alternative proposition is depends not so much on the number of people who already support it, but rather on the quality or persuasiveness of the experience of the execution of this idea (albeit fictional). We could therefore say that the requirement of representativeness does not fully apply to artistic civil actions. Not having to speak in the name of a group, or the members of a union or political party, does mean that one can address 'non-affiliated' groups or members of society. Cultural civil actions therefore also have the potential to reach out to very diverse segments of the population and professional groups throughout society. How that exactly works will be discussed further in our Zagreb case.

Transversal Action

The first surprise we got when starting our investigation into our Zagreb case, Culture 2 Commons, was that it did not exist. Or rather, not in the form of a 'traditional' organizational structure: Culture 2 Commons is in fact a provisional hub or cluster, founded tactically in order to make optimum use of several funding programmes, and consisting of three previously existing organizations, namely the national Clubture network, Operation City Zagreb and Right to the City Zagreb. It operates within a network configuration that addresses issues or initiates actions, thus channelling temporarily accumulated energy. Or, as Teodor Celakoski, one of the key figures of this scene, describes it in an interview with Dietachmair: 'It is like an ecological system and it is not coordinated by one subject, but as a kind of swarm of intelligent knowledge.'

As with Les Têtes de l'Art, we observed some distance between theory and reality in Zagreb. Although the basic emotion from our 'civil sequence' is much easier to point out here than in Marseille, we can however not pinpoint one specific 'irritation' in Culture 2 Commons and the scene around it. What does stand out is one very concrete problem: space for independent culture. A shortage of physical space and accommodation for cultural activities and the lack of visibility of the artistic and cultural expressions that the independent scene represents in the mainstream media, initially formed the core of the civil struggle and generated the basic energy for civil action. The founding of alternative media such as magazines and the occupation of empty factories to give place and face to their alternative culture occur more or less simultaneously. In Zagreb, this tactical fight rapidly expands to domains outside the cultural sector that oppose the privatization of public spaces. Such actions range from protests against the construction of a shopping mall on a formerly public square to resistance against the privatization of the highway network in Croatia.

The activities of Culture 2 Commons thus are spreading out on at least two levels: 1) geographically, the civil actions are soon disseminated across the whole of Croatia, for example via the national network of cultural organizations within the independent scene, and 2) at the social level, we see a widening of the artistic and cultural sector into, for example, trade unions and ecological pressure groups. In other words, the cultural scene joins a broader social movement that connects transversally to many different segments of the population and spheres in life. One example of this is Pravo na Grad ('Right to the City'), which was established as a collaboration between civil society organizations working in the field of culture and youth, and was later formalized as an NGO. All activities of Right to the City are implemented in collaboration with 'Green Action – Friends of the Earth Croatia', one of the most relevant Croatian environmental NGOs. This social broadening is crucial in increasing the power and charging the energy of civil actions. In this respect too, well-known civil activities of traditional representational politics in which for instance trade unions and their members play a central part are forsaken in favour of actions that no longer rely on quantity alone but look for the quality of the singular dissonant voice.

This brings us to an important note: the transversal nature of contemporary civil action should be considered as an expression of the broader socio-economic shifts from welfare state to neoliberalism and from Fordism to post-Fordism in the workplace (see also Gielen 2015a and Gielen 2015b), that have the effect that both social problems and struggles are and can no longer be limited to the sphere of labour or, in classic Marxist terms, be reduced to class relationships. Nowadays, working conditions affect all aspects of life – or become 'biopolitical', to use the phrase by Michel Foucault (1997) – with the increasing flexibility of working hours (the line between work and leisure or private time is less and less strictly drawn) and the increased immateriality of work. It seems therefore almost obvious that civil actions that run transversally through various spheres in life fit better within this macro-sociological evolution. Neoliberalism affects the whole of our personalities, and it therefore seems evident that civil actions too are aimed at this totality of the world with its various life spheres (home, ecology, economy, education, politics, et cetera). Any contemporary civil critique or action will therefore be most productive when it engages in this 'total life sphere', i.e. when it becomes 'cultural'.

The independent scene engages in a struggle for its own culture. That is, a struggle in which artists claim space to signify themselves within a society. Earlier we already stressed that this is the very essence of culture: assigning meaning and sense to our own existence within a certain society. Civil action therefore not only joins a political or economic struggle but is always also a cultural undertaking to represent or 'signify' oneself, one's own lifestyle and values within a certain society. Like art, civil action is a way of breaking open and expanding this container of meanings called 'culture'.

To what extent do the rationalization, communication and, finally, organization of the basic emotions in Zagreb, and Croatia as a whole, follow the civil sequence? That we can learn from one of the organizations there, namely 'Multimedijalni Institut' (MI2) and its Net.culture club MaMa. The founders of this organization play a defining role in inspiring, driving and coordinating the whole scene. Since its establishment in 2000, this organization has been weaving together interests of diverse cultural fields, such as 1) critically infected digital arts, film, music and open access; 2) digital commons; 3) philosophy and theory; 4) cultural networking, advocacy and grassroots organizing, and 5) protection of public domain and struggles for spatial justice. Locally, MI2 is mostly identified with the social and cultural centre MaMa in Zagreb, where it organizes cutting-edge cultural, educational and technology programmes, hosts a local hacker community and provides an open venue for other cultural initiatives. But it is also a co-organizer of a Human Rights Festival, electronic music events, publishing activities and the Croatian distributor of Creative Commons licenses.

It is immediately clear how these cultural organizations operate. To put it simply, we could say that in Zagreb and elsewhere in Croatia they are in fact turning an open access on-line system into an off-line model. In any case, new media and digital network culture are among the most important sources of inspiration for 'real-life' analogue organization. Not only does the virtual world work as a mirror for developing organizational models in the 'real' world, it also provides inspiration for civil actions such as 'hacking' tactics and communication via open access. For example, MaMa was the direct inspiration for founding the Clubture Network of similar-minded local 'clubs' in 2002. Clubture Network brings together over fifty independent cultural organizations that are active in various contemporary cultural and artistic disciplines all across Croatia. It functions as a collaborative exchange platform through which organizations directly collaborate, on principles of mutual decision-making and inclusiveness.

It is again interesting to note how cultural and artistic practices play a unique role in civil actions. In Zagreb we were able to observe how debate converts into hands-on practices and also how artistic skills can help in this. Although none of the people from Culture 2 Commons that were interviewed stated that they are practising art while engaging in civil actions, it can hardly be denied that art, or rather creative practices, do inform these actions in a unique manner. The use of powerful visual as well as theatrical means not only make their actions more visible in the media, but the inventive and sometimes playful character of their actions also makes them contagious and generates positive energy. Their techniques convert initially negative emotions or irritations into action while simultaneously preventing them from being stigmatized as 'sourpusses' or doom mongers. Applying creative methods demonstrates a remarkable optimism, or at least inventiveness and the readiness to approach social and cultural problems in a different manner. For example, submitting a petition with 54,000 signatures as a pile of paper or digitally, has a quite different effect than when you hang those 54,000 postcards physically in the public space, as the activists of Pravo na Grad did. And a protest against plans of the Ministry of Construction comes across stronger when you actually cordon off the ministry's building with yellow crime scene tape than by writing a traditional opinion piece. The same goes for a theatrical performance in which activists dressed as tourists arrived at Kulmer Castle – with media attention – to claim their hotel rooms. Kulmer Castle is registered as a public hotel but has for many years now been used as a private residence by the Todoric family, one of the richest families in Croatia. The caste is built in a green area, where facilities for private housing are not allowed. Underlining its official public purpose as a tourist location, Right to the City

– arriving by tourist coach – demanded access to the non-existent hotel rooms in the building. The original imagination and theatricality of such actions not only pays out in media coverage, but their innovative and playful character also has a contagious effect with other social movements, NGOs and civil action groups.

In other words, we see once again the already mentioned 'mimetic' or 'mirror' effect of forms of artistic expression. In any case, the use of such artistic means and involving the media was replicated nationally in very diverse places in Croatia. And although, as in Marseille, Europe is not at the front of everyone's mind in Zagreb, perhaps here we have an important medium for arriving at a more international support base. Like the Guy Fawkes masks seen all over the world, likewise original forms of expression and performances may at least work as 'carriers' in shaping a wider civil playing field. In order to do this, the cultural sector must indeed demonstrate the will 'to break down its own walls', as Croatian cultural activists mentioned on the spot. This means in the first place that the cultural sector realizes and acknowledges that its own problems are also the problems of others. The issues of a shrinking public space, 'enclosure of the commons', precarious working conditions, but also of a diminishing autonomy or chance of self-regulation, is after all not exclusive to the world of artists and cultural organizations. Today, it is a problem shared by education, health care, the legal system, the press and parliamentary democracy. In short, constituting a transnational civil domain not only demands an international but also a transversal and a 'trans-sectoral' approach. That is perhaps one of the most important lessons so far that we can draw from Marseille and Zagreb.

Towards a Transnational Public Sphere?

We have discussed how cultural organizations contribute to the civil domain and to civil action. To a large extent, our case studies followed the logic of the 'civil chain' we laid out in the first section, although the cases also led us to adapt or specify the model in some aspects. The cultural organizations we studied channel and translate emotions, resulting in interventions and activities in public spaces. The most important lessons from our cases were, in the first place, that the added value of culture in these organizations exists in the 'mirroring' effect of their actions, which communicate the 'spark' that once inspired their initiative. In other words:

the emotion that we situated at the beginning of the 'civil chain' is also its result, intended or otherwise. It was clear that the cases we chose were very much aware of their position and role within civil society, not only at a practical and strategic level but often also at a theoretical level. In the second place, we learned that these cultural organizations are increasingly part of wider social movements. It is remarkable that when asked about the initial 'emotion', 'irritation' or 'frustration' that started the 'civil sequence' for them, both the initiators of Les Têtes de l'Art and of Culture 2 Commons also referred to the obstacles to their artistic practice: for example, an excess of bureaucracy or the lack of a physical space to practise their profession. The comparison with Matryoshka dolls made by one of the interviewees in Zagreb is quite apt: when trying to address a certain issue (for example, the lack of space for cultural activities) you discover other political issues behind it and in order to solve those issues you stumble upon other interests (cultural, political, economic or otherwise), et cetera.

This brings us back, finally, to an issue we already addressed earlier, namely how a civil domain could function on a transnational level. Could these organizations themselves contribute to a transnational civil domain? When asked about this possibility the actors involved proved to be sceptical. They often already have their hands full with activating local citizenship, putting local political issues on the agenda and dealing with local authorities, and hardly have time and energy left to worry about such an abstract entity as, for example, 'Europe'. Still, in the development of these organizations thus far we already observe, in a relatively short time span, an impressive expansion of their network, at two levels: from internal-artistic to social, and from the local to regional level. We have seen, especially in the Zagreb case, that an expansion to the rest of the region and collaboration with other regions in the former Yugoslavia are high on the agenda, but Les Têtes de l'Art too strives for a wider network in the Provence-Alpes-Côte d'Azur. If we extrapolate this trend it is very well possible that their agendas develop in such a way that, sooner or later, a cultural-political network for Europe becomes more concrete. And in fact, both cases we studied are currently part of the ECF-supported Connected Action for the Commons, which tries to extend such initial encounters among local actors towards exploring the possibility for creating a cultural civil agenda on a transnational scale. Within these kinds of networks culture organizations soon realize they are often dealing with similar problems, albeit in their own (local) context, and therefore can also learn from each other.

Furthermore, the notion of a transnational civil domain does not need to be as general or abstract as it is often considered to be. Of course the contexts of the various European cultural organizations and their local civil domains differ, sometimes even radically so, but nonetheless they can find each other on the theoretical and sometimes ideological level, and inspire each other. One example of this was the Connected Action for the Commons workshop that we took part in ourselves during our visit to Marseille. One thing we noticed, was that a discussion about the fact that residents around the 2015 Place à l'Art location and other neighbourhoods could soon not have plants or flowers in front of their houses anymore (because of a pending city ordinance) seamlessly progressed into a discussion about David Harvey's notion of 'commoning the city' (2012) as the claiming or reclaiming of the urban public space. During this discussion the participants from distant locations such as Warsaw, Zagreb, Chişinău and Barcelona had no trouble at all understanding each other. In other words, the sometimes indeed perhaps 'abstract' quality of the notion of a transnational civil domain and of the ideals that we as European citizens might want to see as the foundation of the European Union, can certainly contribute to articulating protest and to channelling and directing political emotions.

But it is not only concepts and theories that bridge transnational networks of civil undertakings. As we have described above, the singular experience of an artistic project or an artwork can let people immediately 'feel' and understand what is going on or what is at stake. It is the *aesthesis* of the artistic that has the potential to touch all of our senses. This quality can make very abstract things very concrete and indeed 'sensible'. Aesthetics as aesthesis can make you grasp an abstract idea without losing its complexity, and allows you to literally 'make sense' of it. Besides, aesthetic forms and actions are very easily mirrored because of the transgressional and transnational nature of their 'methods' such as play, humour, irony and exaggeration or travesty. Last but not least, the singular experience goes beyond the abstraction of theoretical notions, or figures and numbers in scientific reports, because it can touch us directly, provoking our emotions. In that sense, art offers us a wonderful tool to fuel civil action.

Notes

1 Rancière speaks of 'le partage du sensible'. In French, partage means both sharing and dividing.

Bibliography

- Boltanski, Luc, and Laurent Thévenot. 1991. *On Justification: Economies of Worth*. Princeton and Oxford: Princeton University Press.
- Castells, Manuel. 2015. *Networks of Outrage and Hope: Social Movements in the Internet Age*. 2nd enlarged and updated ed. Cambridge: Polity Press.
- Christ, Hans D., and Iris Dressler. 2015. 'Rethinking Institutions and Critique'. In: *Spaces for Criticism: Shifts in Contemporary Art Discourses*, ed. Thijs Lijster et al., pp. 129–149. Amsterdam: Valiz.
- Foucault, Michel. 1997. *Ethics: Subjectivity and Truth*. Edited by Paul Rabinow, translated by Robert Hurley et al. New York: The New Press.
- Fraser, Nancy, et al. 2014. *Transnationalizing the Public Sphere*. Edited by Kate Nash. Cambridge and Malden: Polity Press.
- Gielen, Pascal. 2015a. *The Murmuring of the Artistic Multitude: Global Art, Politics and Post-Fordism* 3rd enlarged and completely rev. ed. Amsterdam: Valiz.
- 2015b. 'A Caravan of Freedom: Mobile Autonomy beyond "Auto-Mobility"', In: *Mobile Autonomy: Exercises in Artistic Self-Organization*, ed. Nico Dockx and Pascal Gielen, pp. 63–83. Amsterdam: Valiz.
- and Thijs Lijster. 2015. 'Culture: The Substructure of a European Common'. In *No Culture, No Europe: On the Foundations of Politics*, ed. Pascal Gielen, pp. 19–64. Amsterdam: Valiz.
- Habermas, Jürgen. 1989. *The Structural Transformation of the Public Sphere: An Inquiry into a Category of Bourgeois Society*. Translated by Thomas Burger and Fredrick Lawrence. Cambridge MA: MIT Press.
- Harvey, David. 2012. *Rebel Cities: From the Right to the City to the Urban Revolution*. London: Verso.
- Luhmann, Niklas. 1997. *Die Kunst der Gesellschaft*. Frankfurt am Main: Suhrkamp.
- Rancière, Jacques. 2015. *Dissensus: On Politics and Aesthetics*. Translated by Steven Corcoran. London, New Delhi, and New York: Bloomsbury.
- Stevenson, Nick. 2003. *Cultural Citizenship: Cosmopolitan Questions*. Milton Keynes: Open University Press.
- Vega, Judith, and Pieter Boele van Hensbroek, eds. 2012. *Cultural Citizenship in Political Theory*. London: Routledge.

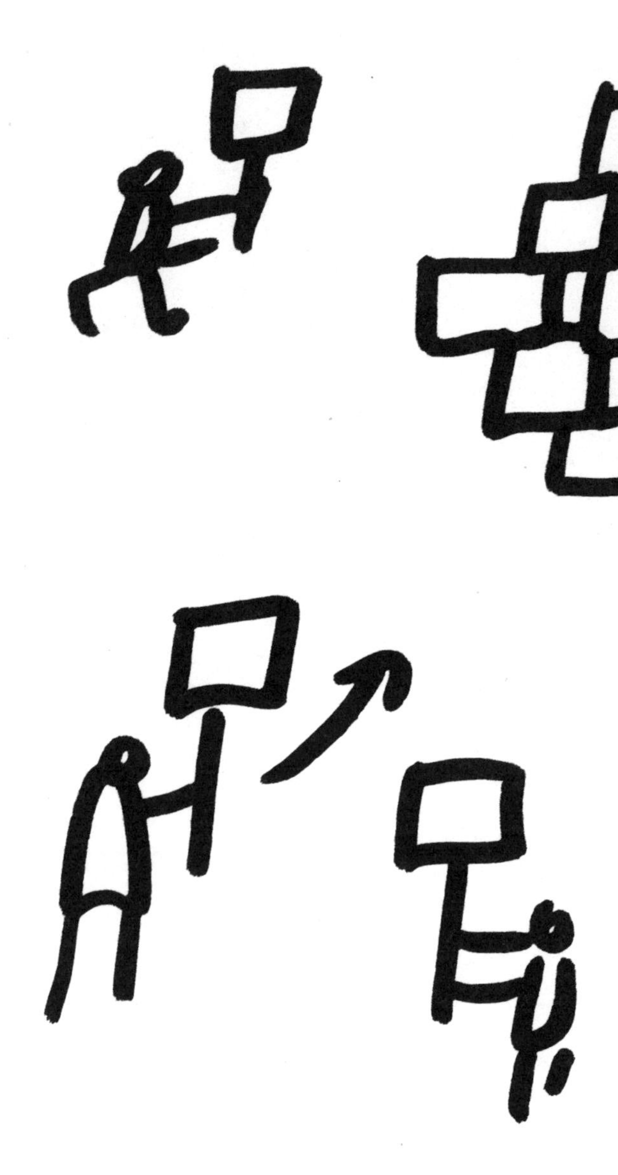

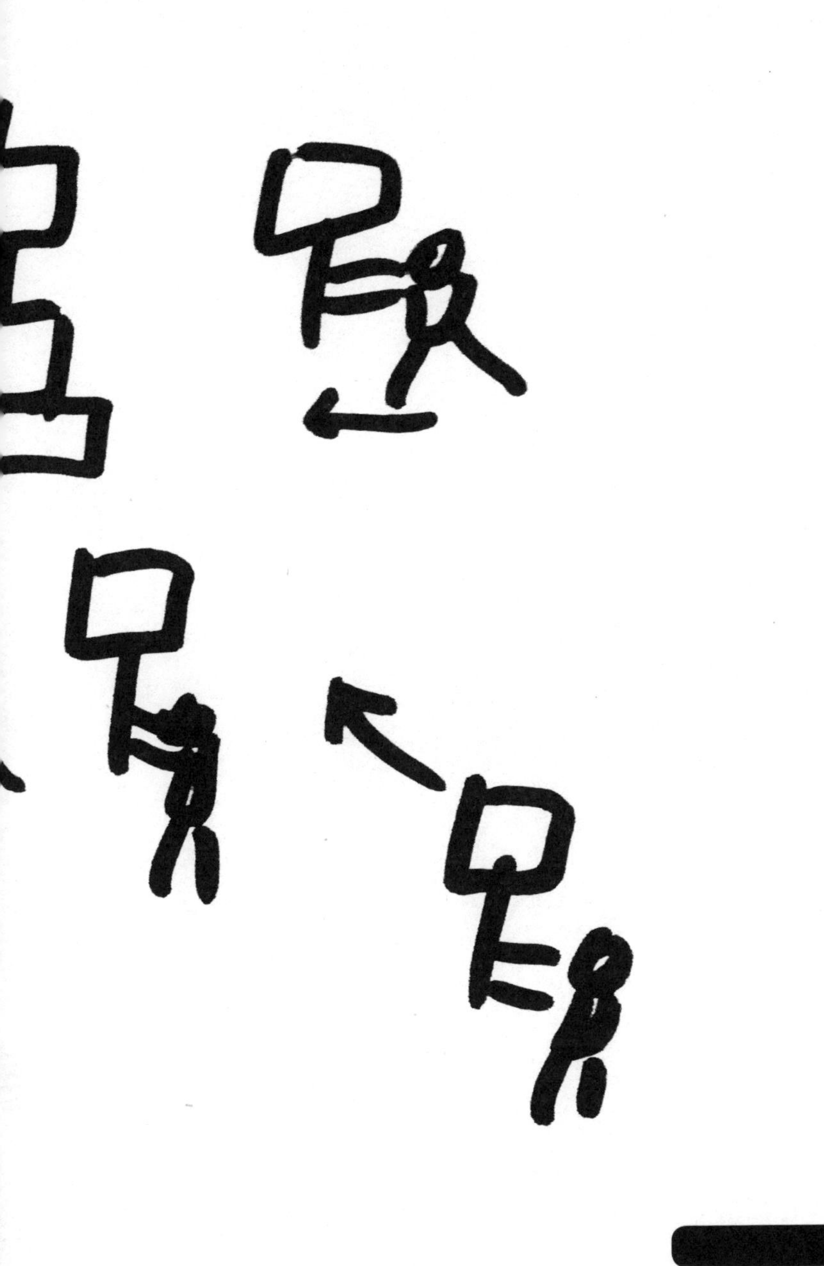

In the Absence of Culture There Can Be No Political Community

A Conversation with Ivan Krastev

Philipp Dietachmair
& Pascal Gielen

Protestors who spoke the language of social poetry left it up to the establishment to translate their ideas into real political prose.

This is one of the conclusions that political commentator Ivan Krastev draws, a few years after writing Democracy Disrupted, his unconventional analysis of the motives that have driven protest movements around the world since 2008.[1] The editors of this publication have invited him for a conversation on the role of cultural questions in these movements and the significance of their specific aesthetics of protest. Ivan Krastev was born in Bulgaria where he founded the Centre for Liberal Strategies in Sofia. He is a permanent fellow at the IWM Institute for Human Sciences in Vienna and founding board member of the pan-European think tank European Council on Foreign Relations.

Philipp Dietachmair – *Democracy Disrupted* was published in 2014. 'The current protests', you wrote back then, 'are a revolt against representative democracy. They mark the disillusionment of the citizen voter. The current protests function as an alternative to elections, testifying that the people are furious.' You also described the protests as 'an insurrection against the institutions of representative democracy but without offering any alternatives within the democratic system'. Since 2015, Barcelona or Madrid provide examples of cities that are governed by citizen platforms that practice direct democracy and have elected activists who have emerged from the local protest movements as mayors. In Zagreb, a new political platform that has formed in and around the cultural ecosystem we have studied for this book won almost 8% of the votes in the local elections of May 2017.[2] How do you perceive these developments? Do you see a change in how protest movements have emerged and progressed since you wrote your book?

Ivan Krastev – After *Democracy Disrupted* was published, two major things happened: from about 2011 to 2013, most of the political activism around the world was connected to the impact of the financial crisis and how to deflect the burden this situation had put on people's shoulders. Many of the activist movements we were talking about back then articulated themselves in a more leftist language – think of Spain, Greece, or Occupy Wall Street. However, a first new phenomenon we have been nonetheless witnessing over the past years and in the wake of the refugee crisis in Europe was a great increase of political mobilization and electoral support on the right. During the last two to three years we have seen many successful right-wing parties in different countries. None of them managed to actually win elections yet, but one of the shared conclusions here is that many blue collar workers have in fact turned to the far right.

Secondly, the very much street-based activism of the first years after the financial crisis had hit Western societies and some of the protest movements that have emerged from these years have meanwhile articulated and organized themselves as new political parties. In Spain we have Podemos, in Greece we have Syriza, for example. What was interesting in these developments was that regardless of the fact that these new political players claimed legitimacy based on the partisan ideals of the protest movements, they were very much organized as traditional political parties, with strongly leading personalities, and not so much along the logic of horizontal networks and leaderless movements. What I find really intriguing is this shift of configurations during the emergence of Syriza and Podemos. Both come from the protest movements, yet in their structures they follow very traditional party models. What came out of the national protests in Greece and Spain was not some kind of flat working model that engages people in hours and hours of nightly discussions about what strategic decisions need to be taken, but organizational structures that are based on a strong political leader and a clear chain of command, which resembles leftist parties that are much older than them.

A third observation is connected to the younger generations, which since last year are taking to the streets again with strong political demands, particularly in parts of Central Europe as we can see in Bucharest, Belgrade, Budapest and other cities. For me these new protests have a lot to do with two factors that define the role of youth in politics today: One is the fact that the core of the young population today is numerically much smaller than it used to be in the times of the 1968 protests. Nowadays, young people in Central Europe represent a very clear minority. Secondly, for those who want to change the way they live, it is much easier these days to change country than to change the government under which one has to live.

Pascal Gielen – Your views, and you introduce similar thoughts in *Democracy Disrupted*, seem to describe a rather pessimistic perspective of the outcomes such protest movements can actually have.

IK – In my book I basically tried to make two points about this: The political movements I described of course have left a strong trace. One of their strengths is the very particular shared experience many people have made by gathering in the streets, through being together and becoming part of collective action. On the other hand, however, I don't believe that these movements have managed to profoundly reshape the way young people and societies as a whole respond to political crisis situations today. Have a look at the new type of illiberal and totalitarian regimes we can find in Russia and Turkey now: to an extent, these developments are also a response to previous protest movements in these countries. We can only fully understand Erdoğan's conservative counter-revolution in Turkey in the context of his response to the Gezi Park protests in 2013.

Then there is of course the example of Putin's third presidency in Russia after 2012. The political mind of the new president Putin, whose decisions led to the annexation of Crimea, has very much been shaped by the severe crisis of political legitimacy he has experienced during the protests of 2011 and 2012. What is interesting here is that a study has shown that the level of popular support for the annexation of Crimea in 2014 was highest in those Russian cities which had the strongest number of supporters in the protests against Putin during the years before. The underlying story was that people initially took the streets in search of and demanding a change. One of the key issues that fired the protests against Putin in 2011 and 2012 was the question of dignity. Citizens who joined the demonstrations in the big cities felt very much humiliated by how the question of who would become the next president had been decided as a put-up affair between the old boys Putin and Medvedev. People demanded to be treated with respect and made strong arguments to reclaim their dignity as Russian citizens. Vladimir Putin then basically took over their notion of reclaiming dignity and in return transformed it into a very strongly emotionalized answer of his own: Russians cannot be dignified citizens, he declared, if they are inhabitants of a country that is not appreciated by other states, and he promised to push the international community to return to properly respecting Russia again. These messages were delivered by means of very much state-controlled media, in particular television, which began broadcasting highly adrenalizing political programmes which had not been seen on Russian TV before. In this sense, the protests managed to generate a lot of strong sentiments that made people feel that they do matter again in some way. This example shows that protests can be very easily hijacked by more powerful political players, which was a major issue in Russia. A good part of the emotional temperature that was created by the 2011–2012 protests was soon instrumentalized by the state propaganda that channelled it towards creating this new patriotic identity framework we see today. This is why I don't believe that the protest movements of the past years have succeeded to translate much of the energy they have managed to mobilize into actual political power that is really changing societies.

PG – Do you see any other undertakings of civil action that work in a more structured way and might have resulted in more substantial effects for our societies?

IK – One of the paradoxes of today's social movements is connected to the new power of social media. It is social media that have allowed protest movements of the kind we discuss here to come out of nowhere. Today, one can have hundreds or thousands of people creating pressure in the streets within only a few hours after a Facebook posting. In a paradoxical way however, this possibility and experience also seems to keep people away from a more long-term and organized type of social engagement. Many are not really prepared to invest in developing new organizational structures because of a prevailing feeling that it's already enough to be on Facebook and to mobilize others when something important happens.

Unfortunately, social media have also done much for the benefit of the Far Right and have helped them to create a sort of public momentum. Look at UKIP in Britain, one of the most telling examples of the in fact often failing structures of this type of political parties. Very obviously capitalizing on the anti-EU sentiment and very strong on social media, UKIP was a critical factor in the Brexit campaign. Institutionally and organizationally very weak, it has nevertheless almost disappeared since then.

One of my main arguments, which I also introduced in *Democracy Disrupted*, is that social media and the new media environment we work in strongly empower the individual. We don't need to be published by a newspaper anymore in order to have our voice heard. Today, our voice very quickly resonates with people who think like us, and that also puts us in a position to start doing things together rather swiftly. At the same time, this straightforwardness of social media has created a problem for real collective action. People believe that getting together is so easy that they are not ready to invest in more structural efforts anymore.

Nevertheless, I believe we still can see some results that these new social movements have achieved. For me the major impact they had is not related to the actual power they have gained but to the extent they have managed to change the political agenda. All these new discourses about social inequality in Europe and the United States have certainly a lot to do with what has been put on the agenda by Occupy Wall Street and other social movements around the world. I absolutely believe in the relevance of this eruption of civil activism in the last decade; this was unprecedented. However, already during this overly optimistic times following the Arab Spring I remained rather cautious compared to voices that saw the emergence of a new type of politics, where old institutional structures would not matter anymore and parties and their ideologies were no longer necessary in times when people can take to the streets. I was much more sceptical and have not changed my view on this since I wrote *Democracy Disrupted.* I do believe that in politics, organizations matter, institutions matter, and if we want to achieve sustainable change we have to invest in creating and transforming them.

PD – In this context, how do you see the efforts then of some of the new political party projects on city level that try to convert ideas and values of direct democracy – something they have acquired inside the local social movements – into tangible political power, but only on the municipal level at first? I have already referred to Barcelona en Comú, Ahora Madrid or Zagreb je NAŠ. Around the world there seem to be a growing number of cities that start to explore governance models and decision-making processes that try to build politics around the immediate concerns of and directly with the people living there.

IK – The most profound question in politics is always how to get to power in order to actually be able to realize a different kind of policymaking. What is interesting is that the protest movements indeed managed to unlock some of the established dividing lines in politics, and new coalitions became possible that were different from before. I agree with you that settings where we can observe a major change of how politics are practised are indeed to be found more frequently on the local levels of decision-making these days. Interestingly enough, such alterations in political practice do not occur so much in small- or medum-sized towns. These new ways of governing in a participatory way are more a phenomenon of large cities and megapolises, which present political players and citizens with totally different types of choices and alternatives. There, we can also find an entirely different set of problems compared to those governments normally have to deal with. We could observe that very well during the most recent elections both in the United States and Europe: there is a major gap between how citizens of the megapolises perceive the world and how the rest of the population in many countries relate to that. The appearance of a totally new type of political community will also push the emergence of a new way of doing politics, as we can already see these days. In the large megapolises of today people understand that the way governments were working before does not function anymore. In these big cities one can, for example, never precisely know how many people actually work there, legally and illegally; there are policies for migrants as well as for tourists to be developed, large numbers of people move in and out all the time and the structure of the economy is very different. This is why I believe that on this city level we can observe a major shift that may lead to a totally different way of governing. Indeed, some of the best ideas in this direction are coming from people that have been a part of the local social movements, which allowed them to develop a much better understanding of how their urban communities, particularly the most active segments of them, are actually composed and what the local population wants. Also during the refugee crisis we could see that mayors around the world framed problems very differently and came up with alternative solutions. I think this is very promising.

On the other side, I do believe it is extremely important that we don't allow the gap between the big cities and the other parts of the countries to widen even further. The risk with this gap between the city and the regions is that it could reinforce and inevitably intensify the polarization in politics we are already witnessing. Let's take the example of the Brexit vote: Nearly 60% of voters in London voted for Remain. It seems that it was not so much the differences in income or education that determined whether one voted for the UK to stay in the EU or not, but rather that the places people live in determined their point of view. Or take the US presidential elections last year: Hillary Clinton won all those constituencies in which the bulk of 54% of the whole US population lives while she lost two thirds of all constituencies outside the large urban agglomerations across the rest of the country, where Trump gained the majority. She used this infamous and very dismissive phrase of the 'basket of deplorables' to describe her competitor's electorate, and I found it culturally very interesting how his supporters in return called for a boycott of the

Oscar ceremony over Hollywood's 'liberal limousine bias', as they described it.

The difference between how residents in the regions and the big cities see the world, how they understand politics and cast their vote has in a very peculiar way become a decisive factor for predicting the totals of election results. Its seems that in cities we can hardly find a social group anymore that still believes that the world can largely be preserved as it has always been. Bigger cities are already so much different compared to ten or fifteen years ago that we may say the great revolutionary days of opening up to the world and fully engaging in globalization have pretty much passed there. These highly populated areas are much more diverse in terms of ethnicity and religion. They are economically more active and prosperous, nevertheless they show an odd combination of very low and very high levels of income, and inequality is often excessive. Statistics from the US by the way show that the socially most unequal municipalities are run by the most progressive mayors. It seems that the big cities have already adapted better to the world that we will see coming. Many are for example already extremely inventive when it comes to using new technologies for solving problems in the fields of public transport, education, and various other fields. Although of course enough of the key issues we discuss here remain unsolved in urban contexts as well. Nevertheless, cities are places where people experiment a lot, where we have communities that act and function as a sort of laboratory. This is not exactly the case when we look at the situation in the less urbanized parts of many countries, in the more traditional places where socio-political and cultural ideals of a nation state are still very much the prevailing name of the game. What may work in Barcelona is probably not going to work in the same way in a regional town of 60,000 inhabitants elsewhere in Spain, or even in Germany. This is why I believe we need to find a way to bridge these two worlds that are emerging as an effect of globalization, but also as a result of two conflicting types of political activism during these past years. We should really look at how we can stimulate civic engagement and social progressivism in areas outside the large metropolitan areas. I believe we need to treat this issue with critical importance in order to maintain a certain level of social cohesion in our societies, especially in Europe.

PD – I recently spoke to the organizers of a rock festival in Eastern Germany who try to resist the take-over of a small place in Mecklenburg Western-Pomerania by a group of neo-Nazis whose leaders have declared their home a model village for its radical political activities in the region.[3] In his text for this book too, Ilya Budraitskis introduces a case that describes how the Nizhny Novgorod branch of the National Centres for Contemporary Art in Russia and its critical exhibitions regularly became the target of a group of 'offended citizens' who were in fact supported by a patriotic movement called 'Great Fatherland'.[4] Do we not have a major issue with that regressive sphere of citizens' activity as well? How do we reach them? How can we avoid the notion of civil action becoming misused for legitimizing repressive and authoritarian political agendas?

IK – In the last few years a lot of attention was paid to the rights and the role of civil activism. At the same time however, and as response to the refugee crisis, we also experience the rise of the so-called uncivil society. Many people in this scene are politically very active – on social media and in the streets where they passionately bring forward their demands. Their political ideas often show visions of a community that is defined in mutually exclusive terms. As we all have learned meanwhile, the most xenophobic segments of the electorate live in places without many immigrants. Those voters often face a major gap of experiences that urban populations have already made, which can't be simply tackled with more education and raising their levels of income. So indeed, the big question here is how do we allow certain values of cultural openness that were framed in urban contexts to spread in rural areas? How do we translate the city experience to a fruitful village experience so that more remote communities can also adapt to the major changes that come with globalization? How do we facilitate communication between these differing experiences and types of perceptions?

When trying to answer these questions, it doesn't make much sense to make moral judgements about personal reactions of people who perceive things emotionally after all. A popular assumption of the 1990s, for example, was that in Central and Eastern Europe younger generations as a rule shall become more liberal than the previous ones who grew up under socialist regimes. This is not supported by data we have available now. While the hypothesis of a more open-minded youth still holds somewhat true for matters of sexual life, we observe the emergence of an actually much more conservatively thinking young generation that seems to experience some kind of shock caused by the speed of change we are facing. As a result many of the right-wing movements in Eastern Europe include very young people.

Nevertheless and despite some totalitarian trends, I don't think what is in danger in Europe today is really democracy. Our citizens are not very eager to surrender their influence to any type of elite, they don't trust elites anymore. What is actually in danger in Europe is pluralism. There is a growing trend to perceive anybody who does not share one's own views and perspective on the world as somebody who should be excluded and antagonized. We can clearly observe this on the far right of course, but also on the liberal left. What we see everywhere at the moment is a major standoff between the very liberal, inclusive variations of activism that have been born in the context of the big cities and a much more restrictive activism that is based on feelings of ethnic solidarity, exclusivity and patriotism, which predominantly has its origins and supporters in rural areas. Of course the ideals and values of these social movements are inevitably bound to clash, but I do believe it is extremely important to find ways that help these opposing groups to talk to each other. I would start with building on some of the strangely coinciding commonalities in their otherwise conflicting views: both sides are preaching change, both are a reaction to the fact that a certain type of institutional structures and understanding of political democracy do not function anymore as they used to do. The overarching goal of whatever we try to do and invent in this direction is to prevent that we end up with two parallel worlds that remain alongside each other and exist without interaction. I find it critically important to tackle one of the most threatening features of the modern world, namely that both the market and digital technologies provide so much encouragement to follow our personal preferences and our own natural choices that people always end up communicating and living with likeminded peers who think and act just like them. Our societies slowly start to look like the landscape of the settlements in Israel, which somebody very accurately described to me as the most international but least cosmopolitan places in the world. Walls surround and separate communities of identical people, whatever conservative, progressive or religious orientation and lifestyle they may represent. The result is that we simply don't see each other anymore. We do not understand anymore why others say what they say and do what they do. This is a very dangerous development. Not only because it affects how people vote, which could lead to an entirely polarized system that becomes incapable of taking any decisions in the end. From my point of view this self-centredness also bears quite a lot of potential for political violence, especially as in the world we live in everything is changing so fundamentally and so fast.

PG – Your analysis appears to confirm what Richard Sennett suggested already in the 1970s with his book *The Uses of Disorder.*[5] Public space, he stated back then, is losing ground in cities while it is essentially the only space where people are still truly confronted with each other. So you say that digital technology, social media and other phenomena of modern public life in fact further deepen the homogenization of communities and build walls around them rather than increasing a fruitful discourse of opposing opinions and social interaction on a global scale?

IK – These developments indeed have been confirmed by empirical studies and we understand more and more about them. Cass Sunstein's book *Going to Extremes* showed that when individuals very actively communicate with likeminded people they develop a tendency to radicalize their views.[6] Let's say, for example, you are initially only somewhat critical about immigration. Becoming part of a Facebook community where everybody shares your only moderate scepticism at first can turn you into a very radical opponent of immigration in the end. This process nevertheless also works the other way round when it comes to supporters of immigration. As a result we really seem to have lost a public space which is defined by a collective reception and debate of all these different views.

PG – I tend to make a more academic distinction between public space and civil space. For me, public space terminologically describes a space for exchanging arguments and for proposing and discussing new ideas. Social media as well, from my point of view, have more and more developed into a type of public space where you express your liking or disliking of something and everybody can see it, but these individual motions don't result in all too much consequential action as a collective. It is very difficult to translate social media activity into real civil acts of shared action, which is what defines civil space for me: growing networks of civil action that strive for common achievements and need to be reinforced and re-institutionalized in a tangible, maybe almost physical way. Finally, we could also distinguish between civil and civic space, but civic for me rather describes state-organized structures than autonomously operating networks of civil action.

IK – I find these distinctions very useful. Public space indeed should exist as a space where we all share and try to understand differing views while we effectively live in a civil space that should allow us to actively participate in things. There are a lot of studies that show how the Internet has nevertheless started to modify and interfere with the functioning of these ideal forms of public and civil spaces we both seem to imagine. Nevertheless, in order to be successful in politics and to change societies one first needs to know and understand what others want. This is why a broadly inclusive and functioning public space is so important. I think we have not done enough yet to understand these new, increasingly gated information communities and how to escape the danger that we all end up communicating solely with fellow citizens who already share our views. I recently talked to a software engineer here in Austria who suggests that all online newspapers should contrast each story they bring on a certain issue by immediately publishing a serious counterargument or differing point of view right next to the original article. I think in times of digital interconnectivity on a global scale it is nonetheless going to be very difficult to restrain people from following their natural instincts of congregating with the likeminded. This is why it is so important to create different notions and forms of social cohesion.

Traditionally it has been the nation state that provided social cohesion by sustaining the framework that pushed groups with differing views to act together. In the 1950s and 1960s we could observe strong efforts for a homogenization of societies by state structures. Particularly in Eastern Europe, where I grew up, we painfully experienced this dark side of homogenization by state-run institutions that tried to push all citizens to read the same books, et cetera, so that everybody would have the same ideas. Today, we have arrived at another extreme: seen from the outside, our societies seem to work in a highly pluralistic manner. However, if we take a look at what kind of information individuals consume today, how increasingly segregated communities frame their issues, we seem to face a substantial loss of ability to understand and develop empathy for positions that are different from our own points of view. This is why I believe that we need to fundamentally rethink how a vital level of social cohesion can be maintained in a world that is much more diverse, where structural homogenization of societies is not an option any longer and where both the market and the Internet make it so much easier for individuals to simply escape any opposing views or people they don't like.

PG – When we talk about the construction of state and the building of nations we of course start to touch upon questions of the political role of culture, which are at the heart of this publication. Michel Maffesoli clearly distinguishes between a structured and organized state and its bureaucracies and the social ambiance of communities that build on sentiment and emotion, something that even the cultural constructions of the nation state and its institutions cannot provide any longer. The modern state is too rational and too much built around economics, he argues, and that is the reason why our societies have ended up in a sort of new tribalism that has replaced individualism with consumerism.[7] From your point of view, is there a more fruitful role that culture could play in the context of these new and global processes, which obviously decrease citizens' abilities to really interrelate and deal with complexity, as you say?

IK – Indeed, the role of culture is one of the most critical questions in this context. In the absence of culture one cannot build any type of meaningful political community, and political community can also not be reduced to institutions only. Studies show that the more diverse communities are the less we can rely on an intuitive understanding of cultural values to be collectively shared inside them. As a result governments tend to use much more forced measures and in some cases even violence to regulate societies and exercise power. The problem here is how to develop a shared cultural understanding at a time when state structures have lost the monopoly of creating common narratives?

When we look back at the nineteenth century, societies and political regimes in Europe established different forms of highly elitist institutions that generated a common history. The base for this common understanding of history was first provided by Roman history, which was taught at gymnasiums and supported the development of generally understandable points of reference among the elites. When the nation states emerged, this elitist notion of a shared Roman history turned into the conception of a universal history whose legitimizing functions in society started to be substituted with new national narratives and histories. Schools and other educational state institutions then helped to define a shared national canon of cultural references such as books, films, et cetera, which provided citizens with commonly understood points of identification and legitimation. These shared references were essential for a state when communicating with its citizens.

I believe we have arrived at a totally different cultural situation today. Had I travelled to the Netherlands twenty years ago and asked somebody about the best Dutch writers I probably would have heard three or four names who were generally accepted to be the most important ones, even if I had asked a very diverse group of people and even if some critics thought the quality of their literature was perhaps still debatable. If you ask somebody for the most relevant writers of a country today, especially young people simply name the authors they read, wherever these are actually from. The state's educational institutions and schools have lost quite a lot of their erstwhile monopoly to determine what its citizens read, learn and how they learn. More and more nation states end up with a mix of cultural communities within their borders that have their own references and narratives, follow their own authorities and represent their own cultural particularities and views, which, on top of that, are all largely unknown to other communities that live in the same territory. Ten years ago, the prevailing and I believe rather naive view was that we should not be too much troubled by the absence of shared cultural references. It was considered fully sufficient to maintain a situation that would allow everybody to read whatever they wanted to read and to do whatever they wished to do. However, I think we have arrived at a point when creating common references also becomes an important factor for sustaining social cohesion within and among our societies.

I believe a crucial question here also is, how to start thinking about social cohesion that is not simply understood as a redistribution of financial resources, as important as this is. In Europe, the crisis of the past ten years has highlighted the limits of exactly this type of an exclusively money-focused solidarity. The question now is, can we identify common references that help us to create the shared emotional space that we need in order to secure our societies' empathy and solidarity on national and pan-European levels. The prominent public stereotyping of 'diligent Germans' versus 'lazy Greeks' during the European financial crisis is just one example of developments that we need to overcome in order to arrive at a political community that exists and succeeds because it is capable of acting in a solidary way, on shared emotional grounds and not only based on fiscal transfer policies. In this context, it is interesting that the protest movements of the past years were quite internationally oriented and pro-European, but nonetheless never managed to engage much in conceptually rethinking the functionalities of the European Union. Citizens in the streets of Madrid and other Spanish cities for example were rather Europe-friendly. Nevertheless, discussions about Europe never seem to have played a larger role in this quite pro-European crowd.

PD – How do you explain this? Why do European questions and common references play such a minor role in these social movements? How would you bridge the gap between what we see politically emerging at local levels and your vision of a more solidary Europe that is based on shared emotional and cultural grounds?

IK – It think one of the reasons why the movements in Spain or also Greece never managed to surpass the city or national level had to do with the fact that their major political concern were questions of the sovereignty of the people. This is particularly strong in the case of Podemos and the movements in the Spanish cities, because questions of democracy are what matters most to them. It is a major justifying factor for their existence, and because democracy is very much exercised on the level of local and national communities, European questions never played a bigger role. When protesters take to the streets one of their most natural claims to voice is We Are The People. We are here to protect and demand our democratic rights! However, they refer to their own people, as Greeks, Spaniards or Bulgarians, not the European people – and that is an important difference.

Europe nevertheless did serve as a very strong symbol in the protest movements throughout the peripheries of Europe and also outside the EU – in Romania, Hungary, Ukraine or even Turkey. Paradoxically, it seems that the more doubts there are about a society's actual political belonging to Europe, the more important it can become as a symbol for political activism. It is interesting to see that in these contexts feelings of loyalty with European values such as democratic institutions, protection of human rights, et cetera can almost develop forms of constitutional patriotism. But this is not enough.

Yet, on the other hand these crisis years in Europe do make its publics much more aware of each other. Germans started to have an opinion about the Greek economy, we were all interested in what's going on with refugees in Hungary, Italy and everywhere along their routes through the Balkans, and Brexit remains a top story for all of us. I think this is a relevant change, as the very first step for any level of sympathy or solidarity among us is developing curiosity in each other. In this context, however, the Far Right in Europe also receives a lot of attention, be that in the Netherlands, in Austria, in France, in Bulgaria and so on. Paradoxically, the really Euroskeptic parties have started to benefit from these pan-European processes as well. Still, I believe that even this absurd phenomenon pushes Europeans to reflect about their joint future much more than they did before. Five to six years ago a potential disintegration of the European Union was something unthinkable. Today, we know that we cannot take the European integration for granted anymore and many EU citizens understand that without making an effort a break-up could happen quite easily. I think this has pushed Europeans to think in essentially much more pan-European terms. Nevertheless, here we come back to a problem we have already discussed before. Political activism tends to be more successful when operating on the local level. When it tries to go beyond the national remit, it often gets lost institutionally, its constituencies disappear and the variety of problems from sometimes very dissimilar European societies and communities lets things usually go astray very quickly. Still, I do believe we need to further explore how social cohesion can work better on all levels of public and political life. First on the local levels, where social inequality in the big megapolises remains excessively high, as I have argued before. If in addition we don't manage to develop a certain degree of social cohesion on the level of the European nation states, we will experience a very strong backlash from the Far Right, I am afraid. Finally, what could be mechanisms that provide social cohesion when we are talking about Europe as whole? Interestingly enough, it is also in times of sensing new external threats that we Europeans begin to realize that we share very particular common interests. The US elections and president Trump's very different views on America's traditional relations with Europe, the rise of Putin's Russia and Erdoğan's post-coup Turkey have started to shape a certain type of new political identity that cherishes our way of life and its institutions and makes EU citizens understand that they should care about them. I don't believe these external threats are strong enough to create a full pan-European identity. However, there has never been a historical process of political identity building where external threats were not at least a formative factor.

There is one more thing in relation to your question, which I consider to be very important: How Europeans and in particular the European elites see the world today has also very much changed. Ten years ago, a vision that really thrilled us was how to transform other societies. What occupied our minds very prominently was further European Union expansion and how Europe is changing its neighbouring countries. We lived in a world in which we knew that we were most probably surrounded by the future EU member states. The past ten years have changed this perception a lot and for many Europeans, I believe the question today is not so much anymore how to transform our neighbours but how to prevent that some of our neighbours actually do transform us. I think this presents us with a situation that inevitably asks for much more political cohesion than we needed before. On the other hand, this carries its own risk: When the European Union from a value-based point of view was in its more expansionist mode, and I mean this in a very positive sense, it tended to be much more universalist and all-encompassing. Today, Europe starts thinking about itself in substantially more exceptionalist terms. We are trying to define Europe in terms of its cultural uniqueness. And here the responsibility of the arts and culture community comes in, in my opinion. We need to find an answer for maintaining this cultural dimension of Europe without making it too exclusive. The task is to avoid that we create a Europe that is so aware of how different it is from others that it actually starts fearing the rest of the world.

PG – Your ideas about the role of culture in the framework of creating more social cohesion seem to build very much on a notion of culture that supports societies in facilitating consensus. However, when we refer to Europe and its cultural diversity as a given, could we not also think of culture as a constructive process of dissent? Could a less harmonious concept of public cultural discourse and activity not also provide us with a proper base for more coherence and solidarity?

IK – For me the cultural empowerment of people that represent minority groups and opinions is of critical importance, particularly in the context of the nation states where different groups that represent the majority always tried to own culture to a certain extent. Nation states traditionally had a tendency to be culturally very dominant and to assimilate their minority cultures in one way or another, but this has limits and can severely backfire. There were certain cultural gatekeepers that often kept minority groups and positions away from the power of mainstream cultural interpretation. However, the dominant public role of cultural gatekeepers, such as the conventional media institutions for example, has been demolished by today's media landscape. Meanwhile, we have ended up in a situation where it is not clear anymore for many societies who and what actually represents the majority and a common mainstream. And I do believe this actually calls for a joint effort to redefine some leading cultural threads, a new common, a canon, which of course cannot be simplistically imposed by the dominant ethnic group. It cannot be taught in schools or distributed by television, because of the diversity of the media environment we have today. Here I would like to return to the example of the five books that everybody who grew up in a particular country used to know and read, we have mentioned this before. My idea would be to move forward to identifying five to ten books again that everybody should know, but then the selection of these books should represent a much more diverse cultural canon than we used to have before. If we don't manage to reconstruct a sort of new and authentic framework of cultural authority, a set of commonly acknowledged cultural references that provides legitimacy from the inside and the outside, a more genuine social cohesion in and among communities and societies is going to be very difficult to achieve. Consequently, we would end up in a post-truth world, a landscape of radical diversities without any type of normative frame, where everybody follows their own alternative facts and Nothing is True and Everything is Possible, as my colleague Peter Pomerantsev has titled his book.[8]

PG – You have analysed many of the protest actions that functioned as public manifestations of the recent social movements in Europe and around the world. What role did the variety of artistic and cultural expressions play in them? How do you perceive this display of a quite particular type of aesthetics in these movements? From your point of view, was there a kind of deliberately applied cultural methodology of protest and did its artistic appearances actually work as a public communication tool?

IK – Indeed, there was a great cultural energy present in these protests and an incredible wave of artistic activities that was very open towards quite unusual forms of aesthetic expressions. Streets were turned into theatres and there was no difference between artistic producers and audience. Everybody turned into an artist, in a way. For me this is also connected to the fact that these protest movements did not have a very clear ideological profile. They were an articulation of abstract notions such as freedom, equality. In addition, the shift to predominately visual forms of expression, something that has been going on in other spaces of public cultural communication for a long time, also determined how these movements looked and felt. These were protests without speeches, at least most of them. We saw a protest of posters and all kinds of other visually powerful performances whose aesthetic symbols were circulated and shared across many different parts of the world. This also added a strong component of worldwide cross-referencing to them, and it even caused a sort of international competition for the funniest poster and the best street happening, which I found very interesting. The physical manifestation of these protests and its aesthetics looked like public cultural events, like street festivals. Instead of developing clear ideological lines of thought and political positions these movements focused on creating emotional communities, which explains this strong emphasis on aesthetics and visually experienced forms of expression. It helped people to momentarily assume a common identity when they took the streets together, regardless of often not knowing each other and despite the fact that many of the groups that protested together had quite different views on many issues.

An interesting effect in this context was that during the protests, different subcultures seemed to temporarily merge in a way. Take the example of the Gezi Park protests in Turkey in 2013. The local LGBT community, which represents a subculture of its own, was protesting side by side with groups of nationalist Turkish republicans and many other usually quite incompatible groups. This was a real opening, because these groups joined the protests coming from often very divergent Facebook pages whose followers had their own genuine jokes, favourite videos, et cetera. When they met in the streets they started to learn and understand each other's cultural references. In a way they started to create and culturally express themselves together and for a short while they shared a commonly recognized cultural space. This heterogeneity of people joining forces in the streets was very important because many of them encountered views quite different from their own. They learned about books they had never heard of before and so on. It would be interesting to study which books the protesters started to read after going through these joint experiences. I find it crucially important that after such encounters people don't just go back home to their own gated communities of mind again.

In all protests of the last years this aesthetically determined type of emotional community helped those who participated in them to assume some form of political identity when they were in the streets. However, the airy visual language many of these protests were speaking also was part of their weakness, in my view. Protest movements that make too abstract claims inevitably leave it up to the professional politicians, who rarely join them in the streets, and their interpretation when it comes to writing things down in tangible policy language. So, basically, we can say that the protesters who spoke a language of social poetry again left it up to the establishment to translate their ideas into real political prose. And here, I think, the supremacy of the interpreter turned out to be too dominant after all. The lack of programmatic identity, which is essential for being recognized as political party and when facing more traditional ideological mindsets, made these social movements less effective when it came to really exercising power and essentially achieving their demands. So it's not by accident that some of these protests also ended up with a lot of frustration and disappointment for those who were part of it.

PD – What do you think will come next in these social movements and how do you see the future role of culture in them? What could be cultural questions that might determine the agendas of new local and global movements and what kind of activism will we see in the next few years?

IK – I do believe that the language of culture is going to be more and more used by very different civil movements and political groups. Up to now, certain ideas seem to prevail, such as that arts and culture and the public discourse about them are a monopoly of the liberal and progressive segments of society. What we are going to see as a trend is that far right and conservative groups will much more articulate cultural questions and speak an artistic language too. Because culture is the only public language that allows all of us to be actively involved in civil space without the constraints of an instantly defined political agenda. This is why I find it extremely important that we try to engage, maybe even mix these different and often conflicting directions of cultural activism with each other. Only by opening up people to each other's truths – and cultural and artistic work provides great tools for this – we can develop empathy for things we don't understand and can escape the gated information communities I mentioned before. We will need to go beyond traditional notions of cultural participation that simply promote participation as an objective in itself and just serve our idea of representing truly participative democracies. New approaches will have to go further than just encouraging citizens to be more active. I believe we are entering a new phase where the task will be to essentially make much more sense of civil activism. It will not be enough to simply empower everybody to say whatever they want to say. The question is how collectively shared demands can reach the next, higher level. This is why I think the coming years will be very much about translating the power of civil action, something that people experience very strongly when they express themselves in an artistic way, into real politics that can produce tangible change.

Notes

1 Ivan Krastev, *Democracy Disrupted: The Politics of Global Protest* (University of Pennsylvania, 2014).
2 See Pascal Gielen and Thijs Lijster pp. 39–63 and Philipp Dietachmair in conversation with Tomislav Medak pp. 211–231.
3 www.forstrock.de.
4 See Ilya Budraitskis, p. 191–207.
5 Richard Sennett, *The Uses of Disorder: Personal Identity and City Life* (New York: Alfred A. Knopf, 1970).
6 Cass R. Sunstein, *Going to Extremes: How Like Minds Unite and Divide* (Oxford and New York: Oxford University Press, 2009).
7 Michel Maffesoli, *The Time of the Tribes: The Decline of Individualism in Mass Society* (London: Sage, 1996).
8 Peter Pomerantsev, *Nothing is True and Everything is Possible: Adventures in Modern Russia* (London: Faber & Faber, 2015).

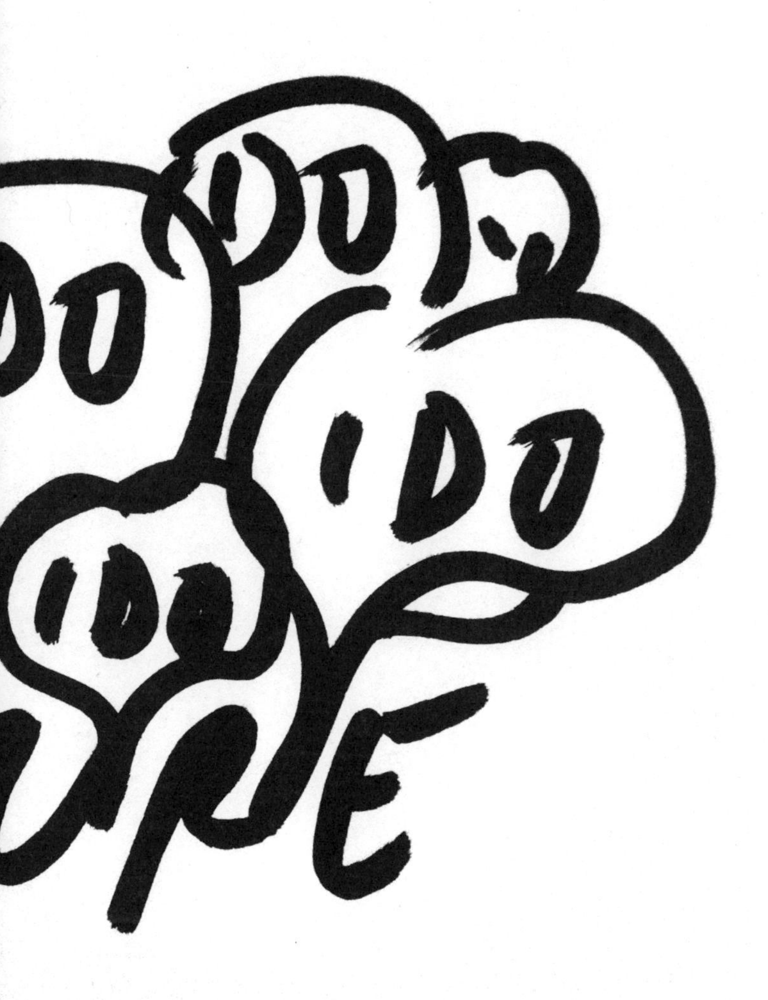

Transnational Activism through the Arts
More a Potential Than a Reality

Yudhishthir Raj Isar

Introduction

Viewing things from a planetary perspective rather than a purely European one, it is difficult to subscribe fully to the assumptions of the editors of this volume. Are artists and their organizations – the actors of the 'arts and culture' whose 'potential' is being explored in these pages – really the linchpins of a 'locally rooted civil society in a globally connected context'? Do artists and their organizations everywhere deal routinely with *global* questions? Are they significant players in the transnational forms of organization that certain sectors of civil society are indeed forging?

To my mind, the answers to all these questions are largely negative. The arts sector has provided no leaders in terms of transnational civil society mobilization in general. There is no artistic or heritage-related cause or movement of global scope that is spearheaded by independent actors in these fields, in the same way that feminism, or LGBT rights, or climate change have been. The defence of artistic freedom is beginning to become such a global cause, but it is still inchoate. Within countries of the global South there are only a few instances of alliance building. The same can be said of the regional level (which is transnational of course, but not global). A notable exception is Africa's *Arterial Network* and for this reason I shall cite its work below.

Mention should be made, however, of the ways in which cultural civil society organizations are mobilizing themselves (albeit at the instigation of the UNESCO Secretariat) in the implementation of UNESCO's Convention on the Protection and Promotion of the Diversity of Cultural Expressions.[1] A recent analysis shows that, at the *national* level, cultural sector organizations and networks are addressing a range of challenges: resourcing for the sector, creative industry development, the status of culture in international trade deals under negotiation, creative freedom, the reform of copyright and intellectual property laws and broadening the remit of cultural policies, including at the community and local levels.[2] Because the Convention's implementation processes are essentially national, the analysis does not have much to say on transnational alliances amongst these national bodies. Yet its author is forced to ask whether models from broader civil society have something to offer the cultural sphere. As he observes,

> mass membership-based CSOs[3] and movements on issues such as the environment and human rights, because they

> are able to secure adequate funds from individual giving, feel free to turn down potential governmental and corporate support, and even make their refusal to seek funds from these sources part of their brand with individual supporters.

Is it even remotely possible to envisage similar movements in the field of culture?

Another set of preliminary remarks is also in order. First, on semantics. The binomial 'arts and culture' is too abstract. It combines analytical categories, not active agents; unless we reify each notion, as we all too often do, neither 'the arts' nor 'culture' has agency as such.[4] Neither 'the arts' nor 'culture' actually does anything. People do. Agency, as far as any form of civil action is concerned, lies with individuals and groups of actors, in this case *artists and their organizations, whether in arts production or in arts delivery*.[5] Surely it is preferable to talk about these actual human and social actors, i.e. artists and arts organizations.

What is more, if we want to capture the content of what these actors actually do, and this is my second semantic issue, 'arts and culture' cannot deliver the goods at the global level. There are two reasons for this. First, because the term 'art' privileges the *individual* creative act or impulse and the mystique of the individual artist that has developed around his or her persona, whereas in many non-Western societies, artistic work is often a collective project, or group manifestation, not just an individual one. For that matter, so it is in the global North: witness the workings of art and design schools or architectural collaboratives, or genres such as film, theatrical and musical performance. The term 'cultural expression' fits the bill better. This is precisely why UNESCO's celebrated Convention of 2005 is devoted to the 'protection and promotion of the diversity of cultural expressions', which it defines as 'those expressions that result from the creativity of individuals, groups and societies and that have cultural content'. Note the reference to 'groups and societies' – this is particularly germane when it comes to tackling issues that affect relationships between communities of people.

A second semantic reason is the fuzziness of the 'and culture' segment of the umbrella term, 'arts and culture'. What does the 'and culture' actually include, over and above artistic expression? People invariably conflate a reading of culture understood as the arts and heritage with the broad ways of life understandings.

But the latter are not particularly germane to the construction of a civil space, for ways of life themselves do not provide the tools for the negotiation of concord and conviviality. The arts *tout court* would suffice, although as I have suggested, the term 'cultural expression' is more apposite worldwide. But since it would be cumbersome to talk of 'practitioners of cultural expression', we may settle for clearly identifying arts and heritage practitioners and their organizations as the sector we are talking about, regardless of the actual terms we use.

A third preliminary remark has to do with the buzzword 'civil society' itself. One wonders what the world's individual creatives and cultural associations were doing until the 1990s, when the term began to be used in its contemporary guise. Were they not addressing democratic potential already? Were they not working across boundaries? The language of cultural advocacy is replete with buzzwords of this kind, which have become talismanic banner heads. 'Civil society' has become such a term, one that has come to be used in such a general way as 'to look more and more like "society" itself and become indistinguishable from it', as the political scientist Neera Chandoke, among others, has pointed out.[6] Witness the very broad definition adopted by the global civil society advocacy organization CIVICUS for its Civil Society Index: 'the arena, outside of the family, the state and the market, which is created by individual and collective actions, organizations and institutions to advance shared interests.'

The term 'civil action' partakes of the 'civil society' mystique as well, regardless of the fact that 'civil society' is not inherently good one hundred per cent. The latter term was for long a 'hurrah' concept, as scholars, activists, and policy-makers began acclaiming the notion in the years immediately after the collapse of the Soviet Union – often for clearly ideological reasons, based upon hostility to the excessive power of the State and its often corrupt and inefficient agencies. But today, as Neera Chandoke has again pointed out, 'there is much more restraint, hesitancy, ambiguity and skepticism amongst those who write about it', not least because some of the most visible and active civil society organizations across South Asia and elsewhere preach and practice intolerance, both ethnic and religious, cultural chauvinism and the persecution of cultural minorities. They too are deploying the 'art' of civil action, but at the service of a toxic politics.

Civil society has also become a suspect category to many across the global South, as a result of the way it was aggressively promoted, during the 1990s, notably by United States governmental and non-State actors alike, not just as a legitimate sector of governance – which it is to be sure – but also as a front for neo-liberal anti-Statist positions, often dominated by western transnational NGOs or loose coalitions of interests pursuing their own agendas. In Northern and Western Europe, lauding the key role of civil society is now *de rigueur*, but it is far from certain that governmental enthusiasm for it is uniformly strong, while outright hostility may be observed in Hungary and Poland. Elsewhere, lip service and political correctness are often as much in play as genuine recognition.

Furthermore, official support is often attributable more to expediency than a belief in the virtues of civil society organizations: with declining budgets and diminished reach, governments both national and local are keen to share the bill with others. This expediency is often reciprocated by the key players in arts delivery as well as production. Both are happy to take on the 'civil society' mantle, for apart from the prestige and aura attached to the term, there are subsidies and grants to be had.

Another form of expediency is to invoke the role of cultural expression, hence also of its exponents, as instruments for the attainment of other, ultimately extra-cultural, ends: causes external to culture itself and to which cultural actors have readily hitched their star, often idealistically, sometimes opportunistically, but not always with the intended effect – and occasionally with perverse consequences. Over the years, these causes have included 'culture and development', 'culture and social cohesion', 'intercultural dialogue', the 'creative industries' and, most recently, 'cultural diversity'.

'Culture in EU External Relations'

There was certainly both idealism as well as expediency behind the European Union's 2013-2014 Preparatory Action entitled, 'Culture in EU External Relations', for which I was the Scientific Coordinator. This mix of motives came out strongly in the report of the Preparatory Action, which we entitled 'Engaging the World: Towards Global Cultural Citizenship'. As the ideas that inspired us then resonate strongly with the goals of this volume today, it seems appropriate to reiterate some of them here.

The report revealed how ties of cooperation and exchange in different domains of cultural expression have been forged with the rest of the world by official as well as autonomous – civil society – actors and institutions in EU Member States. While Europeans have already succeeded in projecting an image of their shared space as one of cultural creativity and diversity, the report argued that the time had come for them to go beyond representation and engage with the rest of the world through stances of *mutual learning and sharing.* Adopting such stances be tantamount to acting in a spirit of *global cultural citizenship* that recognizes shared cultural rights as well as shared responsibilities, hinging upon access and participation for *all* in a framework of cosmopolitan solidarity. How could it be otherwise, the authors argued, in a world in which cultural practice is becoming increasingly transnational and transcontinental, as artists and creative people everywhere remain true to themselves yet have recourse to globalized repertoires, methods and strategies? The challenge for Europe too, in this multi-polar world, is to remain true to itself, yet to position itself more creatively amidst fluid and multiple identities and continuous cultural and social transformation.

The positive forces shaping this transformation include the digital revolution, the exponential expansion of the social media and large-scale political and social changes across the world. Yet there is also a dark side. Cultural actors both in Europe and elsewhere are confronted by the growing concentration of ownership and power in the hands of massive transnational conglomerates, as well as in a small number of privileged cities and regions. This concentration is already limiting cultural freedom and creativity. It will also restrict the scope of transnational cultural exchange unless mechanisms are devised to promote small-scale and local cultural entrepreneurship.

Dialogue through culture, *understanding* through culture, *empowerment* through culture, as well as *prosperity* through culture: these themes were the common threads the authors identified. The four themes, each expressed as mutual processes, emerged from the aspirations and visions of cultural actors in third countries, just as they did from the hopes of their European counterparts.

The banner term '*global cultural citizenship*' encapsulated these four shared horizons. Cultural belonging, cultural rights, cultural voice and cultural inclusion for both individuals and groups are now claims that accompany the demand for economic, political and social rights – claims that were and still are associated with classic notions of citizenship. The cultural citizenship paradigm concerns a far more active engagement, one that is made up of rights as well as responsibilities, whether on the part of individuals or the group to which they belong. It connotes access to and participation in wider communities of commitment and practice. It is not a given, rather it is a horizon of aspiration, a work in progress. It is a process, not a product; it requires mutual learning, notably about living together with others.[7] It concerns both identity and action; it entails both personal and cognitive dimensions; it is both individual and collective; and it is both values-driven and interest-driven.

The notion of *global cultural citizenship* also locates rights and responsibilities at the world scale, in an era when the exclusive link between citizenship and the single nation-state has been greatly weakened. It sees such rights and responsibilities as a horizon to be attained by humanity as a whole. Above all, it seeks the development of a global civil society and public sphere that is able to constructively negotiate difference and foster a spirit of transnational solidarity. As an ideal to be pursued on the world stage, cultural citizenship represents the needs and interests of both Europe and its partners.

For these reasons, we used the term as a metaphor for the kinds of cultural engagements we advocated. These engagements should not be confined to mutual understanding or tolerance. They are based rather on the even stronger values of mutual recognition and empowerment. They also require a rethinking of identity and difference across the world. They make it both necessary and possible to combine concern for social and political rights with the full recognition of cultural diversity. They encompass cultural capacity building, knowledge sharing, professionalization, professional exchange and mutual learning. They require of us as Europeans that we learn to balance a deep and genuine respect for difference with the rediscovery of the art of the common good.[8]

Some of the principles the report advocated are clearly relevant to the purposes of this volume. As regards *value-based principles*, for example, the idea that communication between people and peoples today must take place in conditions of respect and equality. The stances of reciprocity and mutuality, notably mutual learning, embody these fundamental values and should therefore underpin the entire EU approach, the report argued. It is vital to protect and promote the diversity of cultures and the foundations upon which they are constructed. But it is equally vital to eschew all notions of culture as fixed and monolithic or of distinct cultures as homogeneous and monolithic bounded entities, and combat the resulting stereotypes that still persist as a consequence of such notions, both in European countries about third countries and in third countries about Europe.

Europeans need to listen to others as much as they communicate freely with them. Sharing values implies open expression, critical reflection and free debate. It requires free spaces of the mind, as well as physical spaces. Europeans today are critically aware of the legacies of their histories – of both the positive and the negative aspects – including the colonial past in certain cases. Hence it would be simplistic to simply try to export European values wholesale to other regions. We must be ready to learn from the variety of ways in which people elsewhere, notably artists and intellectuals, choose to appropriate and adapt values that originated in Europe, but that have become a legacy for all: gender equality, freedom of expression and human rights. We also need to recognize as well that there are powerful forces and voices that resist or reject those values.

The report stressed the ways in which artistic processes and values played a key role in the nurturing of civil societies in the 'transition countries' after the demise of the Communist regimes in the 1990s. It is now Europe's turn, it argued, to share this experience with civil society cultural actors who would like to position themselves at the forefront of popular mobilization in regions where major social and political transformations are occurring. It is clearly important to deploy more resources through non-governmental channels, at the 'people-to-people' level. This is particularly needed in countries that lack clearly defined state policies or funding. Alternative models of transnational peer-to-peer learning and independent 'eye-to-eye' forms of collaboration would be a form of much desired 'cultural fair trade' and could provide valuable mutual learning experience. These partnerships could bring together artists, cultural managers, journalists, writers, etc.

In this spirit already since 2011, the 'Tandem cultural managers exchange programmes', created and hosted by the European Cultural Foundation and the Berlin-based NGO MitOst, have benefited cultural managers with proven professional experience from countries inside and outside the EU. Tandem has been supported *inter alia* by the Robert Bosch Foundation, Stiftung Mercator, Stichting DOEN, the Dutch Cultural Participation Fund, British Council, Fondazione Cariplo, the Stavros Niarchos Foundation and Mimeta Norway. Local partner organizations in Turkey, Lebanon, Ukraine and Southern Europe deliver the programme's various cross-border collaboration activities to participants in the field. A decisive feature of its success is the equality of power relations in terms of who has the money, the knowledge or the capacity to deliver. Participants work together on the same footing and under the same conditions to co-create and co-produce. Each 'tandem' is completely free to define the project it wants to develop and each member of the tandem is equally responsible for the outcomes. The programme's host organizations function as mentors and facilitators; they do not design projects for the tandems.

One could cite many more examples. In all these areas, however, there is a risk that many cultural activists are reluctant to recognize. This is the risk of asking culture to do too much. Because we have become so used to reifying the concept of culture itself, we tend to overstate the causal and explanatory power of the cultural. We also tend to see it as a panacea: the Dutch anthropologist Jan Nederveen Pieterse has called this the 'add two tablespoons of culture and stir' school of thought... Fifteen years ago already, the literary critic Terry Eagleton called for a much more nuanced view of 'the power of culture' and its relationship with other dimensions of the human condition, arguing that

> ...culture can be too close for comfort. This very intimacy is likely to grow morbid and obsessional unless it is set in an enlightened political context, one which can temper these immediacies with more abstract, but also in a way more generous, affiliations. We have seen how culture has assumed a new political importance. But it has grown at the same time immodest and overweening. It is time, while acknowledging its significance, to put it back in its place.[9]

That said, 'putting culture back in its place' does not mean denying the contribution that cultural expression and its transnational deployment can make in many fields and so it is to this domain that I now turn.

Nurturing the Democratic Potential

Already in 2011, for that year's Culture Forum organized by the European Commission, I had reflected on behalf of the European Expert Network on Culture (EENC) on the links between the empowerment of artists and their organizations for the promotion of democratization processes. My short paper (which has never appeared in print) took up several of the themes of the present volume; the arguments I made then appear to remain valid today. I argued that as democracy and human rights are increasingly placed at the heart of human development, the potential of cultural expression to inform, inspire, and energize aspirations to democracy has come to be widely recognized. I should have also written that this recognition has often been couched in rhetorical or incantatory terms. Realizing the potential is easier said than done, particularly today, when if anything the number of authoritarian regimes everywhere has increased. In the global South, artists and their organizations often struggle against censorship and oppression by both governmental and non-state actors, under conditions of great and often increasing difficulty.

To be sure, things began to change for the better some six years ago, with the 'Arab Spring' and many other civic mobilizations (despite their short lifespan, the reversals and the tragic crackdowns that followed). These developments strongly impacted upon European public opinion. They also and perhaps above all transformed our understandings of what our transnational connections and obligations should be, e.g. by refreshing the meaning of notions such 'Euro-Mediterranean cultural cooperation' or 'culture and human rights in the EU's external policies'. But to seize this opportunity, today even more than during those heady times, we need to be inter-culturally informed in our goals, realistic in our expectations and pragmatic in our methods. We must be ready to tackle visions of and engagements with the ideas and ideals of democracy that differ from our own. We need to demonstrate the creativity of imagination that we claim for ourselves but do not always attain. We also need to be adequately supported by the policies and institutions of the European Union. These are complex challenges.

Most if not all of today's European polities recognize that artistic and cultural expression are constitutive of a free, democratic society – of its diversity, of its liberties, of its openness and of its flexibility. In the living memory of many Europeans as well, artistic expression has provided many vehicles of dissent or rebellion in once totalitarian societies and are once again called upon to do so. Our cultural actors – artists as well as arts-producing or arts-delivering organizations and networks – have generated ideas, works, forms, projects and spaces that have enriched the engagement with democratic governance, fundamental rights and the like. We thus rightly consider cultural expressions to be crucial components of the 'infrastructure' of values and aspirations that underpin the energies of civil society. Beyond our shores such understandings also exist. They have emerged more recently; many are still fragile. Autonomous cultural voice is still work in progress in many instances and we know that it can be and has been manipulated by political forces on several levels. Yet clearly also, cultural practitioners now figure amongst the citizen actors who are acting independently to bring about changes to their lives. Their actions range from Anna Hazare's fasts of 2011 to curb rampant corruption in India, the service delivery protests of poor people in South Africa, the already cited mass uprisings in Tunisia, Egypt and Syria against dictatorial regimes, or the huge protests against rising prices and the cost of living that took place at the same time in Israel. Within the cultural domain itself, there are also struggles under way, for example in favour of ethnic pluralism and minority rights, which go hand in hand with the democratic ethos.

While these are the broad patterns, many local variations exist, each reflecting historical legacies, cultural specificities and different social value systems. For the ideas of democracy and human rights themselves are part of a particular political 'culture', premised on specific values and understandings. Europeans seeking to 'support' democratic movements in other settings need to be sensitive to different readings and priorities, or even to a potential clash of perspectives. Pluralism requires the recognition that there will always be some measure of incommensurable difference. No 'one size fits all' solution can be remotely envisaged: democracy and human rights are certainly universal values, but there is no global formula for their application on the ground. Europeans need to be lucidly self-reflexive about the self-proclaimed mission of spreading the democratic message, lest it resemble Europe's 'civilizing mission' of yesteryear.

The whole point of democracy and democratic discourse is to address such issues openly in the public sphere, to offer constructive critique, to formulate alternatives and to include the excluded – the multitude who are still kept at the margins of political participation and public debate.[10] Hence from the European side, the question is how our cultural operators can best work at the operational level, in a true spirit of intercultural partnership and mutual learning, with their counterparts elsewhere. The challenges here are concrete and include principally the following:

Increased direct support. More resources need to be channelled directly into the hands of third country cultural practitioners themselves. Even small amounts can go a long way, thanks to the volunteering characteristic of the sector. A frequent risk, however, is the over-provision of support to a 'happy few' of individuals and organizations who have learned how to talk the talk and flatter the self-regard of otherwise well-intentioned 'donors'. Support needs to be as multifaceted and broadly based as the pluralism it professes to nourish. Also, it is important to refrain from setting priorities, envisaging strategies or supervising their implementation on behalf of local actors themselves. Many well-intentioned attempts may end up primarily benefiting outsiders, including commercial and political interests, academics, or the funders themselves, ironically reinforcing old modes of paternalism and dependency. Often, the best that an outside partner can do is to find ways to encourage cultural activists and their organizations to carry on their own work for their own purposes and on their own terms. The most enabling approaches stay out of the way, leaving cultural projects the social space and the time they need to be effective.

Organizational and other forms of support. Revolutions can be triggered by a single spark, 'but they can only be sustained and help effectively to transform societies through organization', observed the playwright Mike van Graan when he was running Africa's *Arterial Network*. The organization was created to link artists, cultural activists, creative enterprises, cultural NGOs, etc. at national, regional and continental levels so as to forge a coherent voice for the sector, to provide it space to practice democracy by actively participating in forming in turn its own organizations, electing leadership and holding them accountable, and having a coordinating/coordinated structure that solicits opinions and formulates collective positions that it then represents on behalf of the sector to national governments and in international fora.

An even greater challenge, from the transnational perspective, is the inability of cultural activists to form and strengthen informal networks and formal associations at the local, national, and international levels. European cultural organizations could draw creatively upon their own experience to contribute to such partnership-building processes. Ongoing outbreaks of intolerance driven by religious fundamentalism in South Asia have also seen artists and intellectuals coming out in protest, thereby engaging with key questions of democratization, equity or human rights. There is growing awareness everywhere of how a cultural perspective can help in addressing broader economic, social and political issues. Yet this remains largely rhetorical. Even in Europe the goal of linking cultural policy with other policy domains has been achieved to only a very limited extent. Could independent European cultural actors share the lessons of their own successes and failures with their counterparts in third countries, and in ways that are relevant to the transformations unfolding?

Provision of information and research. Citizens are disempowered when they are misinformed or under-informed or do not have the critical perspectives and tools to evaluate the information they are provided with. Thus *the Arterial Network*, through monthly newsletters, regular news alerts, website updates, etc., has over the years sought to empower activists with information and cultural policy tools that can help them to engage in effective advocacy campaigns at national and regional levels. Such clearinghouse functions can promote improved networking among cultural action groups, counteracting geographic and socio-cultural isolation. Often, the simple awareness that a similar organization exists elsewhere gives a group heart and the renewed energy to face its own challenges. Networking can also facilitate cultural exchanges and the transfer of skills.

Monitoring freedom of expression. Key to creativity is the human right to freedom of expression. While it is advocated in many international and national policy pronouncements, in practice this right is often compromised. Artists are routinely arrested, their works are banned, they are denied access to public funds and opportunities, and are intimidated by extremist, religion-inspired, civil society activists rather than the organs of a repressive State (although in many cases governments collude). Across South Asia, non-State actors, driven by politicized religion, actively subvert the rule of law by harassing or intimidating, often violently, painters, playwrights and filmmakers and thus restricting their freedom of creation.[11] *Arterial Network* provided a response to such threats in Africa by establishing 'Artwatch Africa', which maps the state of freedom of expression in every African country. European actors can give international resonance to the politics of naming and shaming that is involved.

Supporting advocacy campaigns. Democracy is about citizens taking ownership of their lives and interests and engaging in activities to secure such interests; artists and their organizations need therefore to identify issues such as freedom of expression or artists' rights that need to be campaigned for. In 2012 *Arterial Network* was behind the circulation of a petition to stop the Ugandan government from demolishing the Ugandan Museum in favour of a multi-storey office block; it helped buttress the efforts of four national civil society organizations in the arts who took the authorities to court, successfully. Alliance-building is needed for advocacy purposes as well, since the cultural sector cannot bring about social change on its own and many actors now argue that it definitely needs to collaborate with, and be part of broader struggles. European cultural actors need to be parties to these alliances, in the spirit of transnationalism.

Encouraging 'voice'. Artists need to have the freedom to express their views and be encouraged to do so, as the *Arterial Network* has done through competitions in playwriting, filmmaking (with cell phones) and poetry to encourage artists to find their individual and collective voices that reflect the contexts in which they work, and to bring their insights to bear through their creative work that will then be distributed on the continent and internationally. European arts organizations could help give them international exposure.

Conclusion

The recommendations I have just revisited here were made half a decade ago on the basis of evidence provided by the work of artists and their organizations; they reflected shared thinking and common purpose in the global cultural *zeitgeist* at that time. Since then, the needs they responded to have begun to be addressed across continental borders; Europeans have reached out in the right spirit and their counterparts have responded in equal measure. But they have tended to focus on practical and operational needs, in other words the professional needs of the sector itself. Transnational cultural cooperation is not yet driven by any single overriding moral or ethical cause. This is a major gap that needs to be filled. For there are so many cultural 'bads' at work in the world, running the gamut from cultural destruction to cultural closure...

Surely it is high time for artists and arts organizations inhabited by a true spirit of global cultural citizenship, to come together internationally and build a transnational alliance. In one sense, it is their own wellbeing that is at stake, in the face of multiplying threats to the freedom of artistic expression. There are too many rejections in many different places of the very idea that the artist is 'someone whose place is to raise embarrassing questions, to confront orthodoxy and dogma, to be someone who cannot easily be co-opted by governments or corporations'.[12]

Notes

1 It is also true that arts organizations joined forces internationally in the early 2000s to push for the elaboration and adoption of the Convention and contributed decisively to these processes. But once again, they were able to do so only because of the encouragement and funding of the government of Canada, under whose auspices the precursor to today's International Federation of Coalitions for Cultural Diversity was created (see Galia Saouma and Yudhishthir R. Isar, 'Cultural Diversity at UNESCO: The Trajectory Seen Critically', in *Globalization, Culture and Development: The UNESCO Convention on Cultural Diversity*, ed. Christiaan de Beukelaer, Miikka Pyykkonen and J.P. Singh (Basingstoke: Palgrave Macmillan, 2015).

2 This analysis by Andrew Firmin, Editor, Policy and Research, CIVICUS, will be one of the chapters in a forthcoming report on the implementation of the Convention to be published by UNESCO in late 2017.

3 CSO = Civil Society Organization.

4 Reification is the mental process of transforming concepts into things.

5 'Arts production' refers to artists and creatives themselves, while 'arts delivery' covers cultural operators (to use a term favoured in European Union circles), activists and organizations.

6 Neera Chandoke, 'What the hell is "civil society"?', on opendemocracy.net, www.opendemocracy.net/democracy-open_politics/article_2375.jsp (accessed 6 April 2017).

7 Gerard Delanty, 'Citizenship as a Learning Process', 2007, www.eurozine.com/articles/2007-06-30-delanty-en.html.

8 Nick Stevenson, *Cultural Citizenship: Cosmopolitan Questions* (Milton Keynes: Open University Press, 2003).

9 Terry Eagleton, *The Idea of Culture* (Oxford: Blackwell, 2000).

10 Formulations borrowed from Charles D. Kleymeyer's pioneering book *Cultural Expression and Grassroots Development* (Boulder and London: Lynne Riener, 1994).

11 Developments across the world regarding the freedom of artistic expression will also be analyzed in the UNESCO report referred to above.

12 This admirable formulation is taken from Edward Said's *Representations of the Intellectual* (New York: Vintage, 1996).

IAL

ULTY

Beyond the Violence of Colonial Civility
Examining the Art of Raven Davis

Max Haiven

The Genocidal History of Civility in 'Canada'

Canadian civil society as-such transpires within and is part of an unfinished genocide towards Indigenous peoples. This genocide is also a wholesale politicide, where a settler-colonial social and governmental apparatus has sought, and continues to seek, to systematically eradicate every vestige of Indigenous political autonomy in the name of clearing the land for white-preferential settlement and capitalist exploitation.[1]

In what is now the Canadian province of Nova Scotia, where our story takes place, this process began almost as soon as Europeans invaded, and especially after the conquest of the region by the English in the mid-eigtheenth century. Even before they arrived and imposed their legal and political system on the indigenous Mi'kmaq people – quite literally at the point of a bayonet – the previous French colonists had already set out to lethally undermine Indigenous civil society.[2] For instance, French Catholic missionaries explicitly set out to use patriarchal Christian scriptural texts and ideology to attack Mi'Kmaq women's power, authority and respect within their communities, with the aim of saving souls but also eradicating Indigenous modes of political and civil organization and replacing it with what they imagined to be a more 'civilized' order.[3] Likewise, French merchants and fur traders surmised (rightly) that the commercial capacities and territorial authority of Mi'Kmaq people were integral to their forms of self-governance and civil life, and explicitly aimed to dissolve it by using liquor to implant forms of addiction that led directly to social breakdown.[4]

The settler historical record, as well as Mi'Kmaq oral histories, make clear that, like many other Indigenous peoples, the Mi'Kmaq were shocked by the *incivility* of European invaders. As Mi'Kmaq historian Daniel Paul notes in his aptly titled book *We Were Not the Savages*, Mi'Kmaq pre-invasion social and political institutions were based not on the authority, legal codes or might of authoritarian sovereigns, but on multiple interlaced living relationships that valued interdependence and autonomy.[5] As such, what Europeans would term 'civility', in terms of values such as politeness, dignity, respect, persuasiveness, tolerance were central to daily life and integral to the political culture of what Glen Coulthard calls the 'grounded normativity' of Indigenous social reproduction: the complex relationality of humans and the earth.[6] If civility is, to some extent, the ability to coexist in peaceful and mutually enriching ways with one's human and non-human neighbours, the Mi'Kmaq social, spiritual and political system clearly held such a virtue in high regard. In contrast, the crass merchant-adventurer entrepreneurs, the dispossessed and exploited press-ganged sailors, the second-rate political appointees and the missionary zealots European powers sent to the Americas, organized as they were under rigid and lethal hierarchies, surely appeared to the Mi'Kmaq as an unimaginable nadir of civility.

When the British arrived, traditional Mi'Kmaq political and social organization, to the extent it had survived the first waves of invasion, was either directly outlawed or rendered functionally impossible by the imposition of British law, gunboat diplomacy or the theft of land and resources that aimed to make Mi'Kmaq people dependent on the colonial system.[7] This followed decades of intentional and unintentional biological warfare that reduced the Mi'Kmaq population to a fraction of its pre-invasion numbers, and with the dead many of the key political and civil traditions, stories and oral histories that were key to autonomous Mi'Kmaq political life were also lost. To add insult to injury, by the early nineteenth century the British (and later the governments of the Colony of Nova Scotia and the Dominion of Canada) had directly forbade or refused to acknowledge Mi'Kmaq traditional forms of governance and imposed on them a political form that was designed to maximize the potential for corruption, clientelism and the systematic theft of what little Indigenous land remained.[8] As became unavoidably clear when the colonial-settler government began to seize children from their families and place them in the infamous church-run residential boarding schools (where they were subjected to unspeakable forms of abuse and suffered high rates of death) in the name of civilizing people they deemed 'savages', the goal was genocide: the systematic obliteration of Mi'Kmaq and other Indigenous people.[9]

The results and resonances of this violence continue into the present day, and are too numerous to mention here. Indigenous people in Canada now live on less that a fraction of 1% of their traditional lands, under a system of colonial management orchestrated from Ottawa.[10] While legal apartheid policies have been formally relaxed since the 1970s, their impacts have far reaching consequences. At various times since Canada's confederation 150 years ago, Indigenous people were barred from using modern farming technology, from gathering in large groups, from leaving reservations without an authorized pass from the white Indian Agent, from practicing their political, cultural, medical and educational traditions, from hiring lawyers, from owning private property and in some cases from marrying outside their community without losing their status.[11] The Canadian government saw fit (and in some ways still sees fit) to determine who is and is not Indigenous.[12] The destruction of sustainable traditions has meant the entrenchment of a system of deadly dependency wherein Indigenous health and social indicators are dramatically worse than those of Canadian settlers, compounded by a long history of environmental racism and increased exposure to toxins.[13] The Assembly of First Nations (the coalition of state-recognized Indigenous governments) sums up the situation in a few brief (conservative) statistics from 2011:

> One in four children in First Nation communities live in poverty. That's almost double the national average. Suicide rates among First Nation youth are five to seven times higher than other young non-Aboriginal Canadians. The life expectancy of First Nation citizens is five to seven years less than other non-Aboriginal Canadians and infant mortality rates are 1.5 times higher among First Nations. Tuberculosis rates among First Nation citizens living on-reserve are 31 times the national average. A First Nation youth is more likely to end up in jail than to graduate high school. First Nation children, on average, receive 22% less funding for child welfare services than other Canadian children. There are almost 600 unresolved cases of missing and murdered Aboriginal women in Canada.[14]

It is vital to recognize that all of this was done in the name of civility and the expansion of settler-colonial civil society. It was justified with recourse to the work of philosophers of civil society including Locke, Hume, Smith and Rousseau.[15] While much of this genocidal work was carried out directly by the state, a lot of it was franchised out to settler civil society: business, churches, community groups, individual families, universities, all had roles to play in, ultimately, the attempted eradication of Indigenous forms of civil society.[16] And indeed, the sustainability and vitality of these civil institutions depended, ontologically, financially, and in terms of legitimation, on this process of eradication. A fine example is the 1857 *Act to Encourage the Gradual Civilization of Indian Tribes in this Province, and to Amend the Laws Relating to Indians*, passed by the pre-Confederation government of Canada that, under the guise of 'enfranchising' Indigenous men deemed by the state to be 'able to speak readily either the English or the French language, of sober and industrious habits, free from debt and sufficiently intelligent to be capable of managing his own affairs', stripped them of Indigenous status and folded them into the body politic, ultimately severing them from their communities, assimilating them into the settler polity (as second-class, racialized citizens) and abrogating their treaty rights.[17]

As Aileen Moreton-Robinson makes clear, the system of settler-colonialism, of which Canada is a product and project, is a joint enterprise, where settlers and their non-government organizations and initiatives are enrolled into participation in, and profit from, a state-led process.[18] Ideologically and affectively, what ties the state and its citizens together in this project is a weaponized notion of civilization and civility that, as Daniel Coleman illustrates, associates these virtues with a normative (if historically flexible) notion of whiteness. Studying a corpus of early Canadian literature and documentation, he argues that 'white civility' was the mobilizing discourse of a national project that was ultimately predicated on the theft of Indigenous lands, the subjugation of Indigenous bodies and, importantly, the complete erasure or abjection of Indigenous forms of political, social and cultural life.[19]

Sherene Razack and others have shown how Canadian civil society is still predicated on a notion of civility that demands constant reaffirmation.[20] Razack takes up the case of Canada's military and allegedly humanitarian participation in neo-imperialist 'civilizing missions', almost universally in support of NATO or US strategic objectives. In these conflicts, Canadian soldiers, peacekeepers, police-trainers, and aid workers are cast as benevolent angels of civility sent to benighted zones of barbarism. In this way, they draw on and reproduce myths of Canada's colonial foundations: bringing civilization and enlightenment to allegedly savage peoples. Likewise, following her previous research into the racist mythscape of Canadian multicultural nationalism, Eva Mackey has recently turned her attention to the righteous rage awakened in settlers whose lives, communities, and expectations are 'unsettled' by Indigenous protests, arguing in part that the accusation of the latter's 'lawlessness', 'disrespect', and 'barbarism' are thinly veiled racism dependent on a notion of 'civilization' associated with a normative whiteness.[21] Similarly, numerous scholars have illustrated the way that Islamophobia and restrictive laws and security protocols in post-9/11 Canada have depended on coding the Arab or Muslim 'other' as not only uncivilized, but also a threat to Canadian civilization itself.[22]

At issue here is the way the legacies of genocidal settler-colonialism leads to a cultural politics in which 'civility', 'civilization', and 'civil society' continue to function as keywords of power. Particularly, they are keywords by which the project of the state, which has now wedded a logic of settler-colonial extractive capitalism to one of multicultural neoliberalism, built racialized and racializing allegiances with citizens and civil society.[23] The myth of Canadian 'civility', the patrimony of a European 'civilization' and the alleged freedom of liberal 'civil society' all work to erase not only the decidedly *un*civil and violent history and present of Canadian settler-colonialism, but a history and present of racialized exploitation and oppression of non-white people as well. It also serves to smuggle these violent Canadian traditions into the present under the blanket of a set of unimpeachable euphemisms. These terms create an often invisibilized matrix of cultural power that normalizes the economic, social and cultural reality of a nation still very much organized around settler-colonialism and racialized oppression and exploitation.

The Violence of Civility in Today's 'Canada'

An example of the use of civility to normalize settler-colonialism and white supremacy has been the accusations of incivility levelled against numerous recent activist and social justice initiatives that have sought to fundamentally challenge that reality. In the winter of 2012, for instance, a grassroots non-violent uprising of Indigenous people from a wide diversity of nations within Canada, most of them led by young women and genderqueer or non-binary people, manifested as Idle No More.[24] This decentralized but still coordinated movement was most publicly characterized by big marches in all major cities and many towns across the country, as well as Round Dances, where Indigenous people and their non-Indigenous allies came together to occupy public space (parks, streets, shopping malls, government offices) with drums, singing and a signature dance where participants (Indigenous and non-Indigenous alike) joined hands and, facing centre, moved in collective rotation.

While we should not underestimate the degree to which these powerful displays of resilience, conviction, and solidarity shifted the perceptions and ideas of many non-Indigenous Canadians, it also awakened a massive nation-wide racist backlash, much of which was directed at the perceived 'incivility' of protesters who had the gall to disrupt civil space and inconvenience law-abiding citizens.[25] As we have seen, this narrative of Indigenous 'interruption' of otherwise civil space has a sordid pedigree.[26] Further, it erases and normalizes the genocidal violence that rendered that space available for colonization, and also invisibilizes the forms of Indigenous 'civil action' (though we should be careful about imposing this terminology) that might have existed *before* the invasion of European nation-states and the implantation of settler civil-society.

Likewise, as part of the massive uprising against racist police violence known as Black Lives Matter, Black activists in Toronto and other Canadian cities have mobilized to challenge these dynamics in Canada.[27] For instance, in the past decade (and indeed, for decades prior) there have been a number of high profile murders of black and racialized people by police in Toronto, and the Service continues to enforce a practice of 'random' street checks (so-called 'carding') in spite of the fact it has been widely condemned as impractical and, more importantly, racist.[28]

Fighting an uphill battle against a self-satisfied culture that believes Canada to be a refuge of tolerance, peace and multiculturalism when compared to its southern neighbour, the US, Black Lives Matter Toronto activists have made the tactical decision to target liberal and cosmopolitan institutions, rather than only conservative and reactionary ones.[29] In part because of the high number of queer, trans and non-binary participants in BLM, in part because of the very public and high-profile presence of the Toronto Police, one of these targeted institutions was Toronto's annual Pride Parade, one of the largest in the world and a major draw for tourists and locals alike with an estimated attendance of over one million. In the summer of 2016, Black Lives Matter Toronto captured headlines and outrage across the country by staging a demonstration against the police participation in the march and the general exclusion of Black people from the planning and public face of the festivities.[30] The demonstration halted the extremely carefully choreographed march – which included Canada's Prime Minister and other prominent politicians as well as representatives of many prominent Canadian banks and corporations – for over half an hour. Such an action not only drew attention to the importance of Black lives, it also contributed to a recent history of resistance to the corporatization and mainstreaming of Toronto's Pride parade in the service of what Patrizia Gentile and Gary Kinsman call neoliberal homonationalism.[31]

BLM's (ultimately highly successful) action, however, brought down a 'whitelash' firestorm of criticism, much of which, once again, mobilized the accusation of (in)civility.[32] As Rinaldo Walcott, Jared Sexton and others have shown, the character of anti-Black racism in Canada and elsewhere figures blackness as the very antithesis of a notion of civilization coded as European and white.[33] The legacies of the world-defining transatlantic slavery, as well as centuries of oppression and violent representations have fixed in the civic imagination the notion of blackness as the paragon of incivility. Hence, the Toronto disruption staged by BLM arrived to many liberal and reactionary observers as both an unspeakable affront to civil space and also as a justification of what they always already thought they knew about blackness. The online comments sections, letters and editorials of local and national newspapers made this evident: in short, the argument typically implied that the incivil behaviour of Black Lives Matter itself demonstrated something about blackness and black people that retroactively *necessitated* the harsh police treatment of Black people in the first place.[34] A pattern is, by now, surely becoming clear: the hegemonic notion of civility is used in these cases precisely to exclude certain groups from participation in civil space.[35] That these groups are uniformly racialized reaffirms the historical record which demonstrates that, even in an allegedly multicultural nation, the notion of civility, and therefore the legitimacy of civilization and the character of civil space presumes white supremacy and settler-colonialism.[36]

Another example has been the remarkable attack on those who would offer criticism of the policies of the state of Israel on Canadian university campuses, especially on those who propose or defend the campaign, called for jointly by Israeli and Palestinian civil society organizations, for a Boycott, Divestment and Sanctions campaign aimed at pressuring the Israeli government to obey international law. In the United States, much media attention was paid to the recent case of the abrupt termination of Professor Steven Salaita from the University of Illinois Urbana-Champaign after what the university administration called 'uncivil discourse' on Twitter.[37] Notably, Salaita's academic and social media discourse centred around the continuities between Israeli and American settler-colonialism.[38] His firing made international headlines thanks to revelations that the university president had abrogated Salaita's academic freedom and superseded the will of his colleagues after coming under strenuous pressure from donors and Board members.[39]

The accusation of 'incivility' is now being widely used by university administrators to attack and undermine the academic freedom of faculty.[40] While new policies of collegiality, civility and civil speech have the pretence of responding to the very real problem of racism, sexism and other oppressive speech and action on campuses, as well as to rampant (highly gendered and racialized) bullying and antagonism among the professoriate, these policies and orientations serve in actuality to place the university further in the hands of an non-academic administrative elite. The growth (in size, power and remuneration) of this elite has been part and parcel of the neoliberal turn in government policy and, more generally, in governmentality since the 1980s, with universities increasingly seen as semi-privatized zones wherein student-customers are given the chance to (go dramatically into debt to) 'invest' in their own human capital, and where, as a result, academic education is reduced to a rudimentary, skills- and performance-based degree mill devoid (as much as possible) of critical or radical thinking.[41] The (ab)use of 'civility' aims precisely to defend and expand these trends.

Beyond/Beneath Civil Action

It is possible to fathom and analyse all these movements and conflicts within the capacious frame offered to the scholar by the language of civil action. But to do so in this context would elide or erase the very real and deadly complicity of this terminology not only in the historic processes of white supremacy and settler-colonialism, but, as we have seen, in its career in our present moment. If we wish to cultivate the radical imagination,[42] that is to say an imagination that fundamentally challenges the status quo by seeking out its roots, then we should ask questions such as: what forms of political and social organization, which today we might characterize as a form of civil society or civil action, existed *before* the settler-colonial invasion of Canada? What might we learn from them, and from how they inform the struggles of those who inherit their legacies, which is to say Indigenous people. Likewise, if notions of civility and civilization to some extent gain their definition through a fundamental anti-Black history, as always-already gaining their positivity and legitimacy from their abjection or erasure of blackness, what forms of political and social organization, which today we might characterize as a form of civil society or civil action, might emerge from the experience of Black diaspora? What might we learn from them, and from how they inform the struggles of those who inherit their legacies, which is to say Black people?

These unsettling questions are not meant to be answered here; they are meant only to disrupt an impulse we might have to fold the forms of radical action we discussed above into a Eurocentric framework that would domesticate them. The radical imagination, as Alex Khasnabish and I have argued, grows through the incommensurable encounter with alterity, though the irreconcilability of thoughtworlds that demands not only better thinking, but the work of solidarity and transformation.[43] As Yellowknives Dene political theorist Glen Coulthard and Mohawk anthropologist Audra Simpson both argue, in different ways, Indigenous political and social organizational forms rarely translate accurately into European or Eurocentric frameworks because they are intimately bound up with the nexus of land, language, community, tradition, history, and relationships.[44] A good example from the Mi'Kmaq world is the term *netukulimk*, which is translated in many different ways but appears to me to indicate the intricate, living, shifting inter-reliance of human and non-human actors in maintaining equilibrium.[45]

The mere fact that, I, a native-English speaking professor with a PhD in English, have such trouble crafting a phrase to explain the meaning of *netukulimk* (after years of trying) not only indicates my woeful ignorance of the Mi'Kmaq language, it also indicates the untranslatability of the concept when it is severed from the living lifeways, relationships and land of which it is a living part. Yet *netukulimk* might be precisely the sort of term that terms like 'civil action' or 'civil society' or 'civilization' ploughed and paved over. When my proverbial ancestors (not biologically speaking; rather those who handed-down my settler-colonial and white privileges and worldview to me) ripped Indigenous children from their families and incarcerated them in residential schools, when they beat them for speaking Mi'Kmaq or practicing their culture, when they insisted those children name their beloved parents and ancestors as semi-evolved barbarians,[46] all in the name of 'civilization', my ancestors aimed to erase *netukulimk* from the world.

For the theorists of the Frankfurt School, especially for Herbert Marcuse, the role of art was to refuse what they called the 'reality principle': the idea that things need to be the way they are, that the capitalist system can potentially satisfy all our desires.[47] The cultural industries, as well as the broader network of relations and institutions of capitalist modernity don't simply exploit and oppress us, they also shape our imaginations into believing that this state of affairs, this order of desire and pleasure, this form of social and political organization is all that could possibly exist. It is a civilization in which progressively everything is instrumentalized, where everything and every person is judged and valued based on its or their capacity to serve other ends, archetypically the ends of productivity for profit and the reproduction of state authority. For these thinkers, art was one of the few spheres of activity that still maintained a degree of autonomy from this logic, an irreducible kernel of purposelessness that resisted any expediency. For Marcuse, art needn't be explicitly political in its form or content; good art (which is to say thoughtful, careful and transformative art) has the latent ability to make us question the reality in which we find ourselves, to light a spark within us that, for a moment (or possibly longer) believes that nothing needs to be as it is.

For Khasnabish and I, this spark is the radical imagination, and we have suggested that it is not something that we own but something we practice, and something that is not experienced primarily as an individual, but in collective and collaborative settings.[48] Art can awaken it, but it is also awakened in social movements and collectives that struggle against injustice and oppression. In my own work, I have even suggested that this spark is always with us, pregnant even in the most oppressive and exploitative conditions: it is a holographic shard of human cooperative potential lodged within each of us.[49] As Cornelius Castoriadis suggests, this is really the substance of the world: all social institutions are composed of the solidification of the imagination into durable forms.[50] Marriage, royalty, the nation: all are abstract concepts given force by the conscription of the imagination that affords them legitimacy. While they may manifest as material objects or be held in place by violence, they are fundamentally formations of the collective imagination which, in turn form the imagination because it shapes social actions. Institutions only remain durable until such time as the radical imagination, that tectonic force within us and at work in society, emerges to challenge this solidification. Castoriadis likens it to a volcanic magma that erupts in liquid form and cools into rock, only to be swept away in the next liquid eruption.[51]

In this sense, the role of the artist is, from one angle, to quicken the flow of the magma, to awaken the eruption, to erode or dislodge the petrified imagination, and to hold open the door for something *else* to arrive. Yet while those of us who work in the Eurocentric tradition hold open a certain door to the future, still hoping in some way for the promise of a Western progressive modernity, many Indigenous artists hold open a different door.[52] It is not only a door to the pre-colonial past because, as numerous authors have shown, Indigenous modes of temporality are not so simple. It is a door held open to a word like *netukulimk*, which overflows the categorical borders of my imagination and of the settler-colonial thoughtworld. And in that overflowing, such a notion might help reconfigure the world otherwise.

The Work of Raven Davis

To elucidate this discussion, we now turn to the work of Raven Davis, an artist and activist working in Halifax, the capital of Nova Scotia. Davis, who was raised in Toronto (Canada's largest city) is Anishinaabe and their work encompasses media including performance and relational art, graphic design, painting, and sculpture and installation. Much of Davis' recent work has involved placing their body in public and gallery settings in order to create a moment where the past and present of Indigenous and colonial history can become visible and to instigate critical questioning and reflection among invited guests and passers-by.

In the Spring and Summer of 2017, for instance, Davis presented a series of works aimed at disrupting the state-funded celebrations of Canada's 150th anniversary. Thanks in large part to the charisma of its sanitized and romanticized British colonial heritage and architecture, tourism remains one of Halifax's key industries, with visitors from around the world flocking to the city especially in the summer and fall.[53] As part of a commission by the Mayworks Festival for Working People and the Arts (an annual week-long cultural event funded by the city's trade union movement and dedicated to social justice), Davis staged participatory performances at a number of the city's key colonial landmarks. These included Citadel Hill, the colonial-era fort built by the British to wage war on the Mi'Kmaq and French populations of Nova Scotia, and the controversial downtown statue of Edward Cornwallis, the British aristocrat who is credited with founding the city (on stolen Mi'Kmaq land), but who also is infamous for placing a bounty on the severed scalps of Mi'Kmaq children, women and men.[54] Davis explains that Cornwallis' actions were consistent with, and helped reinforce, the methods of colonial violence that were implemented and resonated well beyond Mi'Kmaqi: in a sense, he is synecdoche for a much larger process.

During their performance, Davis had themselves bound with ropes to these landmarks, asking audiences to consider how the civil and orderly spectacle of Halifax's and Canada's history and built environment are bound up in a violent colonial history. This history in turn binds up the bodies and fates of Indigenous (and, in different ways, non-Indigenous) people and acts as a constant and visual reminder of the genocide Indigenous people have endured and continue to face. Facing the landmark, Davis placed, for the duration of the performance, two pieces of furniture. One was a custom-built church pew, designed by Davis, complete with a pad for kneeling in prayer. However, upholstered on the kneeling pad was the image of the Canadian flag, inviting the audience to question the national project of 'civilizing the Indian' as the (literal and figurative) basis and support for their own hopes, aspirations and prayers. It also called attention to the ways in which religion was used as an oppressive force against Indigenous people to separate them from traditions, community and land. To compliment this intention, Davis created replicas of an actual 1971 prayer book titled *Look and Live*, which was originally customized specifically to proselytize to Indigenous people in Canada and featured stereotypical and demeaning images and text that implicitly and explicitly denigrated traditional Indigenous cultures and spirituality. Beside the pew, a small table also held a box of a dozen white eggs, each emblazoned with a red maple leaf, the symbol of Canada that appears at the centre of the nation's flag.

As Davis explained, the audience was invited to make a choice about how to respond to their Indigenous body bound to the nationalist monument: would they react violently and throw the eggs, acting on hate and racism in a public forum? Or would they take a moment for a deep, spiritual questioning of the way the impacts of historical injustice 'ripple' through the present? Such turbulence is part of the shared context of power and resistance that defines contemporary Canadian society and shapes the audience and the performer as subjects. Here, Davis insists, they are interested in transforming the audience into the performer to highlight the fact that colonialism is not merely an over-and-done history, but a series of ongoing performances of which settlers are typically unaware.

For Davis, this moment of a spiritual reflection is central, and emerges from a history in which, as they explain, foreign religion and spirituality were forced on Indigenous people in the name of colonialism's 'civilizing' mission. Identifying as a queer and Two Spirit person (an umbrella Indigenous designation for those who do not identify with the colonial binary gender and sexuality system, long part of many traditional Indigenous societies in the Americas), Davis notes that reclaiming an Indigenous spirituality is key to reclaiming and rebuilding resilient community in the face of continued violence, especially as it targets Indigenous women, girls and Two Spirit people. Such a spiritual practice is one that is not confined in space to a house of worship or in time to one day a week. Informed by discussions with Indigenous elders, Davis understands spirituality as a practice that can happen in any place, that is located in the body, and that is a force of transformation. This means that political art can also be forms of prayer: 'Every protest is a prayer, every fight is a prayer, in a way', they informed me. 'Prayers don't necessarily mean being in a church.' Davis speaks of art as also a tool of healing and communicating a different sort of civility in a gallery space. 'It is often safer than performing on the steps of Ottawa's parliament buildings. Activist art is also a tool of healing and protest, and can also include prayer.'

Hence a year prior to the Canada 150 performances Davis staged a four-day event in Halifax's main town square, named Grand Parade, which is located between the city's oldest building, an Anglican Church (an institution central to British colonial power, and which ran many of the nation's notorious Residential

Schools), and its city hall, and which contains several war memorials. Here, Davis temporarily renamed the square Grand Pray, lit and maintained a Sacred Fire to honour and commemorate those Indigenous youth lost to an epidemic of suicides, largely due to lack of mental health and other infrastructure on remote reservations, poverty, the intergenerational effects of residential schools, isolation, and also the mass neglect of Indigenous youth in cities across the country. By bringing this spiritual tradition of a scared fire, practiced by many different nations, uninvited, to the heart of Halifax Davis boldly asserted the persistence of autonomous and 'unauthorized' Indigenous presence on Canadian land and forced the colonial-settler state to accept the right and sovereignty for an Indigenous person to pray and practice ceremony anywhere on the land. Meanwhile, it invited passers-by in this busy thoroughfare to engage with an performative act of politicized grief, mourning, and questioning. Davis also notes that this was an 'opportunity to hold sacred space in memory and prayer for those who are still alive and suffering from a lack of mental health services and access to traditional ceremony'.

Once again, Davis' ambitions with this piece were multiple and complex. On one level, this assertion of Indigenous presence directly defies a notion of civil space that is coded and presumed as normatively white, and that assumes that an unruly Indigenous presence can safely be relegated to the colonial past. On another level, it is a direct challenge to the increasing policing and surveillance of public space that has ratcheted-up in recent years thanks to the politically expedient spectre of terrorism; as Davis explains, art can and must be used to fight back against the hyper-masculine militarization of culture and the increasingly authoritarian politics of security. On still another level, this work supplants or re-occupies the colonial realm of civil society and civil discourse – which erases the perpetuation of anti-Indigenous violence – with an autonomous, renegade and grassroots temporary zone of encounter and discourse. Uninvited and technically 'illegal' (such manifestations typically require permits from City Hall, and open fires are almost all forbidden), Davis' spiritual event and art performance challenged the colonial ordering of space, time and authority. Finally, on still another level, Davis' piece countered the civil order of mourning, insisting that the suicides of Indigenous youth across the country needed to be grieved and accounted for in public, not merely in the private realm of family and friends.

It would be overly simplistic to ascribe works like these only to the realm of public art, performance art or participatory art within civil space and civil society. They are not contributions to but *interruptions of* the colonial ordering of civil space and time. They do not exist to be consumed within a capitalist multicultural society but to reveal the shared historical, conditions of colonial violence on which that society rests and on which it continues to depend. Davis' work, like that of many Indigenous artists working today, carefully weaves together artistic practice, spiritual resurgence and activist energies to manifest a resurgent Indigenous thoughtworld in the midst of the colonial norm. Davis take care to create circumstances where Indigenous and non-Indigenous bodies and minds must meet on a new social terrain, which is also always-already the denaturalized terrain of history and colonialism, and craft their social relations anew. These acts, rather than simply provoke and antagonize, implore us to recognize that *other forms of civility are possible* and waiting to be (re)discovered, and that the settler-colonial (white) civility that rules today is, in fact, deeply uncivil, even by its own skewed standards.

Davis reflects that the institutions of the Canadian colonial settler state, including the institutions they target in their work (historical sites, government bureaucracies, etc.), are keen to 'include' Indigenous work they presume will be amenable to their expectations. They are eager to incorporate traditional Indigenous dance, drumming and regalia into civil spectacles. Davis suggest that, while the beauty and gravity of these performances should indeed be honoured, this hunger for 'tradition' can be used to erase the lived and political realities of Indigenous people. Likewise, Taiaiake Alfred, among others, has noted that key to the particularly Canadian forms of settler-colonialism is the *cultural* 'inclusion' of Indigenous people, so long as this inclusion is seen as one aspect of a multicultural fabric of Canadian civil society. At the point when Indigenous culture and spirituality challenge the bedrock of the Canadian colonial settler-state – for instance, when Indigenous people reclaim stolen land, or defend the land from capitalist ecological terrorism, or insist on making ongoing colonial violence an unavoidable public issue – the much-fabled tolerance, politeness, and civility of Canada and Canadians disappear, often replaced with virulent anger. Eva Mackey refers to this moment as one of 'unsettled expectations' where settlers' presumption of their right to continue to enjoy the lands, resources and 'peace' promised by the settler-state is imperilled by the actuality of Indigenous presence and protest.[55]

I read Davis' work as aimed precisely at using the space and power that the field of art provides to unsettle expectations. By placing their Two Spirit Indigenous body in allegedly civil space, but resolutely insisting that the silenced history and present-day reality of colonial violence be addressed, and by crafting ambivalent, agent-driven public spectacles, Davis aims to quicken a form of radical questioning. While this occurs *within* the spaces and architectures of colonial civil society it is not *of* that civil society, but poses deeper question about what, precisely, society, community and civility might mean on stolen lands.

Yet Davis also notes that the objective of their intention is not only to speak to and disrupt the expectations of settlers. They insist that the most vital aspect of their work is to reach Indigenous people and people of colour in Canada and in their community, especially to youth. The parent of three teenage sons, Davis reflects that 'anything I do is, in some way, for my children, and for the future generations'. They continue that 'It doesn't bother me if a middle-aged person comes to the gallery and loves the work or hates it. I want to know: what does a young person seeing themselves reflected in the work think?' Davis is critical of many conventional galleries that are not welcoming to or interested in young BIPOC (Black, Indigenous and People of Colour) people and what they have to offer.

At work here, I would suggest, is a challenge towards the role of art in colonial social reproduction. Appreciation of art is encouraged by the colonial school system, but largely in ways that use the gallery to compel young people to be civil subjects: dutifully filing past famous works of art in silence in galleries, not so much casting their gaze on the artworks but having the artworks and the institution as a whole cast its disciplinary gaze upon them, insisting they behave and conform. This resonates with Davis' observations about the way conventional religion has been used as a disciplinary force to 'civilize' young people, especially Indigenous youth. Davis' work, on the other hand, encourages a different form of engagement between young (and not young) people and art, one that incites a moment of anti-colonial recognition. For Glen Coulthard, this moment of (dis-)recognition is key.[56] Drawing on the work of Frantz Fanon, he argues that the revolutionary moment comes when the colonized subject ceases to look to the colonizer for recognition and, instead, begins to look to their own traditions and struggles for a sense of power, solidarity, and value. For Coulthard, a rejection of the 'colonial politics of recognition', which extends to the political realm where Indigenous people and nations are encouraged to seek standing with and rights within the colonial-settler legal and financial apparatus, is central to the survival of Indigenous people. As the late Patrick Wolfe explained, once they abandon the politics of direct genocidal elimination of Indigenous people, colonial-settler states turn towards an equally but more subtly genocidal politics of 'inclusion' that aims to subsume Indigenous people into a body politic and supplant them by appropriating, claiming and appointing itself the 'protector' of Indigenous culture.[57] To accept such a status would undermine the forms of relationality to land and 'grounded normativity' that is at the heart of Indigenous life and thoughtworlds. Hence, for Coulthard, the need to struggle, on the cultural and the material level, for autonomy, solidarity, and collective power – indeed, in ways that reject the separation of cultural and material realms.

I see Davis' work as precisely operating at the fraught juncture of recognition politics. Not only does it disrupt and reverse the conventional politics of vertical 'inclusion' of the category of 'Indigenous Art' within Canadian multicultural capitalist civil society, it also holds open a space – a spiritual, material, artistic, and activist space – for new forms of horizontal recognition to occur. This is the artistic manifestation of a living Indigenous sovereignty, which should not be mistaken for a sovereignty on the model of the colonial European nation-state, nor the sovereignty of the white masculine subject germane to Western liberal philosophy. Rather, this is, as Joanne Barker suggests, a sovereignty of living, place-based relationality.[58] In this sense, the model of civility and civil action at the core of Davis' work, and at the core of Indigenous resurgence and resistance to colonialism in Nova Scotia and beyond, cannot simply be incorporated into or subsumed under the reigning Eurocentric and colonial models. Not only do they occupy the same usurped space (anathema to the colonial model of sovereignty), they also do not speak the same language.

In our conversation, Davis elucidated a key point: Canada is (grudgingly, and belatedly) a signatory to the 2007 United Nations Declaration on the Rights of Indigenous People, the landmark international document that sets forth protections for

Indigenous life, culture, spirituality, economic vitality, and land rights. Yet the reality of the Canadian economy (based in large part on extractive industries and the expropriation or poisoning of Indigenous lands, both domestically and overseas) and society (which is disproportionately physically, bureaucratically and culturally violent towards Indigenous people) are constantly in violation of this declaration. For Davis, this renders the Canadian state and society in a constant – one might say ontological – state of incivility and disrepute. While the nation may be based fundamentally on a myth of (white) civility, the reality is the opposite. It is precisely in and at this contradiction that Davis aims their interventions.

Notes

1 Glen Coulthard, *Red Skin, White Masks: Rejecting the Colonial Politics of Recognition* (Minneapolis and London: University of Minnesota Press, 2014); Patrick Wolfe, *Traces of History: Elementary Structures of Race* (London and New York: Verso, 2016); Leanne Simpson, *Dancing on Our Turtle's Back: Stories of Nishnaabeg Re-Creation, Resurgence and a New Emergence* (Winnipeg: Arbeiter Ring Pub, 2011).

2 Daniel Paul, *We Were Not the Savages: Collision between European and Native American Civilization* (Blackpoint, NS: Fernwood, 2006).

3 Ruth Holmes Whitehead, *The Old Man Told Us: Excerpts from Micmac History, 1500-1950* (Halifax, NS: Nimbus Pub, 1991).

4 Andrea Smith, *Conquest: Sexual Violence and American Indian Genocide* (Cambridge, MA: South End Press, 2005).

5 Paul, *We Were Not the Savages.*

6 Coulthard, *Red Skin, White Masks.*

7 Paul, *We Were Not the Savages.*

8 Taiaiake Alfred, 'Colonialism and State Dependency', *Journal of Aboriginal Health* 5, no. 2 (2009), pp. 42-60.

9 'Honouring the Truth, Reconciling the Futre: Final Report' (Ottawa: The Truth and Reconciliation Commission of Canada, 2015), www.trc.ca/websites/trcinstitution/File/2015/Honouring_the_Truth_Reconciling_for_the_Future_July_23_2015.pdf.

10 Arthur Manuel and Ronald M. Derrickson, *Unsettling Canada: A National Wake-up Call* (Toronto: Between the Lines, 2015).

11 Pamela D Palmater, *Indigenous Nationhood: Empowering Grassroots Citizens* (Blackpoint, NS: Fernwood Publishing, 2015).

12 Brenna Bhandar, 'Status as Property: Identity, Land and the Dispossession of First Nations Women in Canada', *Darkmatter* 14 (2016), www.darkmatter101.org/site/2016/05/16/status-as-property-identity-land-and-the-dispossession-of-first-nations-women-in-canada/.

13 Alfred, 'Colonialism and State Dependency'.

14 www.afn.ca/uploads/files/factsheets/quality_of_life_final_fe.pdf.

15 Robert Nichols, 'Indigeneity and the Settler Contract Today', *Philosophy & Social Criticism*, 16 January 2013, 0191453712470359.

16 Emma Battell Lowman and Adam J. Barker, *Settler: Identity and Colonialism in 21st Century Canada* (Winnipeg, Manitoba; Black Point, Nova Scotia: Fernwood Publishing, 2015).

17 'Act to Encourage the Gradual Civilization of Indian Tribes in This Province, and to Amend the Laws Relating to Indians' (1857), http://caid.ca/GraCivAct1857.pdf.

18 Aileen Moreton-Robinson, *The White Possessive: Property, Power, and Indigenous Sovereignty*, Indigenous Americas (Minneapolis: University of Minnesota Press, 2015).

19 Daniel Coleman, *White Civility: The Literary Project of English Canada* (Toronto: University of Toronto Press, 2006).

20 Sherene Razack, *Dark Threats, White Knights: The Somalia Affair, Peacekeeping, and the New Imperialism* (Toronto: University of Toronto Press, 2004); Sherene Razack, *Dying from Improvement: Inquests and Inquiries into Indigenous Deaths in Custody* (Toronto: University of Toronto Press, 2015).

21 Eva Mackey, *Unsettled Expectations: Uncertainty, Land and Settler Decolonization* (Halifax and Winnipeg: Fernwood Publishing, 2016).

22 Sherene Razack, *Casting Out: The Eviction of Muslims from Western Law and Politics* (Toronto: University of Toronto Press, 2008); Mehdi Semati, 'Islamophobia, Culture and Race in the Age of Empire', *Cultural Studies* 24 (March 2010), pp. 256-275; Michael Connors Jackman and Nishant Upadhyay, 'Pinkwatching Israel, Whitewashing Canada: Queer (Settler) Politics and Indigenous Colonization in Canada', *WSQ: Women's Studies Quarterly* 42, no. 3-4 (2014), pp. 195-210.

23 Richard Day, *Multiculturalism and the History of Canadian Diversity* (Toronto: University of Toronto Press, 2000); Himani Bannerji, *The Dark Side of the Nation: Essays of Multiculturalism, Nationalism and Gender* (Toronto: Canadian Scholars Press, 2000); M. Nourbese Philip, *Frontiers: Selected Essays and Writings on Racism and Culture, 1984-1992* (Stratford, ON: Mercury Press, 1992).

24 Kino-nda-niimi Collective, ed., *The Winter We Danced: Voices from the Past, the Future, and the Idle No More Movement* (Winnipeg: ARP Books, 2014).

25 See for example Christie Blatchford, 'Judge Slams Ontario Police for Not Breaking Up Idle No More Protests', *National Post*, 7 January 2013, http://news.nationalpost.com/news/canada/canadian-politics/judge-slams-ontario-police-for-not-breaking-up-idle-no-more-protests; John Iveson, 'Whatever the Canadian State Cedes to Theresa Spence, It Will Never Be Enough', *National Post*, 7 January 2013, http://news.nationalpost.com/full-comment/john-ivison-whatever-the-canadian-state-cedes-to-theresa-spence-it-will-never-be-enough; Colin Perkel, 'Aboriginal Leader Fears Idle No More Backlash against Native Students', *Huffington Post Canada*, 1 October 2013, www.huffingtonpost.ca/2013/01/10/aboriginal-leader-fears-i_n_2451254.html. For a broader analysis of this trend, see A.L. McCready, 'Redressing Redress: The Neoliberal Appropriation of Redress in the Anti-Native Backlash at Caledonia', *ESC: English Studies in Canada* 35, no. 1 (2009), pp. 161–190.

26 Adam J. Barker, '"A Direct Act of Resurgence, a Direct Act of Sovereignty": Reflections on Idle No More, Indigenous Activism, and Canadian Settler Colonialism', *Globalizations* 12, no. 1 (2 January 2015), pp. 43–65; Mackey, *Unsettled Expectations*.

27 Phillip Dwight Morgan, 'How Activism Has Evolved for Black Canadians', *Macleans*, April 27, 2017, www.macleans.ca/news/canada/how-the-nature-of-activism-has-evolved-for-black-canadians/.

28 Sandy Hudson and Yusra Khogali, 'City Must Eliminate Carding Data: Black Lives Matter | Toronto Star', *The Toronto Star*, 2 June 2016, www.thestar.com/opinion/commentary/2016/06/02/city-must-eliminate-carding-data-black-lives-matter.html; Jonathan Goldsbie, 'Police Carding: Racist, Anti-Black, and Useless', *NOW Magazine*, 13 May 2015, https://nowtoronto.com/api/content/82a2c486-f9a5-11e4-a027-22000b078648/.

29 Paul Barrett, 'Black Pride Matters', *The Walrus*, 7 July 2016, https://thewalrus.ca/black-pride-matters/.

30 Desmond Cole, 'Pride Has Divorced Blackness from Queerness', *The Toronto Star*, July 7, 2016, www.thestar.com/opinion/commentary/2016/07/07/pride-has-divorced-blackness-from-queerness-cole.html.

31 See Patrizia Gentile and Gary Kinsman, 'National Security and Homonationalism: The QuAIA Wars and the Making of the Neoliberal Queer', in *Disrupting Queer Inclusion: Canadian Homonationalisms and the Politics of Belonging*, ed. OmiSoore H. Dryden and Suzanne Lenon (Vancouver: University of British Columbia Press, 2015).

32 Desmond Cole, 'Don't Mistake Responses to Violence for Violence Itself', *The Toronto Star*, 7 April 2016, www.thestar.com/opinion/commentary/2016/04/07/dont-mistake-responses-to-violence-for-violence-itself-cole.html; 'Blackness under Scrutiny', *The Varsity*, 28 July 2016, http://thevarsity.ca/2016/07/28/blackness-under-scrutiny/; John Ibbitson, 'Pride Controversy: Gay, White Men Were Once on the Outside Too', *The Globe and Mail*, 5 July 2016, www.theglobeandmail.com/opinion/pride-controversy-gay-white-men-were-once-on-the-outside-too/article30760916/; Ashley Dryburgh, 'Some Basic Tips for Discussing Black Lives Matter and the Toronto Pride Protest', *Vue Weekly*, 13 July 2016, www.vueweekly.com/some-basic-tips-for-discussing-black-lives-matter-and-the-toronto-pride-protest/.

33 Jared Sexton, 'The Vel of Slavery: Tracking the Figure of the Unsovereign', *Critical Sociology* 42, no. 4–5 (2014), pp. 583–597; Rinaldo Walcott, *Black Like Who? Writing Black Canada*, 2nd ed. (Toronto: Insomniac, 2003); Philip, *Frontiers*.

34 On this trend elsewhere, see Jordan T. Camp and Christina Heatherton, eds., *Policing the Planet: Why the Policing Crisis Led to Black Lives Matter* (London and New York: Verso, 2016); Stuart Hall, ed., *Policing the Crisis: Mugging, the State, and Law and Order* (London: Macmillan, 1978).

35 For a more indepth analysis see David Theo Goldberg, '"Killing Me Softly": Civility/Race/Violence', *Review of Education, Pedagogy, and Cultural Studies* 27, no. 4 (October 2005), pp. 337–366.

36 On the poisonous ways in which 'inclusion' is mobilized, see Sara Ahmed, *On Being Included: Racism and Diversity in Institutional Life* (Durham, NC, and London: Duke University Press, 2012).
37 'Academic Freedom and Tenure: The University of Illinois at Urbana-Champaign', *American Association of University Teachers*, 2015, www.aaup.org/report/UIUC.
38 Steven Salaita, *The Holy Land in Transit: Colonialism and the Quest for Canaan* (Syracuse: Syracuse University Press, 2006); Steven Salaita, *Inter/Nationalism: Decolonizing Native America and Palestine*, Indigenous Americas (Minneapolis: University of Minnesota Press, 2016).
39 Steven Salaita, *Uncivil Rites: Palestine and the Limits of Academic Freedom* (Chicago: Haymarket, 2015).
40 James Turk, ed., *Academic Freedom in Conflict: The Struggle over Free Speech Rights in the University* (Toronto: Lorimer, 2014).
41 Marc Bousquet, *How the University Works Higher Education and the Low-Wage Nation* (New York: New York University Press, 2008); Randy Martin, *Under New Management Universities, Administrative Labor, and the Professional Turn* (Philadelphia: Temple University Press, 2011), http://public.eblib.com/EBLPublic/PublicView.do?ptiID=717052.
42 Max Haiven and Alex Khasnabish, *The Radical Imagination: Social Movement Research in the Age of Austerity* (London and New York: Zed Books, 2014).
43 Ibid.
44 Coulthard, *Red Skin, White Masks*; Audra Simpson, *Mohawk Interruptus: Political Life across the Borders of Settler States* (Durham: Duke University Press, 2014).
45 Martha Stiegman and Sherry Pictou, 'How Do You Say Netuklimuk in English? Learning through Video in Bear River First Nation', in *Learning from the Ground up: Global Perspectives on Social Movements and Knowledge Production*, ed. Aziz Choudry and Dip Kapoor (London and New York: Palgrave MacMillan, 2010), pp. 227–242.
46 Isabelle Knockwood, *Out of the Depths: The Experiences of Mi'kmaw Children at the Indian Residential School at Shubenacadie, Nova Scotia*, 4th ed. (Halifax: Fernwood Publishing, 2015).
47 Herbert Marcuse, *The Aesthetic Dimension: Towards a Critique of Marxist Aesthetics* (Boston: Beacon, 1978).
48 Haiven and Khasnabish, *The Radical Imagination*.
49 Max Haiven, 'Are Your Children Old Enough to Learn About May '68?: Recalling the Radical Event, Refracting Utopia, and Commoning Memory', *Cultural Critique* 78, no. 1 (2011), pp. 60–87.
50 Cornelius Castoriadis, 'Radical Imagination and the Social Instituting Imaginary', in *The Castoriadis Reader*, ed. David Ames Curtis (Cambridge and New York: Blackwell, 1997).
51 Cornelius Castoriadis, 'The Logic of Magmas and the Question of Autonomy', in *The Castoriadis Reader*, ed. David Ames Curtis (Cambridge, UK and New York: Blackwell, 1997), pp. 290–318.
52 Janette Armstrong and Douglas Cardinal, *The Native Creative Process: A Collaborative Discourse* (Penticton, BC: Theytus, 1991).
53 Max Haiven, 'Halifax Nocturne versus (?) The Spectacle of Neoliberal Civics', *PUBLIC: Art, Culture, Ideas* 45 (July 2012), pp. 79–93.
54 Jon Tattrie, *Cornwallis: The Violent Birth of Halifax* (East Lawrencetown, NS: Pottersfield Press, 2013).
55 Mackey, *Unsettled Expectations*.
56 Coulthard, *Red Skin, White Masks*.
57 Patrick Wolfe, 'Settler Colonialism and the Elimination of the Native', *Journal of Genocide Research* 8, no. 4 (2006), pp. 387–409.
58 Joanne Barker, ed., *Critically Sovereign: Indigenous Gender, Sexuality, and Feminist Studies* (Durham NC and London: Duke University Press, 2017).

Part 2

Getting on the Ground

Artistic Spaces of Civil Action

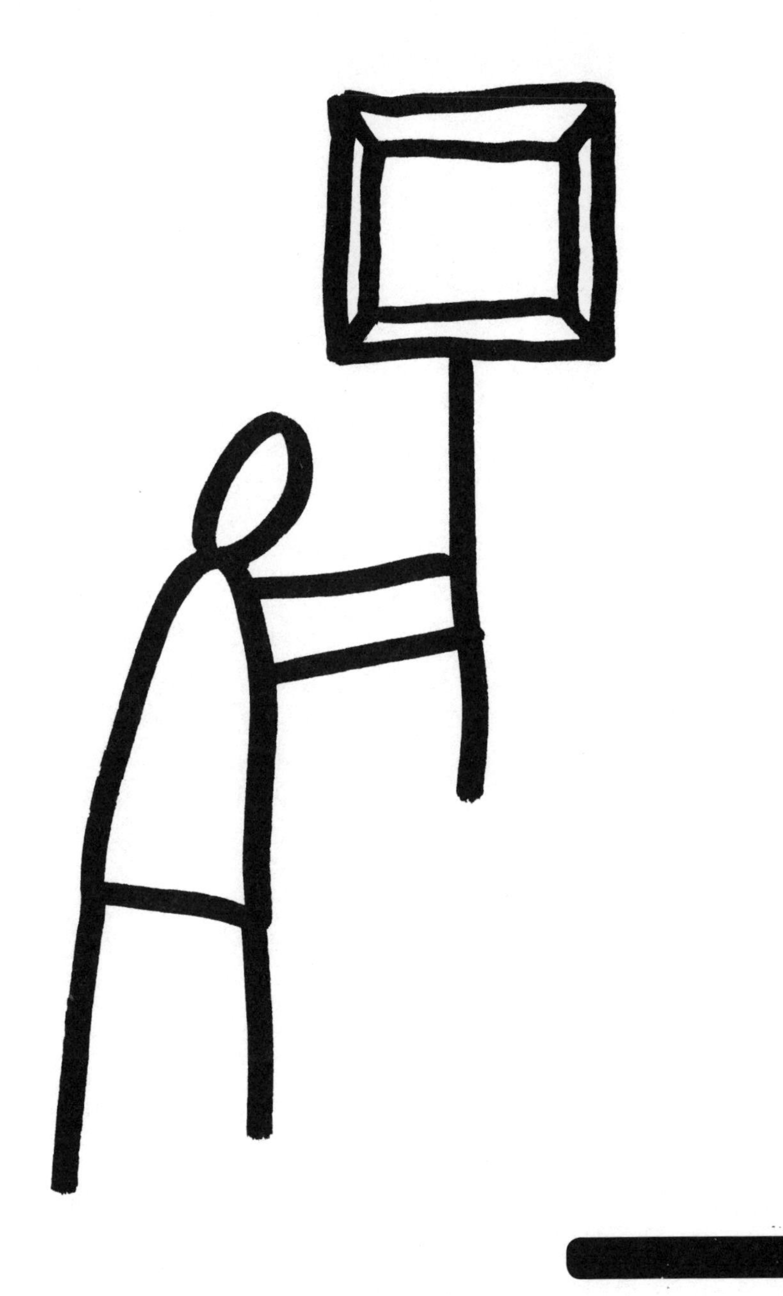

To Give a Voice
A Conversation with Stefan Kaegi of Rimini Protokoll

Giuliana Ciancio
& Pascal Gielen

Rimini Protokoll are a theatre collective based in Berlin. The three founders, Helgard Kim Haug, Stefan Kaegi and Daniel Wetzel, extensively work on installations, site-specific projects, large-scale immersive performances, and public art. Active under the label Rimini Protokoll since 2002, they are pushing the boundaries of western theatre placing political issues and people's stories centre stage throughout their practices.

From the involvement of hundreds of citizens for a *qualitative* representation of a city to a simulation game for twenty people, they 'outsource', as mentioned by Stefan Kaegi, their ideological positions from their artistic point of view to the people. A venue can be a public square, a theatre, an art gallery or a Parliament and, according to their practices, these are not just places of representation, but become arenas in which people are allowed to perform themselves, to meet and to be engaged.

Rimini Protokoll redefine the theatrical event by reintroducing art in the public sphere. They have conferred a civil dimension to the contemporary art creation suggesting a shift from the notion of cultural consumption to a participative democratic engagement.

In December 2016 we held a Skype meeting with Stefan Kaegi while he was working in Chili on the project *App Recuerdos*. He told us more about Rimini Protokoll's practices and tools, the challenges and the values that move their work.

Giuliana Ciancio – Can you tell more about how you create your projects and how you develop them? What is the starting point? When do you feel the need to organize a project around a subject matter?

Stefan Kaegi – One main gesture that goes for many of our projects is that we try to give a voice to the people that are not the most prominent or canonical voices to be heard. It is not the mainstream voices that we try to bring to life in our projects. At the moment I am in Santiago del Chile where we are creating a new project called *App Recuerdos*. *App* stands for Application and *Recuerdos* refers to a very specific concept. *Recuerdo* doesn't mean 'memory' because that would be *la memoria*, which is a very ideological term used to describe what happened in the past. For example, here in Santiago there is the Museo de la Memoria, which is the museum where the dictatorship is being looked at from the victims' point of view and where it is presented as an official statement referring to what happened after all those years when in school students wouldn't hear about people disappearing because of the dictatorship. *Recuerdo* is a term that is much more subjective. *Recuerdo* can be just something that happened yesterday and that I think of. It can be something that is not about the sufferance. It can also be much more simple. That is why we have chosen this term.

The project works like this: we have about 120 contact points all over the *micro-centro* of Santiago del Chile. This area used to be the important downtown area when Santiago grew at the beginning of the twentieth century, where the central market was and where the people from the Andes came to sell their products. During the Pinochet era, the city grew very much in this direction. I can see it out of my window now. Actually, *Las Condes* is a whole new neighbourhood that is for all the banking centres, the shopping malls, the modern infrastructures and where the more wealthy people live now. On the other side of downtown you can still find the palace where Allende was bombed out by the fighter planes at the time. In this area, there are hundreds of such very subjective memories that are brought together.

Here, we are collaborating with artists and scientists from Chile who have been gathering, over the course of one year, subjective recordings about what happened on this very corner. Some recordings can sound like, for example: 'I lived up there in that house. I was looking down at the street when the Pope visited the city. It was s a very important visit in the 1980s when the Pope came here and justified and tried to a little bit to criticize Pinochet'; or 'this is a bank where I work now, and at the time, I was working for the Ministry of Pinochet, and I believed in the neo-liberalism that the Chicago Boys installed in this country'; or 'I was here on the street when suddenly I was taking part in the demonstration when the police stopped, and they arrested me.'

GC – How do you expect that people will see the project? How does it work?

SK – The people will be standing in the middle of a public space, but they will be there with something that is private, the headphones. They will hear something that is a mixture of the private memory of one person and the history of the country. All of these narrations are from the 1970s and 1980s. We present precisely curated situations. We have selected and edited all these memories. We have worked with these people on how to represent their memories of that time. It will be accessible for free and available forever (until the software changes). People can just download the app on their smartphone. For the people who don't have a smartphone, we have places where they can go and borrow one for one day for free. The entire project is totally for free. It is an invisible museum, in a way. You stand on that corner, and now maybe the place of torture is not there anymore. Maybe in the same place there is a hotel now, or you stand in front of the Palacio de la Moneda, and you don't see the tanks anymore that attacked, but you see just the tourists standing in front of it. You hear this story or some of the original recordings that we made, a speech again from that time, and somebody tells you why that speech was very important to him.

Coming back to your first question, this is a concrete example. We don't have a general strategy. For each project the strategy is different, but what we generally do is to try to give a voice to the people that are normally not heard and to foster the subjective narration going beyond what the people post on Facebook every day. We aim to create something that has a political meaning because it's brought together from carefully chosen points. For instance, here we had to fight quite hard to convince our collaborating artists to also include many voices of people who idealize Pinochet. These people are still present in this society. Our point is that it is interesting to present contradicting memories, as they exist in this society. The project is a curated kind of symposium of the city talking about its past.

Pascal Gielen – When you refer to a specific project, you point at a specific concern, emotion or something that you experienced. I was wondering, when you started with

Rimini Protokoll, did you have a kind of general concern or a specific value you decided to point at?

SK – At our beginning, first of all, there was a very big distrust of craft. We didn't understand why theatre should be something made by people that are geniuses in imitation or by geniuses with good techniques. We were saying: *no techniques*.

We were saying that *form* could not be the only interesting key of access. If we zoom back into late 1980s and 1990s, a lot of people in the avant-garde scene were taking very erratic formal decisions about the body (for example look at Grotowski), about the light (Bob Wilson), or about the space (Anna Viebrock). These were very formal approaches.

I came from journalism. That was my first job. And when we started, we didn't want to speak about reality through techniques or only through *form*. We wanted to find new ways. Nowadays, we clearly see ourselves as communication designers. I wouldn't have said that at that time. Theatre has had some phases where it was seen only as a place of representation and of one-way communication. We started saying that communication is good if it has multiple directions.

PG – Can you say a little bit more about that? Because, for example, communication design sounds very technical, but you also have an ideological intention about how this communication should be organized. I was wondering, were there also other concerns? One concern you point out is about the function of theatre at that specific moment in time. Am I right?

SK – Obviously you can say that the *form* shouldn't be the starting point, but still, you will need a form at some point. Often we tried to identify a form that existed and use it as a copy-frame. For example, if we look at the *World Climate Conference* project, it was a very clear and simple thing. We said, 'Let's try to make a World Climate Conference happen as if it is being organized by the UN.' We will shorten it. We won't have two weeks, but three hours, and we'll do it with our audience. 500 people, 600 people came together, and we distributed roles. The form, on the one hand, came from the climate conference format and, on the other hand, from these simulations where students step into the role of a politician for a day. These were the two main decisions. Obviously you have hundreds of details to consider, you have to collaborate with scientists to solve those, and so the whole production came about. I won't go too much into details, but this is to say that we didn't invent a completely new form.

We dis-trusted the gesture of invention by the artist; we rather said let's try to copycat and rearrange existing forms. Another example would be the form of the telephone conversations that take place every day between call centres in India and European businesses or individuals. We have used that format with a different purpose, and from there the whole *Call Cutta Project* came about. Or we decided to use the form of the shareholders' meeting, the annual meeting of the board of Daimler, who own Mercedes and many other car companies. This meeting is held every year at the headquarter of the Congress Centre in Berlin. 5,000 shareholders come together and re-elect the board. This event is so interesting theatrically that we just said. 'We don't need to adapt this form and transfer it into theatre, we just bring people there and call it a piece of theatre.' We wanted immediacy.

Theatre always tries to speak about reality. Even Shakespeare, probably, would have said that, but there were a lot of techniques and interpretations installed in between. If Peter Brook would have made that play about the 'World Climate Conference', he would have rewritten a text that actors then would have studied. He would have given an interpretation of it which then would transfer his ideological understanding of this place.

You might blame me for using a neo-liberal term, but we 'outsourced' the ideological positions from our artistic point of view to the people. We want this ideology to be heard and reframed in a different context.

PG – How do you choose your subjects? What is your drive and what are the main concerns that guide your work aesthetically and politically? Was there a conscious decision when you started with your company?

SK – I don't think I can wrap this up in a general talk. When you are 26-year-old and just coming out of university, you don't have a clear vision of where you are going. We never thought of such a long-term working relationship together. Generally, when you are young, you don't start after school thinking, how can I organize the rest of my life in a very reasonable way. You rather think, how can I do the most non-reasonable things.

The very first project was with people living in a home for the elderly next to the theatre we were working in. There were all these young, fancy artists doing exciting avant-garde creations, and. next door there was this home for the elderly. We thought that these old people were much more interesting than the hipster's interpretation of art with some crossover with electronic music. We went to talk with these old people. Our question was how to bring them on stage to talk about their problems. They were 80 years old and had to deal with things such as breaking a leg when you stand up very fast, or, the in-ear amplification system that doesn't work well because you hear better what is happening behind you than what happens in front of you. We thought that these were interesting concerns to be heard, especially in a crowd that is young and fancy and thinking of art.

PG – Were there some projects you couldn't realize because of obstacles that you encountered? How did you develop strategies to overcome the problems and find your way? Or, did you realize all the projects you wanted?

SK – With *Deutschland 2* we were trying to copy what was going on in the German Bundestag in Berlin and to live-sync it to Bonn in 2001. It was just a few years after the Capital was moved from Bonn to Berlin. Our idea was to copy these discourses made by the politicians and re-enact them with common citizens. The place would be the former Parliament, the Bundestag, *a* building that still exists even today, and it looks like the one in Berlin. We rented it for one day, which was quite expensive. But, before the event took place, the head of parliament – at that time Wolfgang Thierse who still had the possibility to decide what will happen and what not in that building in Bonn – decided to revoke our contract for the rent of the space. He forbade us to proceed, because, as he wrote in his letter, he was afraid we would harm the dignity of politicians.

It was strange because politicians always represent citizens. Why shouldn't citizens be allowed to represent the politicians for one day? Why would politicians be so afraid that citizens would harm their dignity? If you look at who wanted to participate in the project, you could see that they were people who had a positive image of the politicians because they had been in Bonn for so many years – during the period in which the city was the capital of West Germany – and they had seen the politicians from close-by. We didn't intend to harm the dignity of the place with our performance. Anyway, the project was cancelled for the former Bundestag and we could not realize it there.

In the end, we decided to realize the project in a large neutral space, which was rented by the theatre, at the time. We installed a simplified version of a German Bundestag. We put some blue chairs and a large eagle (which is the symbol of the Bundestag). Then, we did our performance there, which took 18 hours. It started early morning and it ended only after midnight. It was a live copy of the debate happening in Berlin. Our speakers had in-ear monitors of what the politicians were saying. 200 citizens of Bonn did this with us.

PG – And examples of specific tactics? In your work you generally deal with people who are not strictly connected to the art field: you have to convince a politician or a lawyer for example. Can you give us examples of how you convince people to make this step into your projects?

SK – Sometimes it is surprisingly easy, sometimes it is a very difficult process in which first you have to identify people, then talk to them and convince them to take part in the project. For instance, right after our interview, I will have a Skype meeting with an insect researcher that I want to convince to take part in a project. The main topic is why Germany has so many big problems in making huge constructions happen, especially when they are publicly organized. For example, the new Berlin Airport BER or the Opera in Berlin, which both are never being finished, or the Stuttgart train station that will cost three times as much as foreseen. The insect researcher can give us interesting insights, because ants are the most successful builders of huge constructions, because of their particular non-democratic model of society. This is theoretically very interesting. So now I will have to convince him to come, bring in his knowhow, spend many days in Dusseldorf (where we are rehearsing) and to donate a lot of his time to our project. This will be the challenge: a very practical one.

On other occasions, you have to face content problems. The latest project we started in Munich: *Top Secret International.*[1] It is about secret services. You can imagine that the people working in this sector sometimes have great difficulty in speaking in public. So, in this case, we made an audio-based interactive system that we set up in a museum space where you can hear those voices. You can imagine that many people, especially in countries such as Egypt, China, Iran, or Russia did not want to speak in front of a microphone about what we were discussing behind the scenes with them.

Reality imposes obstacles. You have to deal with this. When you let real people speak, then they also will implement their censorship on you, on what to say and what not. It is their lives and they have to live with it afterwards as well. It is much more complicated than just giving an actor the text, and he or she will recite whatever you want them to. This friction is interesting to us because the friction often produces more reality than the total freedom in an empty artistic space.

PG – Do you sometimes use your position as an artist or the position of art as an 'excuse' to convince people or organizations to do things they maybe would not do otherwise? Do you sometimes use the argument like 'we just make art' or 'it is fiction, don't mind or don't care'?

SK – To use that argument in front of the people that are part of one of our projects would be cheating them. We never try to make only fiction. An exception may be 'Remote X' for the way in which it is performed. It is science-fiction, not a documentary.

In our view the artistic space, even while knowing that it has a documentary reality of itself, is still giving ordinary people a feeling of... 'okay, here I can say things that I wouldn't say in a political speech in front of Parliament', or '...this is something I wouldn't say in front of my boss. Here I can say it.' Sometimes participants change their names so that they are a bit more protected. These are all techniques that we can then use to mediate, but as I said before, we are not so interested in techniques and mediation. We try to avoid those.

I did a project in Egypt, which was realized with the muezzins that are calling for prayer every day. Obviously they had a lot of constraints about what they could or could not do on the stage. Some of them told us that they cannot play Domino on the stage, others had other practical issues, for example they could not show their feet or the sole of their feet on stage. Things that you learn while doing. You respect, you ask, but still you want them to talk about particular things. It's a long process of negotiation and, of course, of building trust.

GC – So, in this negotiation, what is the role of the theatre that invites you to realize a project? In the negotiation with the people you involve, are they supportive? Do they help you in the mediation? Do art institutions, theatres, who invite you in their programmes, backfire when you go into the field? And perhaps sometimes restrict you?

SK – The relationship with the institutions is maybe not so different from the one with all the others on the artistic team. They will all make their suggestions; it is not just all coming out of our mind. We work with the technicians, the sound designers and find our mediation with them. Obviously, when you choose with which producer you are going to work, you also take a common decision about whom you trust more to make this happen in a good way. In some way, the producers will choose to work with you because they respect your work, and they will try to make things happen, but sometimes they are also good at pointing out problems that they will have. Sometimes they will see difficulties where there are none. So you have to convince them.

An example that I can use for this case is the project *Nachlass*. In the very beginning, I just wanted to place an announcement that said that the theatre was looking for people who were soon going to die and who would be willing to talk, very simple. Panic! It took me months and months to convince the theatre to find a way. I had a lot of difficulties to understand what the problem was, but it seemed that they, as a theatre, didn't want to be associated with the notion of death, or they were scared of invading people's privacy. After, we tried many other ways to find people and finally we convinced them to find a solution.

PG – For example, thinking of a city theatre, let's take the Arts Centre deSingel in Antwerp, which is subsidized by the Flemish Government. Often, in a direct or indirect way, you also criticize the politics of such a government, or of what is happening in the society they are governing. Are art institutions sometimes afraid of what you will do there? Or do they just embrace you, and easily say, 'Okay, let's go for it'?

SK – From that point of view, I think they may be more afraid of artists who live on creating scandals. Perhaps they want these problems because they know that it may generate a lot of press attention. This is really not Rimini Protokoll's attitude. I don't think we have an intention of having this kind of process where you will have a law suit afterwards and make the headline of the main newspaper. These are not the kind of projects we go for.

When you look at China and Russia, you have a certain number of artists that do try to make something radical against their government. Then they run away. And sell this piece, the picture of it or the story around it, to a Western gallery, and they become the kind of radical artists that have had the guts to do it. That way maybe will grant you a place in art history, and you will probably sell well in the West, and it may inspire people to have the courage that they don't have in their normal life. But it may also create a fronts with people who have no idea about art and who are perhaps shocked in a way that they will not trust. It will, for example, mobilize all the Catholics or the politicians against your show, and they will from then on never trust theatre again because they have been insulted in one particular aspect. Basically our idea is quite different, we believe more in seduction than in provocation.

GC – Observing your 100% city format and Home Visit Europe, you use a subjective lens for telling stories about the complexities of a city or for creating a discussion around Europe. In addition to this qualitative approach, with both projects you also register data and statistics. What do you do with all this information? Will you use these data or are they just an artistic output?

SK – It is a tricky question. We are living in an age of big data, just look at how Mr. Trump won his election through these algorithms. Simplifying the complex experience that you have in a theatre performance and shrinking it to the data output of it was never really interesting for us. We did one try, and I am half-satisfied with it, which is the website about the project *Home Visit Europe*. There you can see a lot of data. It gives you a picture of hundreds of households. You see how thousands of people have taken part in an interaction in very different rooms, from poor students' flats to high-class apartments or little hostels, Italian gardens to Norwegian farms to Czech hospitals. They all have played 'Home Visit Europe'. I like this part very much because of its diversity.

Then, on the website, you also have the numeric results which might produce a misunderstanding. For instance, it is mentioned there that 0% of Polish people are interested in political parties or that 40% of Norwegians are afraid of the future. This is a bit dangerous; we are obviously having very specific audiences that are not representative of an entire city. We hope that our website clearly comments our critical view on this.

If you look at *100% Show*, the experience you have is not to say 10% of our city are gay or 15% are unemployed. The experience you have is that you see one person who – I'm just making up an example – may have said in his monologue (at the beginning of the performance) that he works as a policeman; during the show he says that he has also smoked dope, and then later he says he is against foreigners. Through him and all the stories that are part of the performance, you can follow a very subjective trajectory and you can do that because you shared a physical space with these people for an hour and a half, which is the complexity that a theatre piece allows.

By contrast, the quick communication of simplified data is a reduction of what might be an interesting decision, knowing the background and the trajectory of a person is very important, it makes the difference. I believe that very soon we will see theatre performances that will have been informed by this age of big data, which we are just about to enter, and it will be interesting to see where it will lead us.

A Few Thoughts after the Interview...

Burzynska and Malzacher (2017), following Jacques Rancière's *The Emancipated Spectator* (2009), open their book arguing that '...the nineteenth century was a century of actors. The twentieth century was a century of directors. The twenty-first century is a century of spectators'. This is the century in which we are facing different forms of participation in the arts, of political activism and social engagement. 'Theatre has the potential to become a kind of "rehearsal space" for democracy, a place where one's encouraged not only to observe, but to be critical, active, and responsible for what is happening' (p. 9), as Burzynska and Malzacher suggest.

An important shift is taking place from representation towards a multilevel co-creation process that is engaging spectators, communities and citizens, opening up new political narratives. This approach is redefining the relationships between the audience and the artists, the cultural organizations and their way of producing. Rimini Protokoll are actively contributing to this debate. Through their art practices they are offering new perspectives on how producing theatre and democratic engagement. Starting from the interview a few thoughts come to mind about theatre practices and the innovative aspects that Rimini Protokoll have introduced into the sector.

To begin with, we should underline the process of 'formatization' of a theatre performance. Rimini Protokoll intervene in transforming the classical structure of a theatre piece, bringing the idea of 'form' into the sector. For them 'form' is a format that exists and that is used as a copy-frame (as Stefan mentioned above), as the case of *World Climate Conference* project. Maintaining the uniqueness of the artistic experience, they create theatre projects that can be duplicated at the same time in different places across the world, travelling as luggage (as the case of *Home Visit Europe).* The formats created are reproducible and this reproducibility creates the exceptionality.

Secondly, *Home Visit Europe* or *Remote X* or *100%*, are 'forms' that foster the idea of active participation of the audience in the show. The participation is not only consumed in the moment of the performance, but is the creative ingredient of the art project itself. The performances are realized without the presence of actors on the stage, they are built-up according to a participative dramaturgy where the experiences of the people (and the narration of those experiences) are the means for speaking about what is Europe or what are global cities nowadays.

Thirdly, in this process of engagement, the spectator becomes a *prosumer.* The notion of prosumer refers to the digital practices when the consumer and the producer are the same person. Popular books such as *We-Think* (Leadbeater 2009) and *Here Comes Everybody* (Shirky 2008) popularized the idea of a society that was moving towards a greater, bottom-up democracy made possible by digital media. For instance Facebook or social media experiences are 'places' that are filled with content by its own users. Rimini Protokoll brought this perspective into the live performing arts playing with the notion of an open and non-linear dramaturgy.

The venue changes its role, becoming a place of expression and experience. The main focus is the 'reality' that is brought by the attendees. The critical perspective on the reality is provided by the collaboration with experts. They bring a more sophisticated and critical perspective to the creation process, enriching the observation of the pure reality. 'What they want to reveal, by using the experts, is not to capture reality but rather to constitute a typology of this reality that cannot be reduced to the banality perceived by the naked eye' as Katia Arfara (2009) suggests. A 'format' allows the artist to create a *meta-place* where the venue is a terrain of encounter between artists, citizens or experts or shareholders.

Rimini Protokoll create a process-oriented, documentary theatre, that has transformed the notion of 'venue' in a civil space and is able to foster the notion of democratic engagement. Their practices bring to light what is invisible. For example, *App Recuerdo* is an invisible museum that is realized in a public space, placed in the 'air', based on a long process of research and analysis across generations in Santiago de Chile, open to all citizens. They co-write their artistic works with citizens and their practices are transforming the way of producing theatre while enlarging the notion of civil sphere and bottom-up political debate.

Notes

1 Top Secret International is a teatrology that insists on the role of secret services, the growing number of whistle-blowers and the condition of post-democratic phenomena (as mentioned by them on their website). The visitors, thanks to the use of the headphones, can move through the museum playing the role of politicians or secret services, choosing and listening to the audio segments that are the result of interviews with real whistle-blowers or secret services.

Bibliography

- Arfara, Katia. 2009. 'Aspects of a New Dramaturgy of the Spectator'. *Performance Research* 14, no. 3, pp. 112–118.
- Biehl-Missal, Brigitte. 2012. 'Using Artistic Form for Aesthetic Organizational Inquiry: Rimini Protokoll Constructs Daimler's Annual General Meeting as a Theatre Play'. *Culture and Organization* 18, no. 3, pp. 211–229.
- Bishop, Claire. 2012. *Participatory Art and the Politics of Spectatorship.* London: Verso.
- Burzynska, Anna R., and Florian Malzacher. 2017. *Joined Forces: Audience Participation in Theatre.* Berlin: Alexander Verlag.
- Leadbeater, Charles. 2009. *We-Think: Mass Innovation. Not Mass Production.* London: Profile books LTD.
- Rancière, Jacques. 2009. *The Emancipated Spectator.* London: Verso.
- Shirky, Clay. 2008. *Here Comes Everybody: The Power of Organizing Without Organizations.* London Penguin Group.
- Walmsley, Ben. 2013. 'Co-creating Theatre: Authentic Engagement or Inter-legitimation?' *Cultural Trends,* 22, no. 2, pp. 108–118.

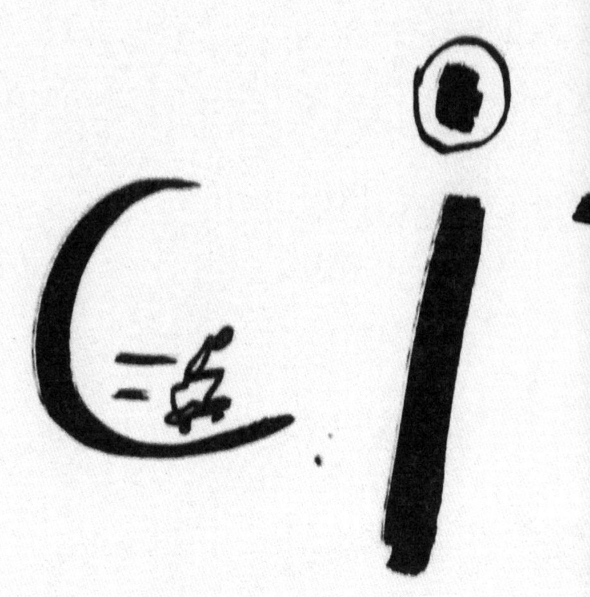

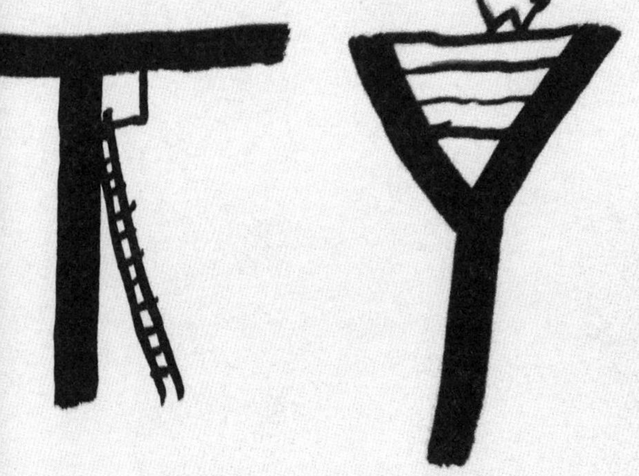

Recetas Urbanas
'Urban Recipes' for an Active Citizenry

Lloreç Bonet

Recetas Urbanas, the architectural studio set up by Santiago Cirugeda in 1996 and run jointly with Alice Attout since 2008, has been known from its beginnings for its capacity to subtly rearrange or subvert the established order, working in the spaces between, in the interstices of the planning regulations, to put forward unexpected urban situations and construction solutions that encourage us to think afresh and act in favour of the common good. The studio's constructions can be thought of as citizen actions that engender a civil space emancipated from the state, not in the manner of Hakim Bey and his famous Temporary Autonomous Zones, where emancipation is understood as a time and a place of exception outside the State,[1] but rather as the emancipation of a group that constitutes itself as an active subject capable of engaging with the authorities and disputing their power as a conscious and proactively purposeful citizen. All of these citizen actions propose an idea of common city, of and from the street, with citizens able to use their power directly, in consensus with other agents.

Recetas Urbanas does not regard its projects as finished architectures, objects that are built and set down in the world. Instead, as the name 'Urban Recipes' suggests, it envisages a project as a recipe, a more or less variable set of ingredients and methods that, as in cookery, have been improving over time, patiently, by trial and error, in the various 'Urban Situations' in which they have found themselves.[2] These are open source recipes, and as such are shared on the team's website, guidelines for anyone to follow and apply in any context, adapting them to their particular situations and personal tastes to develop their own actions and constructions. For the Recetas Urbanas team there is no more satisfying achievement than to see visitors, readers or users of their works going out onto the street and putting their own versions of these recipes into practice.[3]

From the dozens of projects that the studio has carried out, we have chosen the following seven for our analysis of the evolution of their way of working and to show how the construction of an urban building in the community is directly linked to the creation of a civic consciousness in relation to the common, communal space.

Rubbish-free Skips

For decades, the historic centre of Seville had just one children's playground, despite the fact that, from the late 1970s on, various neighbourhood associations had been calling for the provision of more recreational areas. In 1997, Cirugeda applied for City Council permission to temporarily place a skip in the public highway – a very simple permit for an architect to obtain. But instead of the usual rubble container, what he installed was a concrete-filled skip that contained a children's seesaw. By the end of that spring, customised skips began appearing in different parts of Seville with different configurations: a flamenco *tablao* dance platform; a roulette wheel, with pockets marked not with numbers but with urban planning terminology, to stimulate thinking about the public space; a cut-out silhouette in the form of a stylized house, raising the possibility of skips even being used as dwellings, and a series of information panels explaining how the 'skip game' was done, so that anyone who wanted to could take the initiative of installing their own.

This example can be taken as a somewhat schematic synthesis of the kind of approach Cirugeda was already taking in the first stage of his career, which consisted in carrying out an unexpected action that subverts and transforms the customary uses of the public space, with two clear purposes: to construct an object that is actually used for a certain period of time, and to contribute to the creation of an active consciousness in the citizens. The playful, ludic tone of what was in fact a very serious proposal aroused the interest of local residents and the media – and of the neighbourhood children, who wasted no time in making the play facilities their own.

Living on Scaffolding

In 1998, Cirugeda applied for a Seville City Council permit to put up scaffolding from which to clean a façade of some graffiti (which he himself had painted), a perfectly routine administrative procedure for builders. The City Council gave the go-ahead, and Cirugeda legally set up the scaffolding on calle San Luís, on the corner with calle Divina Pastora, in the old town of Seville. The resulting space was then occupied on a temporary basis by young people visiting the city.

A few days later, Cirugeda called a press conference at which he explained that this could be a way of temporarily extending a dwelling, among other possible ephemeral uses. Drawing attention to the fact that the public space could be occupied for four months in order to clean off spray paint, yet it was considered inconceivable that this mechanism of temporary occupation should be used to mitigate the acute problem of access to housing. It was an act of provocation with which the architect sought to spark reflection on one of the most important social problems in Spain at that time.

The press duly picked up on the action, with headlines such as 'Extend your house with scaffolding', but none of the journalists bothered to reflect in any depth on the question Cirugeda had raised, or even realized that the house on calle San Luís was not the architect's, or any of his friends'. He had chosen it simply to test his proposed system on an old listed building with a high level of official heritage protection.

Like other Cirugeda projects, this one engaged with serious issues by means of a gesture that may at first seem jokey or ironic. This citizen action was carried out at a time when the official discourse insisted that the country was doing well, was prospering, when the reality for a very significant part of the population was that they could not afford to pay their rent, and this problem was especially acute among young people, for whom it had become increasingly difficult to move out of the parental home and rent even a modest apartment of their own. What to some may have seemed like a joke was intended to open up debate on a problem that neither the academy (the architecture schools and universities) nor the critics had managed to perceive, let alone resolve. These projects – and here we are simplifying again – replaced the old battle cry of the 1980s, 'squat and resist', with a less heroic approach the slogan of which might be 'build playfully and let them resist you'. The strategy of communication with the media, in equal parts defiant, proactive and witty, served as a hook or a magnet that began to catch and hold the attention of some people in academic and artistic circles.

A Host of Temporary Uses

In 2004, Recetas Urbanas presented the city of Seville's urban planning department with a proposal to place vacant lots at the disposal of local people for use as temporary public parks, for as long as the owners had no need of them. After carrying out a preliminary study of a hundred unused spaces, the team put forward a shortlist of ten possible candidates for the project. Of these, the City Council agreed to cede two publicly owned lots in the centre of Seville as pilot sites. The work of adapting these had already begun when a private citizen turned up at the Council offices with deeds of ownership for one of the lots (thus revealing the somewhat chaotic state of the municipal archives). However, the other site was duly cleared and equipped with old street furniture salvaged from City Council storage, effectively completing an operation in which not a single cent of investment from the authorities was required.

A couple of years earlier, in 2002, Recetas Urbanas had pulled off an even more difficult feat in using a vacant private lot for temporary housing. With the consent of the owner, Cirugeda built *la casa rompecabezas* on calle Barco in Seville, and this 'jigsaw puzzle house' was occupied for a year and a half, until the owner decided to build on the plot himself.

One of the many interesting things about these and other comparable actions – whether the occupations be illegal, agreed with the owners, or existing in a legal limbo – is that all of them stem from a radically proactive attitude that dares to imagine new models for bringing disused spaces to life. Amsterdam's urban plan, which since 1947 has enabled Aldo van Eyck's famous playgrounds to be built on both public and private lots, has been widely celebrated – by Dutch politicians, architecture critics and users, among others – but no European institution has taken up the challenge of exploring or promoting its possible development; for example, by considering the possibility of drawing up a plan for temporary housing as a means of containing price inflation in the continent's major cities.

Although they have not always enjoyed the most cordial relations with the authorities, the Recetas Urbanas team aims to ensure that their actions have repercussions in the city, and with this in mind they are fully aware that agreements with the authorities can bring about real improvements in the long term. In one of these accords the authorities invited Cirugeda to take part in the review of Seville's Urban Plan in 2006, which is still in force today, and which now has a provision that entitles any citizen to ask for the temporary use of a plot (Article 3.3.13). There have been only a few applications so far, but the existence of a legal framework of this nature has supported citizens' initiatives in cases such as La Carpa, the marquee of the Varuma theatre association, and led the authorities to be more amenable to such temporary uses, as in the case of the occupation of the Huerta del Rey Moro.

University Trenches

In 2005, the University of Málaga invited Cirugeda to carry out an architectural intervention in the recently inaugurated Faculty of Fine Arts. The first-year classes were being held in poorly lit ground-floor rooms, and Cirugeda proposed that the students themselves construct classrooms totalling 225 m^2 and a 600 m^2 terrace on the flat roof of the Fine Arts building. The construction system was simple, and based on the repetition of easy-to-learn operations in short working shifts, giving the student workers plenty of opportunity to talk, discuss and get to know each other better. This made it possible for these new students to constitute and relate to one another as a group, and during the construction they began to debate the possible uses of the building and how it was to be managed. Once the work was finished, the students decided that they would use the new space as workshops, in which they would carry out a cultural programme complementary to that of the university. Since they had the key to the building, they managed it as they wished, even on Sundays, when the campus was closed. After a few months, the rector's office started to question the use of the space and to ask whether responsibility for its running should be in the hands of the students or of the university, which had paid for the materials and had hired Cirugeda as a tutor and the professional construction workers who carried out the most complicated tasks. Aware though they were that the building did not belong to them, they also felt that having made it with their own hands might give them a right to play an active role in its management.

The young people who took part in this do-it-yourself construction process learned in a practical way what it is and what it means to build a common space: the only theory was that which was generated in the conversation between the people involved in the work. Even the students who signed up for the course with no other objective than to join in some construction-related work ended up forming part of this informal permanent assembly.

Visually, the classrooms looked like two wartime trenches made of stacked rows of filled sacks, although in construction terms they were more like a tent: a timber frame covered with a tautened awning. The wooden walls were covered with sacks of jute fibre (recycled), filled with shavings of cork bark (waste residue from the manufacture of wine corks), two extremely cheap natural insulation materials. Designing a 'trench' for students to take refuge in is a manifest statement of intent, but the irony does not end here, because what looked like a massive defensive structure with no interior was actually lighter in weight than a tent and had an interior lit by diffused natural light, perfect for visual arts studios.

This construction, designed by Recetas Urbanas, is one of the few of the studio's projects to receive so much formal premeditation. In most cases – whether as a result of budget restrictions, the reuse of existing materials, having assigned part of the formal decision-making to the users, or two or more of these at once – the design worked with is more open, and will end in one form or another, depending on the conditions on site, but in every case the participants develop a personal attachment to the object: the pleasure of doing and making, and of valuing what they have created with their own hands, which fosters the sense of individual and collective belonging and facilitates the good maintenance and ongoing reconfiguration of spaces by their users.

Collaboration with Art Institutions

In 2016, Recetas Urbanas was invited to build House of Words – HoW – in the context of the Göteborg International Biennial for Contemporary Art, organized by the Röda Sten Konsthall arts centre and curated by Elvira Dyangani Ose. HoW was to be a temporary space adjacent to the arts centre, and would be used to host a collective experience activated by the artist Loulou Cherinet. The operative capacity of Recetas Urbanas in the process of self-construction was exemplary: up to seventy people of different ages and backgrounds worked together to create a space from metal structural elements to prop up façades and reused materials, mostly from the city's Municipal Recycling Station.

This being a building commissioned by an institution, the 'action' was itself part of its programme: there was the artistic-cum-political action activated by Cherinet on the artistic/art-expository plane,[4] and there was the construction with the help of volunteers of the building that was to contain the art action. In this case, however, the supposed citizen action was in fact a simulacrum, since there was no authentic group of citizens manifesting a genuine civic demand.

The undertaking of initiatives on the part of universities and arts institutions to promote active citizenship is a relatively recent phenomenon and one that has not always worked.[5] Since the early days of his career, Cirugeda has given innumerable lectures and workshops in academic and art centres around the world. For the architect, these situations outside of his day-to-day activity 'on the ground' are breaks, moments of 'pause', remote from the work of the activist subjected to the pressures of often tense relations between the different parties involved. These 'exceptional' situations allow him to work in a different way. On the one hand he can concentrate on the material aspects of the work, he can experiment and try out new techniques or new materials, a type of testing that would perhaps not be advisable in more difficult situations where children are involved, or where there are tight constrictions of timescale or social conflicts to engage with. On the other hand they give him access to budgets with which to construct prototypes that can then be reused in real situations (often with the support of the institutions involved). These active 'pauses' also allow him to reflect on his own practice in rapport with specialists from a variety of fields, and the sharing of experience in this way often helps him define and enrich his practice, while the reciprocal benefit for the theorists is to find in Recetas Urbanas the practical application of their theoretical paradigms, in real cases that put to the test their thinking about the possibilities of transforming the city and citizenship. Theory and practice have the potential to transform urban planning in our cities and foment policies that bring institutions closer to the people.

Skips and Collectives: An Iberian Road Movie

In 2007, after listening to him give a lecture in Zaragoza, a city planning official approached Cirugeda to congratulate him on his work. He explained that the City Council had needed to relocate a number of families for a short time, pending completion of the public-sector housing where they were going to live. Once the work was completed, the twelve container-type transportable buildings that had been used as temporary prefabricated dwellings would be left vacant, and redundant, and the City Council would have to dispose of them. The official then offered Cirugeda the opportunity of recycling these containers for free if he would cover the cost of transporting them from Zaragoza. Cirugeda had spent years working with groups all over Spain with whom he shared ideals and practices, and he decided to contact them to see who needed that kind of material and could take advantage of the opportunity. He shared out the containers around the Iberian Peninsula and with them the responsibility of managing them, and they have since been recycled and used – some several times over – in various places for a variety of citizen actions. Some have gone to cultural associations: Alga in Pontevedra, M-txea in Pasaia, Straddle 3 in Arbúcies, Nautarquia in Torelló, LaFundició in Esplugues de Llobregat and Asociación Luna Serena de Castuera; some to collectives of different kinds: in conjunction with Todo por la Praxis in Cañada Real the containers have been used in collaborative ventures with social services associations; some to the university groups Trincharte in Málaga, Abierta in Granada and the ESD design school in Madrid; some to the V de Vivienda housing collective in Madrid, and one even ended up in the Bòlit contemporary art centre in Girona.

These containers, which had appeared like manna from heaven, turned out in some instances to be a mixed blessing, since managing collectives and projects is not always an easy task. A number of projects were cut short for one reason or another – such as the container going up in flames or being stolen – but most difficult of all were the projects that failed to obtain sufficient support to achieve their goal. One of those that seemed to be going well was an initiative by the Proyecta group to create a cultural space in Benicàssim. Six containers were adjoined to a small abandoned warehouse at the railway station to create more than 400 m^2 of classrooms for workshops and meeting spaces. The initiative had the backing of the local council and was financed with funds from the European Union. However, a serious mistake was made: no document was signed for cession of the space; all of the agreements with the local council were verbal. After the work was completed there was a local election, a change in the party in power, and the new cultural space was taken over by the council and renamed Proyectalab. The grassroots association was never able to carry out the cultural programme for which it had been created.

One of the most interesting outcomes of the whole Zaragoza containers project was that in 2007, as a by-product of their involvement in it, the various collectives held their first joint get-together, from which has emerged an organized network of self-managed collectives committed to the mutual pooling of resources, both theoretical – information on legal issues, procedures and construction systems – and practical: distributing materials and helping in each other's projects by providing labour. What started out as an informal gathering of local groups went on to include open workshops in its second assembly and, since its third, free open days for anyone interested.[6]

In spite of setbacks and failures, the sum of experiences has genuinely strengthened the network and the groups and made it possible to refine strategies and devise increasingly sophisticated tactics with which to construct self-managed spaces that are effective and feasible in the long term. It has also given rise to new projects, such as GRRR, the Group for the Reuse and Redistribution of Resources, which has created the grrr.tool and made it openly available to collectives across Europe for the exchange of materials; meanwhile another group from Madrid is now developing an equivalent mobile application to make the exchange of resources even more fluid.

La Carpa: The Most Active Cultural Space in Seville

In 2010, Jorge Barroso, a founder-member of the Varuma theatre company, widely acclaimed for its special mix of street circus and flamenco, signed an agreement with ICAS, Seville's Institute of Culture and the Arts, for the cession of an unused plot of public land on the outskirts of the city for four years, with the option of a further four, on which to put up a Big Top circus tent (La Carpa) and embark on an ambitious cultural programme. Friends and acquaintances lent Barroso small sums of money to finance the project until the promised public funding came through (it never did). Barroso had more than ten years of cultural production at his back, and had won numerous awards, notably the prestigious Giraldillo prize in 2006 for the best flamenco show. In four years he turned that vacant lot into a community, a home for some fifteen different groups. The space worked without any kind of subsidy and offered a programme combining flamenco, theatre, circus, cabaret, concerts and more. It had the fullest and most varied daily programme in Seville and became the cultural centre with the highest number of visitors in the city.

The Big Top tent was a 'cultural city', designed to comply with the strict requirements applying to venues for public performance, with emergency exits and access for the disabled. It regularly provided space free of charge to associations and groups whose applications for a small permanent or temporary venue had been turned down by the City Council. It was a focus for theatre people of all kinds, from stage designers and scene-shifters to wardrobe and makeup specialists, and also for artists and activists, such as photographers and architects, which created synergies for everyone, in work and in culture.

Recetas Urbanas worked with several groups to put up the tents and build six more structures, which provided workshop spaces and bases for the collectives and associations that met there, and also erected a pergola for much-needed shade. Most of these constructions were made with recycled materials from previous projects, such as the Spider, a container raised off the ground on six angled 'legs', thus providing an enclosed space and at the same time freeing the space below it as a perfect setting for open-air shows.

By 2014 La Carpa had become the most popular theatre venue in the city and was at the centre of an electoral debate. Although all political parties had claimed to support it, in the aftermath of the elections the City Council was not willing to extend the initial cession of the site. La Carpa had clearly grown too strong and was beyond their control. In the end they preferred to pull the plug on it, while defusing potential opposition with misinformation and false promises. They offered to move it to a smaller alternative site, and raised the possibility of an agreement to cede the 6,826 m^2 Pavilion of the Fifteenth Century, constructed for the 1992 Expo, and unused since, between CaixaForum and the Centro Andaluz de Arte Contemporáneo (CAAC), part of the city's new zone of cultural facilities. This cession was blocked on the pretext that the building was destined to become the CAAC's future visitable warehouse, a project that had stalled for want of a budget. Beginning in 2015, as one institutional promise after another came to nothing, the groups were forced to disperse and relocate elsewhere, and the project was gradually deactivated. Jorge Barroso currently lives in Germany and what was in its day La Carpa is now a parking lot.

Jorge Barroso could have chosen to put on his shows in a conventional theatre. He would have been rewarded with hits and prizes in a conventional setting, and everything would have been much easier, but he wanted to try out a new way of managing the creative space and, by extension, a different way of living in the city. Specifically, this took the form of running a *public* space, which complied (in full) with *public* regulations but did not employ *public* workers.

This citizen action generated an 'emancipated civil space' and it was possible because the participants positioned their work

outside the conventional labour market. They did not look for direct remuneration; rather, what they wanted was to *make* city, to invest that work in constructing a new reality. The remuneration would, in any case, come from the activities generated there, but the first thing was to decide that that *civic space* would exist and make it exist. In exchange for work, the capacity for agency is achieved, or, to put it another way, freedom to act in the city. Deciding to do unpaid work in order to build a circus, a classroom or a school makes it possible to extend and open out the capacity to decide what takes place there, and places the authorities in the position of having to negotiate rather than unilaterally control everything that happens there.

A *Direct Action* Agreed with the Town Council

The Europa primary school in the town of Dos Hermanas (Seville) had no dining room, so the school library had been adapted to feed the pupils in turns, with the result that some children were starting lunch at four o'clock in the afternoon. This situation was evidently bad both for the children's eating habits and for the school timetable. The parents' association had been calling on the education authority to resolve this situation for more than eight years, but at a time of economic crisis and austerity, cuts in public spending meant that the Junta (the Regional Government of Andalusia) was unable to make the budget allocation needed to undertake work that would cost, according to the official estimates, something like 480,000 euros. A group of mothers, sick and tired of this situation of impasse and impotence, formed a pro-dining room platform, and in their search for alternative solutions they contacted Recetas Urbanas. Together they examined various technical solutions to reduce the cost of constructing a dining room that would nevertheless meet all the technical requirements and specifications for a public school dining room. Once it had been demonstrated that the scheme was technically feasible and complied with the relevant specifications, and in view of the urgency of the situation, the town council proposed financing the project, even though it was not competent to do so, schools being the responsibility of the Junta de Andalucía. In due course this problem of competences was resolved by expanding the designated function of the new construction, which in addition to a dining room would be a 'Classroom of Coexistence', something that the town council was competent to finance.

The project by Recetas Urbanas significantly cut costs, mainly by using second-hand public (and some private) materials for the partitions and by reducing the number of paid working hours. Those parts of the work required by law to be carried out and signed off by registered professionals were entrusted to qualified plumbers and electricians, while the do-it-yourself construction was organized in the form of workshops, in which volunteers, both adults and children, worked relatively short shifts on adapted tasks that they could could carry out, even potentially risky procedures high off the ground. Developed out of years of experience, Recetas Urbanas has a protocol by which participants can start working at their own pace and in accordance with their abilities, age, experience and other commitments (and always with accident insurance). The protocol is backed up by safety guidelines, checklists, and explanatory sheets that facilitate communication between everyone involved in a very direct and visual way, so that the construction of a classroom becomes an educational activity in which to learn everything from manual skills to the benefits of teamwork.

This project is a very good example of how Recetas Urbanas works today: its role now is very much like that of a technical consultant, accompanying a process that is started and directed by an already existing collective. It was the group of mothers that had the necessary strength to commence this 'citizen action' and used it, though to carry it out they needed technical, architectural and legal expertise that neither they nor the head of the primary school nor the council technician possessed. Once they had a project that complied with all the regulations and a viable plan of work they could go along to a meet with the authorities and demonstrate that it was their input – their knowledge and their work – that made it possible for the dining room to be built, and therefore they could decide together how that public facility should be.

Without Recetas Urbanas the school dining room would probably still be on the list of facilities waiting to be built: resources that 'society' needs and petitions for but are not provided. Beyond the concrete action of engaging in a successful citizen's struggle, in this case study it is interesting to see how a group of citizens resolved not to submit to the authorities' intransigence and in assuming an active role obliged them to fulfil their obligations. Citizens decide to take on a responsibility and work to address a social issue for which they have no authority, shouldering the risks involved without any kind of payment. In this reversal of roles between administrators and administrated there is an evident process of emancipation from the State, in which the town council and the Education Department recognize their need of this third agent – this 'other power' – to create a facility.

Although it may seem to be a local example that responds to very specific interests, it is worth noting that it was not only parents of the school's pupils who worked to make this 'common good' a reality, but also the parents of former pupils and other politically active citizens with no direct link to the school: friends, neighbours, citizens who decided to get involved because they liked the project and wanted to share in constructing a society of this kind (and not another kind). The strength of this project is clearly apparent in the involvement of the council technician: when someone who has spent years working with bureaucratic rigidity is willing to approve and participate in this kind of project, it suggests that it is indeed possible to change the way of doing things in the public space.

In this, as in other projects of the Recetas Urbanas studio, we recognize an insubordination that is basically all about recovering a measure of freedom: our freedom as citizens to envisage, propose and decide upon new solutions, the freedom to think positively and to use the capabilities of the community to invent new forms of living through which to rescue and adapt the welfare state to the twenty-first century.

How We Govern Ourselves

Although in almost all the situations presented here we have spoken of Recetas Urbanas as a studio that puts forward alternatives to the *status quo* of the city, almost always on a small scale in order to address specific problems, they have no interest in swimming against the tide just for the hell of it. What they set out to do is to draw attention to and correct, as far as possible, the oversights and abuses of the authorities, and always with a view to building a better society, seeking to reach agreements with the authorities, to change legislation and to open up their experience, achievements, and insights to others so that they can be used by the greatest possible number of citizens.

To date, several authorities have attempted to work with Recetas Urbanas on larger-scale problems such as the reconstruction of a Roma village at As Rañas, A Coruña (2010) or the unsuccessful attempt to rehabilitate thousands of rent-protected homes in the Canary Islands through a do-it-yourself construction process. However, whenever the studio has worked with government institutions it has been all too evident that the public authorities in Spain lack the agility and flexibility so essential to the processes proposed by Recetas Urbanas.

The work of Cirugeda and Attout embodies a change in the way of understanding the city and citizenship, at the same time as it provides a set of tried and proven tools for acting in the urban space. Architecturally, they propose an efficient and sustainable way of reusing existing architecture, in most cases piecemeal, although on occasion they have also intervened in whole buildings. In urban planning, their work does not generate capital gains, because it is an architecture of use, and this has very clear implications for the processes of gentrification of our cities, and in social terms their artefacts empower their users as active political agents. Significantly, all of these planes – architectural, urban, social and so on – are present in the same action. How do we want to be governed, how do we let ourselves be governed and how do we govern ourselves? These questions are asked each time Recetas Urbanas is involved in resolving a new urban situation in collaboration with a new group of citizens.

Notes

1 Hakim Bey, *TAZ: The Temporary Autonomous Zone, Ontological Anarchy, Poetic Terrorism*, 2nd ed. 2003 (New York: Autonomedia, 1991). This book by the American anarchist also known as Peter Lamborn Wilson became something of a counterculture reference in the mid-1990s, but although it had considerable influence, its essentially individualist ideology failed to take root in a Europe more inclined to favour collaboration between agents, from the Situationist International to the squatter movement. The most visible expression of Hakim Bey's ideas is the annual Burning Man summer solstice event in Nevada's Black Rock Desert.

2 We explained these recipes ten years ago. See Llorenç Bonet, Santiago Cirugeda and Joana Teixidor, *Situaciones Urbanas* (Barcelona: Tenov, 2007).

3 The Recetas Urbanas team collects versions of its projects, sent to them by people from all over the world.

4 For more information on this piece and on the artist, see the essay by Katherine Finerty at: www.gibca.se/index.php/en/gibca2015/house-of-words/1how.

5 In 2007 Manuel Borja-Villel conceived and ran the 'Agencies' programme at MACBA, Barcelona, in an attempt to create a space for dissent in which institutions and militants could engage one another. The hoped-for coming come together proved not to be possible, but the experiment sowed the seed of today's PEI Independent Studies Programme, which has become a benchmark of the cross between activism and art. See Marcelo Expósito, *Conversación con Manuel Borja-Villel* (Madrid: Turpial, 2015), and *Fundación Macba 30 años* (Barcelona: Fundación Macba, 2017).

6 See the website arquitecurascolectivas.net for more on the activities of these groups. To date they have held the following assemblies: First Collective Architectures meeting. Cordoba, 17-21 September 2007; Second Collective Architectures meeting, Sant Pere de Torelló, Girona, 23-26 September 2009; Third Collective Architectures meeting, Pasaia, Guipuzkoa, 19-25 July 2010; 'Comboi a la Fresca', Valencia, 18-24 July 2011; 'On the right to enjoy the city: housing, public spaces, productive spaces', Seville, 5-8 December 2012; 'Hybrid spaces for urban innovation', Bilbao, 20-25 November 2013; 'The city is not sold, it is lived', Barcelona, 6-13 July 2014; 'PorkinPogress', Santos de Maimona, Extremadura, 9-11 September 2015; 'Tools for an open city', Madrid, 14-18 September 2016.

Regional Experiences of Cultural Activism

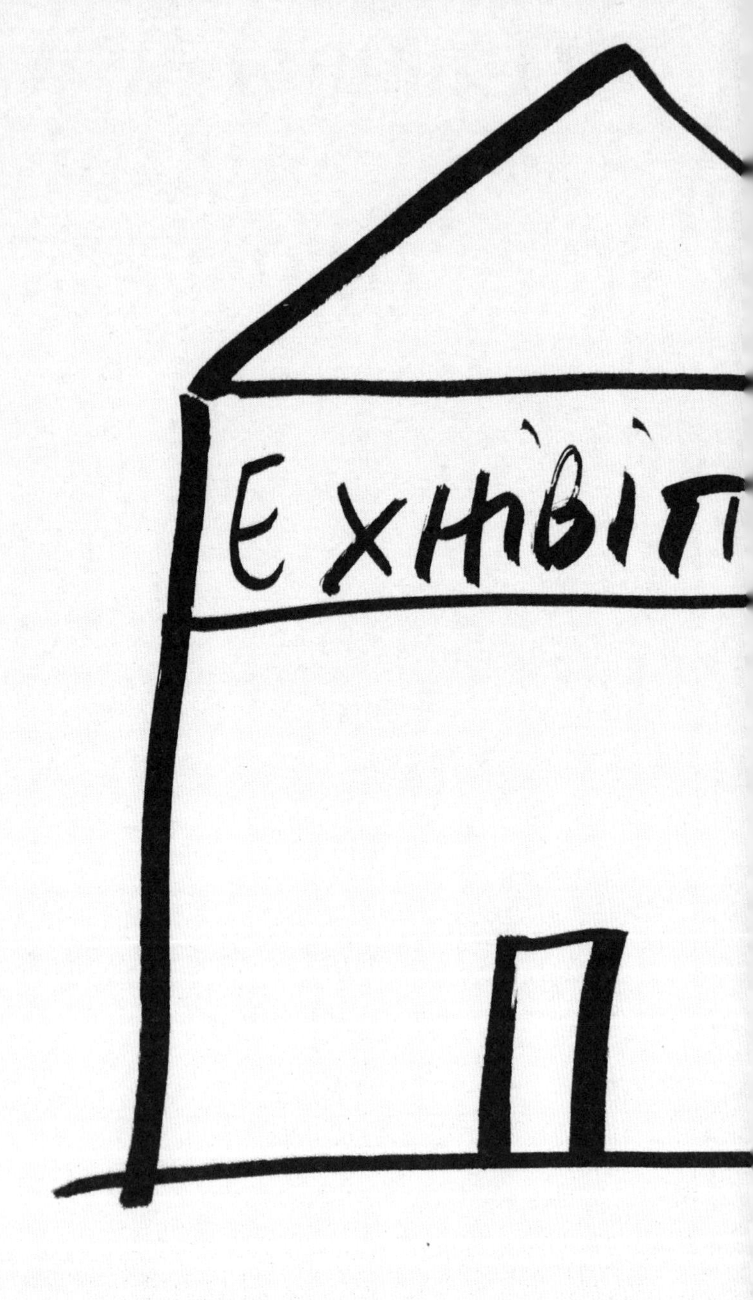
EXHIBIT

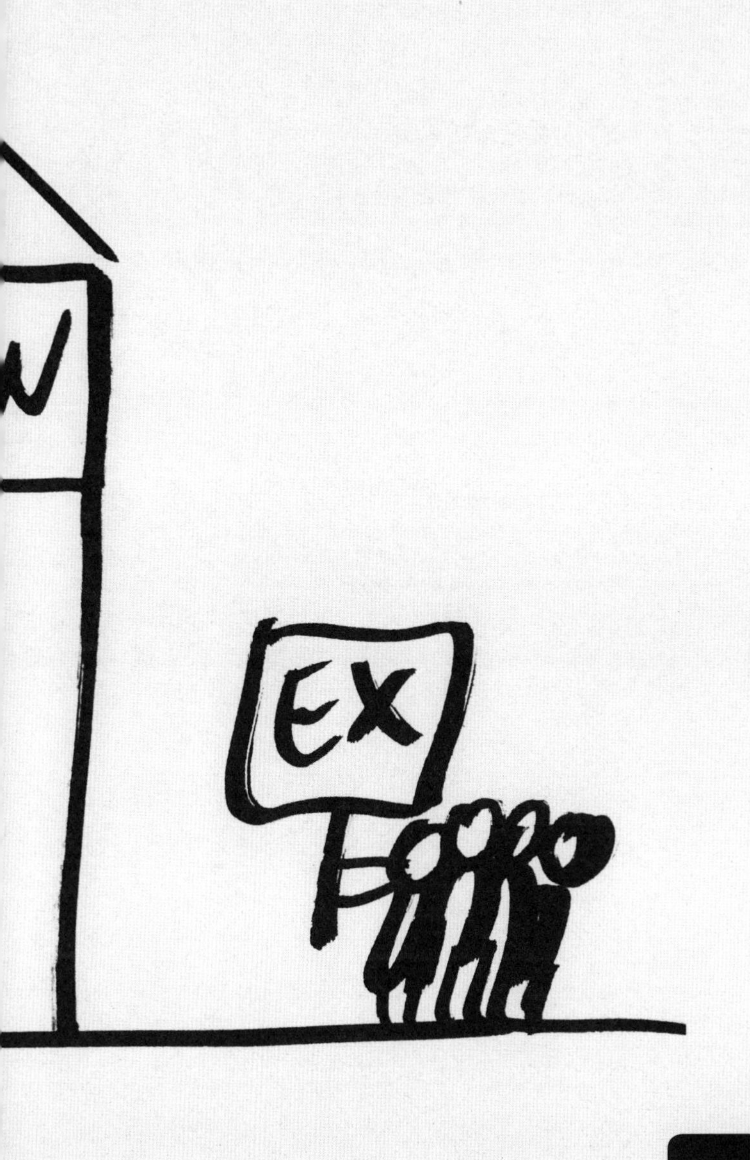
EX

Contradictions in Russian Cultural Politics

Conservatism as an Instrument of Neoliberalism

Ilya Budraitskis

Today, it is accepted to contrast the contemporary Russian state with the Western neoliberal order, which is based on the idea of that political and economic freedom go together. European journalists and experts discuss Putin's Russia as though it were a revisionist state that is not only ready for military aggression, but is also driven by internal destructive forces: a 'populist international' of right and left parties, attacking an imaginary 'establishment'.[1]

Indeed, the idea of Russia's 'special path', that which distinguishes it from Western Europe, has throughout recent years been one of the main elements of Kremlin propaganda within Russia. In numberless public appearances and in official documents, the authority's representatives (including President Putin) have reaffirmed this difference between Western 'individualism' and Russian 'collectivism'. The latter is widely presented as prioritizing common interests over personal ones, which continues to be one of the principle components of the Russian 'cultural code'.[2] However, this 'collectivism', contrasted with materialistic egoism, appears not only as specifically Russian, but also as a universal part of the corpus of 'traditional values'. In defending these values, Russia not only struggles for its own sovereignty, but reminds the West of its own Christian heritage.

Nevertheless, the conservative rhetoric holding sway in Russia today, including attacks on market 'individualism', is organically combined with neoliberal practices in the Kremlin's socio-economic policies. Isolationism, clericalism and authoritarian political methods do not meaningfully contradict the neoliberal principles of subordinating all spheres of social life to the logic of competition and market effectiveness, but create an overall hybrid ideological construct.[3] The cultural domain in Russia in recent years has been both the place in which this hybrid ideology has been produced, and the place of its application. The growth of ideological pressure on state cultural institutions has been combined with the active introduction of the principles of 'economic austerity' and the model of 'public-private partnership'. This situation creates a new challenge for those working in the cultural domain, who must defend their independence in the face of conservative ideological offensives and the logic of the market, guided in equal measure by an authoritarian state. Below, I intend to analyze the particular features of cultural politics of Russian authoritarian neoliberalism, the changing place of contemporary art in the existing ideological set-up, and also the possibilities for new points of resistance for cultural employees in Russia.

The Logic of the Swing Towards Conservatism

The beginning of a swing towards conservatism in Russia is generally seen as being linked to the political crisis provoked by the election of Vladimir Putin for a third presidential term, in March 2012. If during the 2000s the Russian regime preferred to appear publicly as leading a technocratic society, completing its 'normalization' process after the social cataclysms and 'shock therapy' policies of the first post-Soviet decade, then by the beginning of the 2010s, it was faced with the necessity of finding a new ideological foundation for its self-legitimation. In December 2011 there were mass protests in Moscow and a series of other large cities, provoked by the proven falsification of parliamentary elections, and for the more general reason of growing dissatisfaction with a political system that was virtually opaque and unaccountable to its citizens. The position of Vladimir Putin in these circumstances could no longer be designated as one of depoliticized consensus, nor his political regime as a form of continuing transit towards global capitalist 'normality', in which market competition in the economic sphere would organically extend to democratic competition in the political sphere. It became necessary to find a new political language that would continue to preserve the regime while assuming other practices supporting hegemony.

In February 2012, on the eve of the elections, Putin appeared at a 200,000-strong meeting of his supporters who had been brought to Moscow from the whole country for the occasion. The reasoning behind his address was based on confronting a minority that was attacking the historical foundations of the Russian state with the 'silent majority', which was interested in stability, continuity of power, and respect for tradition.[4] In his speech, Putin quoted some verses from Mikhail Lermontov's poem 'Borodino' (dedicated to the battle outside Moscow between Russian and Napoleonic armies in 1812), emphasizing the theme of age-old resistance to the West, whose aim had revealed itself, throughout the ages, always to be the destruction of Russian independence. Thus the authentic source of the protests lay not in internal contradictions, but in external ill will, of which the conscious or unconscious agents turned out to be the oppositionists. In this way, the confrontation became not political, but historic and cultural. It is significant that at the height of the election campaign, the media under Kremlin control had conducted an aggressive campaign against Pussy Riot, who had given their well-known performance in Moscow's Cathedral of Christ the Saviour a week before Putin's speech.[5]

Now support for Putin in the elections was shaped not only by political arguments (the main one being fear of destabilization), but also by the idea of the fidelity of the nation to itself, to fundamental values (of orthodoxy and state authority), without which it would be impossible to protect Russia in the future. Thus, right from the beginning of Putin's third term, questions of culture, history and morals were identified as the essence of politics – its authentic, deeper substance. In such a conservative interpretation, culture becomes 'a new national idea in which the past is experienced as the present'.[6] In the new government structure, put together in May 2012, the post of Minister of Culture (previously non-political) was assigned to Vladimir Medinsky – a public politician, the author of popular patriotic brochures, and a businessman and publicist.

Culture, Security, Competition

In his many appearances and articles, Medinsky comes across as an engaged historian,[7] attacking 'myths about Russia'. From Medinsky's point of view, throughout its history, Russia has been continually subjected not only to open attempts by Western countries to subordinate and deprive it of its independence, but also to a hidden 'information war'. The history of the formation of the national state turned out to be possible only thanks to professional propaganda opposition: 'Without using PR-technology, there would have been no baptism of Rus, no unification, no victorious wars, no transfer of the capital city to Moscow, nor the repulsion of the Mongol invasion.'[8] Thus, Russia's historic choice always not only corresponded to truth ('to the cultural code'), but also turned out to be the result of completely rational decision. This fact, that Russia was able to withstand the pressure of a multitude of enemies is linked with the high competitiveness and effectiveness of her particular cultural and moral values. The principle of 'historic fate' which has constantly, from epoch to epoch, placed the country and nation before external threats to its originality is organically united in Medinsky's approach with the neoliberal analogy of 'effective management'.

History and culture, according to the Minister, represent a place of conflict between the technology of 'myth' creation, with some myths working for the destruction of the state, and others, by contrast, strengthening it. These technologies of 'useful myths', like various other useful tools, must be continually perfected. Or, as Vladimir Medinsky likes to repeat, 'if you don't feed your own culture, you'll be feeding someone else's army'.[9]

This notion of the interdependence of culture, historical knowledge and current issues of national security constitute the basic political strategy of the Ministry of Culture under Medinsky's leadership. In a situation of rapid growth of military expenditure in Russia, the persistent presentation of culture as an important weapon in contemporary open or hidden wars has strengthened the lobbying position of the Ministry of Culture in the fight for distribution of budgetary resources. On their part, Russian military functionaries, right until the beginning of the Ukrainian conflict, actively developed the notion of a 'hybrid war', which included 'non-military' methods in its arsenal along with 'humanitarian measures' 'of a hidden character' which the state should be ready to deflect.[10]

The first practical instrument of such a militarization of culture was the establishment, by presidential edict in December 2012, of the 'Russian Historico-military Society' (RVIO), whose official co-founders were the Ministries of Defence and of Culture. Despite the development of traditional forms of 'military-patriotic education' (youth training camps; costume reconstructions of historic battles), the 'Society' in fact initiated a new stage of 'monumental propaganda'.[11] In recent years, dozens of monuments have been erected all over the country, primarily commemorating military glory. The culmination of this campaign was the unveiling in Autumn 2016 in the centre of Moscow of a large-scale monument to Prince Vladimir, who converted to Christianity in the 10th century.[12]

RVIO, whose chairman turns out to be the very same Medinsky, embodies both the continuity of historical propaganda forms (its very name emphasizes a link with the pre-revolutionary 'military-historical society', founded in 1907), and a model of 'public-private partnership', in which patriotically oriented cultural policies show themselves able to attract private sponsorship. So, alongside high-level officials, the 'Society' includes among its trustees a group of powerful businessmen. Private contributions to patriotic cultural policies appear here in both the category of the virtue of civic participation and long-term investment.

The Crimean Consensus and 'Cultural Sovereignty'

In 2014, after the annexation of Crimea and the beginning of political confrontation with the West, a new stage of the Russian swing to conservatism emerged. From the very beginning, events in Ukraine appeared as not only an internal political challenge, but a direct threat to internal stability. In accordance with officially adopted anti-revolutionary conspiracy discourse, the danger of a 'regime change' was linked with the importing of 'mendacious values' that destroyed the unity of state and society. This hidden internal aggression can be opposed only by a morally healthy nation in which the arbitrariness of individual or group interests is overcome through a commonality of unifying principles. Unity in the face of threat, affirmed through ethics and culture, constituted both the justification for curtailing social expenditure and a general policy of 'economic austerity', imposed by the Russian government in conditions of international sanctions and deepening economic crisis.

The demonization of a destructive 'export of revolutionary technologies' provides universal arguments against any local social protests, with the intrigues of internal enemies being given as authentic justification. In accordance with the decree on the 'Foundations of state cultural policy' adopted at the end of 2014, the vulnerability of the country in the face of internal conflicts is linked with the possibility of a 'humanitarian crisis', which is characterized by a 'devaluation of generally accepted values', the 'deformation of historical memory', and the 'atomization of society'.[13] The threat of such a crisis can become real if a culture is still understood not as an 'integral part of the strategy of national security', but as a sphere in which individual artistic ambitions are realized. However, in principle, in the sphere of culture the state acts not as a disciplinary and punitive force, but as a rational client, whose decisions are determined exclusively according to personal interests. Patriotism, moral values and unity in the face of enemies – these are the sole qualities which the state demands of producers of culture. The logic is simple: if the works do not meet the needs of the state, then it will decline to pay for them.

State interest in culture as one of the key instruments of ensuring security not only does not contradict the neoliberal ethos of 'effectiveness' but, on the contrary, it finds here a natural internal fulfilment. One element affirming this construct is the idea of competition, which determines the attitudes of the state as well as of individuals. Characteristically, culture in the 'Foundations' is perceived as a resource, which, like natural wealth, is advantageous for Russia in the natural state of struggle of world powers for influence.

In his programmatic article 'Cultural Sovereignty',[14] Sergei Chernyakhovsky, a member of the conservative, close to the government 'Izborskii club', defines culture as 'a space for the competition of information and ideas', and state politics in the sphere of culture as a part of global competition for resources and influence. Resorting to the rhetoric of denouncing the 'soullessness' of the West and its 'consumer society', Chernyakhovsky sees these as principles with which it is necessary and fitting to compete. In a paradoxical way, true values must overcome the false not only by the strength of their substance, but also via quality of form. The concept proposed by Chernyakhovsky, is founded on the struggle for quality: primitive Western 'mass culture' must be confronted by Russian 'mass culture of a high standard'. Minister Medinsky expressed this market equivalent of a battle of civilizations in a clear formula: 'a cultural, ideological attack can be countered in the same way as always – with a quality product.'[15]

The time-proven quality of high Russian culture is bound to educate the nation which in turn affirms its accordance with national 'spiritual values' by buying massive numbers of tickets for exhibitions and performances. An example of combining 'high culture' and commercial success in this way can be seen in exhibitions of the classics of Russian art (such as Valentin Serov and Ivan Aivazovsky) at the State Tretyakov Gallery. Serov's exhibition, on from October 2015 to February 2016, had almost half a million visitors. Part of the publicity campaign for the exhibition was a special visit by President Putin. In Medinsky's words, Serov's exhibition bore witness to the 'psychological phenomenon' of the 'limitless attraction of art for a Russian', regardless of 'crises or sanctions'.[16] Classical Russian art stands out for its power of national consolidation, uniting nation and government, higher and lower classes, owing to their common aesthetic and moral convictions. This is an historically proven, guaranteed investment in 'the mass culture of high models', the triumph of the will of the majority, empirically expressed by the masses of ticket-buying visitors.

Here, genuine democracy resists inauthentic pluralism, signified by a right to the equal representation of absolute cultural values and the warped experiments of aesthetes who are distant from the people. Questionable experiments in the sphere of contemporary art not only threaten 'cultural sovereignty', but also directly damage the state.

Conservatives in the Battle for Resources

In this context, moral arguments constitute an important weapon in the struggle for the redistribution of state resources. Significant in this regard was the exhibition 'Na Dne (The Lower Depths)', organized by the 'Art without Borders' Foundation, which is close to the ruling 'Yedinaya Rossiya (United Russia)' party. This consisted of a series of photographs taken from performances at a number of state theatres that challenged 'traditional values' in a variety of ways (nudity, acts of violence, or profanation of Christian symbols). Each photograph was accompanied by precise figures giving the amount of state support received by the show in question. The shocking effect that this exhibition was supposed to have on the viewer was contained in the contrast between the scale of lost resources and the lack in meeting the needs of the majority in a similar art form. The organizers of the exhibition positioned themselves not only as adepts of 'traditional values', but as concerned consumers and tax payers who do not wish to support art that contradicts their moral convictions.[17]

Public actions or legal suits against various exhibitions or shows, initiated by groups claiming to act in the name of an offended 'moral majority', are more and more often accompanied by proposals for an alternative distribution of budgetary resources. In fact, protests in the name of the 'moral majority' constitute part of the 'competition of artistic projects', to which functionaries of the Ministry of Culture constantly appeal. For example, at the beginning of 2015, on the wave of anti-Ukrainian hysteria, having received state funding, a programme to create a network of centres of 'innovative culture' transformed itself into an idea for patriotic clubs, oriented towards the propaganda of 'traditional values of patriotic culture' and a 'wholesome life approach'. A group of conservative cultural activists, effectively hijacking this project, stated frankly that the former concept of 'innovative culture' was ideologically alien and instead of educating loyal citizens, it produced the future participants of 'Maidan'.[18]

The National Centre for Contemporary Arts (NCCA) – an organization created back in the 1990s to support contemporary artists and traditionally characterized by its independence and spirit of pluralism – also confronted attacks on the part of conservative lobbyists at this time. Despite its profile, the NCCA was in fact wholly financed by the Ministry of Culture, managing to create a group of important cultural centres in several regions of Russia. One of the most notable of these was the NCCA branch in Nizhny Novgorod, located in the enormous historic Arsenal building in the very centre of town. After the first exhibition was held in the Arsenal, almost immediately a picket of 'offended citizens' appeared at its walls. Behind the protests against the exhibition was a patriotic organization: 'Great Fatherland', proclaiming its main task to be the 'battle against a repetition of the Ukrainian scenario in Russia'. Its leader, the odious writer-composer Nikolai Starikov, produced an extensive article in which he exposed the leadership of the Nizhny Arsenal as direct agents of Western influence. Nevertheless, the main conclusion of this piece was by no means a call for repressions – Starikov was concerned primarily with the question of the fate of the building in which these outrageous exhibitions were taking place. For the protection of state interests he proposed to the Ministry of Culture and local authorities that the Nizhny NCCA property should be handed to people who could fill it with 'images and ideas directed towards the dignity of the Russian nation'.[19] Despite the fact that this direction remained fruitless, the NCCA as an institution continued to be subjected to attacks from conservative critics. In 2016, the Ministry of Culture carried out a restructuring of the NCCA as a result of which it lost its independence and was combined with another state cultural organization, ROSIZO, and the director appointed was a former functionary of the ruling 'United Russia' party.[20]

One recent striking manifestation of patriotic lobbying was the establishment of the 'Russian Art Union', in May 2017. The new organization, whose main public leaders are the writer Zakhar Prilepin and the theatre director Eduard Boyakov, see their task to be the struggle for 'traditional values' in the cultural sphere. Prilepin openly declares that there is disproportionate state support for projects not serving the interests of the majority: 'The country is living in an imperialist, patriotic passion, and in the sphere of culture, at its basic points of influence on society, nothing is happening.' In Prilepin's opinion, the state in its inertia was continuing to support art that not only directly opposed the interests of Russia, but turned out to be financially unprofitable. Increasing budgetary support for patriotic culture would correspond to the 'principles of democracy', that is, it would respond to the tastes and convictions of the majority of the population.[21] In practice, immediately after the establishment of the 'Russian Art Union', Prilepin and Boyakov were received by Minister of Culture Medinsky who assured them of his support for their initiative.[22]

There is no doubt that from the beginning of the 'swing to conservatism' in 2012, the discourse of 'traditional values' was completely absorbed into the logic of 'creative projects' taking part in the competitive struggle for public funding. The objects of attacks are precisely those individuals and collectives that also take part in the mechanisms of funding distribution. For example, in May 2017, the deputy from Crimea, Natalya Poklonskaya, known for her conservative and monarchical views, submitted an official request for a tax inspection of the production of the film *Matilda*, which was due to appear on screens in the autumn of that year. The film portrays the love affair between the young heir to the Russian throne, the future Nicholas II, with a ballerina from the Petersburg Mariinsky theatre. Ignoring the fact that the film had received state support, or that its director, Aleksei Uchitel was known for his loyalty to the political direction of the Kremlin, *Matilda* became the object of criticism from conservative groups. From their point of view, the image of Nicholas II, officially recognized as a saint according to a decision of the Orthodox church back in 2000, would be discredited by the portrayal of his intimate union before marriage. All the same, deputy Poklonskaya, repeatedly criticizing the film, chose to attack it using the argument of financial opacity.[23]

At the same time, against this kind of background, private institutions – museums or theatres – look like oases of freedom and experimentation, restricted only by problems of self-sufficiency or the preferences of their owners. Thus, the centre for contemporary art 'Garage' or the 'Victoria' foundation (recently opening its own gallery in the centre of Moscow) had not experienced the obvious pressures of censorship or public attacks from patriotic lobbyists over the last few years. Their exhibition policy goals correspond to the standards of Western private galleries (although there are attempts to avoid the most provocative themes, capable of triggering complaints on the part of the police or the Orthodox church). It may seem that the practice of these institutions completely conforms to the place allotted by the above described logic of the conservative swing: the preserve of a minority where it can satisfy its own aims alien to the cultural needs of the nation, and not on the state account.

However, in this capacity they present not an alternative to the state, but an organically composed neoliberal model of 'cultural economics, or culture organized like economics'.[24] In the existing hegemony, the place of contemporary art is determined by a constantly growing social inequality, a current abyss between the majority of the population and a decreasing megalopolitan middle class: if the cultural preferences of the former are voiced by a conservative state, then the critical stance of the latter looks legitimate only thanks to their buying power. The opposition between state and private cultural spheres in actual fact becomes a loss across the whole expanse of culture, which differs from the logic of the market.

Corporate Solidarity and the Subjectivity of Cultural Employees

In this context, the principle issue becomes the subjectivity of cultural workers, their capacity for self-organization and reflection on their own social position. One could say that today in Russia elements of such self-organization in the sphere of culture are characterized mainly as a reaction to direct repressive challenges by the state, without affecting the actual foundations of the hybrid model of neoliberal-conservative politics described above. Thus, the artistic community quite actively took part in a campaign of solidarity with the arrested members of Pussy Riot or the struggle to free Pyotr Pavlensky (after his well-known action at the headquarters of the Federal Security Services in Moscow in November 2015). These campaigns were motivated fundamentally by the demand for freedom of artistic expression, which cannot be evaluated according to political or moral criteria (and accordingly be the object of criminal investigation).[25] Such an approach generally reproduced the pattern familiar from Soviet times of conflict between the repressive state authorities and the heroic individual, confronting conditions of social un-freedom. In the framework of this approach state and society appear as a uniform grey mass, forming a background of absurd 'kafkaesque reality',[26] and opposing it was exclusively moral in character. This reduced picture of reality, continually reproduced by cultural sphere activists, paradoxically does not enter into serious conflict with the fundamentally mendacious conservative cultural politics of an ideological figure claiming the organic unity of nation and government. Despite impressive examples of self-organization, these campaigns are not based on active doubt in the fixed character of conflict between a social minority, interested in artistic freedom, and the majority, silently supporting a repressive response on the part of the state. It turns out that the rights of the critical artist are defended only by those who are interested in their existence (completely in accordance with the cultural theory of Medinsky).

Another example of this contradictory position can be seen in the situation surrounding the raids and arrests at the 'Gogol Centre' Theatre in Moscow, which took place on 23 May 2017. The main suspect, the famous director Kirill Serebrennikov, had in recent years become the benchmark for successful management in the sphere of culture. It is notable that in 2012 Serebrennikov was appointed by the Moscow authorities as director of the Gogol Centre Theatre, as the previous leadership and company were dismissed in response to the theatre's low attendance rate (that is, its 'inefficiency'). An experimenter and opponent of 'forbidden themes' in the theatre, Serebrennikov nevertheless managed to skilfully integrate into the circumscribed model of cultural politics: his productions at the Gogol Centre were popular with the young, educated and well-off Moscow public and demonstrated high levels of attendance. It is in this sense that the characteristic retrospective evaluation of Serebrennikov in the Russian liberal media appears: 'the director's work and that of his theatre in recent years served for many as a space of internal emigration, an escape from increasingly persistent mass cultural trends with their emphasis on blind statism.'[27]

The reason for interrogating Serebrennikov (as a witness) was the charge of misappropriation of funds granted to him by the Ministry of Culture for a creative project. Even if we are to assume that this criminal case turns out to be a falsification, there is little doubt that its cause is in some way or other tied up with the position of Serebrennikov in a state cultural institution and reflects a change of balance of power in the struggle for the distribution of resources. As a representative of the liberal flank, Serebrennikov showed himself to be vulnerable in conditions of increasingly severe competition in the cultural sphere. This was instantly evaluated in moral categories, the pressure of 'an atmosphere of fear' and a return to the time of mass Stalinist repressions. Well-known actors and directors, coming out in defence of Serebrennikov, while familiar with the internal situation in the cultural sphere, thus reveal themselves also as its actors.[28] However, their strategy of defending Serebrennikov turned out to be completely determined by corporate solidarity. Declarations of support for the director did not reveal the real attitudes of the competition behind the prosecutions, but presented it exclusively as a question of censorship and an attack on creative freedom. Thus the well-known cinema director Andrei Zvyagintsev in his emotional piece characterized the persecution of Serebrennikov as 'a blow to freedom of thought in all areas – from political thought to current thought in the area of art'. Behind this blow stands the ill will of the authorities, based on 'archaic consciousness' 'of traditionalists which a huge part of the country reveal themselves to be'.[29] In accordance with the logic of Serebrennikov's defence campaign, his work should not be appraised according to political criteria or moral motives, but should be a public acknowledgement of his talent and the popularity of the theatre he has headed. In this way, the very model of culture as a sphere of competition not only fails to be called into question, but is unconsciously reproduced.

Rooted in the Russian intellectual tradition, the dispute between 'Westernizers' and 'Slavophiles' is today transformed in the cultural sphere into a competition between 'projects' that aspire to acquire public or private funding. In this capacity, the conventional 'Western' cultural project is based on ideas of experiment, is sexually emancipated and hostile to the 'archaic consciousness' that is characteristic of both the state and the majority of society. Its performances make it a target for criticism from the standpoint of 'cultural sovereignty' and make it vulnerable in the struggle for public funding, while at the same time attracting the sympathy of the educated urban middle class, for whom involvement in such art symbolizes belonging to 'the contemporary'. This quality of 'modernity', acquired via culture, represents an important competitive advantage in professional self-realization for the educated middle class.

Contemporary art also continues to present the most successful examples of 'public-private' partnership, and also helps to build up Russia's international image as a developed country that permits criticism and pluralism in the sphere of the arts. One could say that despite conservative criticism from the liberal-elite line, the Ministry of Culture continues to financially support both directions – the conservative and the liberal – whose co-existence and competition ensure the production of cultural products that can be consumed by various social groups. The situation in which the social institution of art itself is transformed into a powerful means of political division of society into a moral 'majority' (organically connected with the authorities through shared values and traditions) and a 'minority' (asserting its cultural superiority over the majority), is completely in the interests of the ruling elite.

The attempt to question the neoliberal model of culture itself, as well as the political manipulations based on it, could proceed from a re-examination of the position of cultural workers as subjects of the capitalist economy. Such a formulation of the question could make cultural issues part of the agenda of the movement for social and labour rights, including employees in other fields. To date, examples of self-organization of cultural workers, centred on criticism of inequality and competition, have been exceptionally rare in Russia. In this regard, we should mention the important, though not serious initiative of the conference of cultural workers in May 2010, in which about a hundred artists, writers, and academic researchers took part. The Congress' programmatic declaration stressed the need to 'be in solidarity with the whole spectrum of struggle against the exploitation of unprotected labour – let's say "hired labour" in factories or supermarkets'.[30] It is noteworthy that after the Congress had finished, its participants went out in a separate column for the 1st May trade union demonstration. The further decline in activity of the Congress was connected not only with the complexity of self-organization for cultural workers, many of whom were not in continuous employment, but with the general crisis in Russian social movements and independent unions in recent years.

Today, Russia is gradually entering a period of political turbulence, which makes the prospect of the rise of a mass civil movement very real. Inevitably, the issues at the centre of such a movement will concern not only fighting corruption or defending citizens' rights, but also the all-important problem of colossal social inequality. This means that in conditions of social upswing, there will inevitably be a growing interest in a variety of alternatives to the very model of Russian post-Soviet capitalism, with its specific combination of authoritarian political practices, conservative ideological hegemony and neoliberal principles of state and business. In such a situation, the cultural sphere, able to critically evaluate its own place in society, can become an important space for discussion of social alternatives.

Notes

1 This idea is, for example, one of the main theses of the expert paper: 'Post-Truth, Post-West, Post-Order?', presented at the Munich security conference at the beginning of 2017. www.securityconference.de/en/discussion/munich-security-report/.

2 'Основы основ: О смыслах государственной культурной политики' [Foundations' foundations. The meaning behind state cultural policies]. Комментарий Института им. Лихачева. http://mkrf.ru/info/foundations-state-cultural-policy/.

3 For example, on the paradox of Russian authoritarian neoliberalism: I. Matveev, 'Неолиберализм с российскими характеристиками' [Neoliberalism Russian style], www.opendemocracy.net/od-russia/ilya-matveev/rossiya-inc.

4 Text of Vladimir Putin's speech at the Moscow meeting, 23 February 2012, https://ria.ru/vybor2012_putin/20120223/572995366.html.

5 The circumstances of this appearance are described, for example, in Julia Ioffe, 'Pussy Riot v. Putin: A Front Row Seat at a Russian Dark Comedy', *New Republic*, 6 August 2012, https://newrepublic.com/article/105846/how-punk-rock-show-trial-became-russias-greatest-gonzo-artwork.

6 Ilya Kalinin, 'Праздник идентичности. Культура как новая национальная идея' [Festival of Identity culture as the new national idea]. 'Неприкосновенный запас' [Emergency Rations] no. 101 (3/2015), www.nlobooks.ru/node/6379#_ftnref17.

7 In 2016, a group of eminent Russian historians, members of the Academy of Sciences, made an appeal for Vladimir Medinsky to be stripped of his doctorate of historical sciences. The basis for this demand was the presence of plagiarism, incorrect research methods, and also Medinsky's adherence to the 'pseudoscientific' view of the precedence of historical myth over fact. Open address: 'О методах научного исследования и диссертации В. Мединского' [On the scholarly research methods in the dissertation by V. Medinsky], http://www.1julyclub.org/node/122.

8 Vladimir Medinsky, Особенности национального PR. Правдивая история Руси от Рюрика до Петра [The peculiarities of national PR?] (Moscow: OLMA, 2011, cop. 19?).

9 Interview with Vladimir Medinsky, *Izvestia*, 17 June 2015. http://izvestia.ru/news/587771

10 Valery Gerasimov, 'Ценность науки в предвидении' [The value of scholarship with foresight], www.vpk-news.ru/articles/14632.

11 More information on the programme of monumental propaganda Military-historical Society can be found here: http://rvio.histrf.ru/activities/monumentalnaya-propaganda.

12 It is noteworthy that the notion of efficacy and market competition as the fundamental driving force of Russian history was also adopted by the Patriarch of the Russian Orthodox Church, Kirill. Thus, in his speech marking the unveiling of the monument to St Vladimir, he declared: 'Prince St Vladimir approached the question of choosing a faith very pragmatically: he sent his envoys to find out where and how God was served', http://rvio.histrf.ru/activities/monumentalnaya-propaganda.

13 'Основы государственной культурной политики РФ' [Foundations of state cultural policy of the Russian Federation], http://mkrf.ru/info/foundations-state-cultural-policy/.

14 Sergei Chernyakhovsky, 'О культурном суверенитете' [On cultural sovereignty], https://izborsk-club.ru/3354.

15 Interview with Vladimir Medinsky, 'Культурная политика должна быть яркой и убедительной' [Cultural policy should be vivid and persuasive], AiF, 23 May 2017, www.aif.ru/culture/person/vladimir_medinskiy_kulturnaya_politika_dolzhna_byt_yarkoy_i_ubeditelnoy.

16 'Мединский назвал успех выставки Серова политическим феноменом' [Medinsky declares Serov's show a political phenomenon], http://tass.ru/kultura/2616910.

17 'Москвичам показали дно современного российского театра' [Muscovites shown the dregs of contemporary Russian theatre], www.ridus.ru/news/185588.

18 ‘Инновационные культурные центры переделают в патриотические’ [Innovatory cultural centres recast as patriotic ones], *Izvestia*, 9 February 2015, http://izvestia.ru/news/582797.

19 Nicolai Starikov, ‘Современное искусство должно быть патриотичным’ [Contemporary art should be patriotic], http://nstarikov.livejournal.com/1534239.html?thread=44477471.

20 ‘РОСИЗО подчинило ГЦСИ’ [ROSIZO taken over by GTsSI], *Kommersant*, 25 May 2016, www.kommersant.ru/doc/2996137.

21 Interview 3, Prilepin, *Komsomolskaya pravda*, 17 May 2017, www.kp.ru/daily/26679/3702725.

22 Prilepin and Boyakov enter into a Russian artistic union, 18 May 2017, https://ria.ru/society/20170518/1494574872.html.

23 ‘Кремль отказался считать проверку компании Учителя “методом давления”’ [The Kremlin declines to consider the investigation of the Uchitel’ company as a ‘method of pressure’], *RBK*, 26 May 2017, http://www.rbc.ru/politics/26/05/2017/5927fa429a7947d007c42818?from=main.

24 Aleksandr Bikbov, ‘Культурная политика неолиберализма’ [The cultural policies of neoliberalism], Художественный журнал [Art journal], no. 83 (2011), http://moscowartmagazine.com/issue/14/article/187.

25 After Pavlensky’s arrest 128 art experts and artists sign a diploma in which they specially attested his status as an artist. For the text of the diploma see: http://archive.is/MYRDY.

26 Direct quotation from one typical reaction to Serebrennikov’s interrogation. Andrei Arkhangel’skii, ‘Невыносимая атмосфера’ [Intolerable atmosphere], *Col’ta*, 24 May 2017. www.colta.ru/articles/theatre/14905.

27 ‘Пришли за Гоголем’ [They came after the Gogol]. Gazeta.ru., 23 May 2017, www.gazeta.ru/comments/2017/05/23_e_10688063.shtml#page1.

28 Деятели культуры выступили в поддержку Кирилла Серебренникова [Cultural activists come out in support of Kirill Serebrennikov], www.colta.ru/news/14920

29 Andrei Zvyagintsev’s commentary on the Serebrennikov affair, https://thequestion.ru/questions/268540/chto-delo-serebrennikova-znachit-dlya-vsekh-nas.

30 The manifesto of the May Congress of cultural workers, https://maycongress.wordpress.com

NON INSTITUTIONAL

CULTUR

From Independent Cultural Work to Political Subjectivity

A Conversation with Tomislav Medak

Philipp Dietachmair

Tomislav Medak is a cultural organizer and researcher interested in political philosophy, media theory and aesthetics. He is an advocate of free software and free culture. He is part of the theory and publishing team of the Multimedia Institute/MaMa. Medak is an active contributor to the Croatian Right to the City Zagreb. He is also an author and performer with the internationally acclaimed performance collective BADco. based in Zagreb.

In 2016, the editors of this book carried out field research with cultural activist groups in Marseille and Zagreb. Our findings from these case studies have substantially informed the text of Gielen and Lijster at the beginning of this publication. Tomislav Medak is one of the many key figures of the independent cultural scene in Croatia we interviewed for our study. Another discussion held in June 2017 complemented insights collected in 2016 with most recent events around the 2017 local elections in Zagreb. Both conversations examined the 'evolutionary or even organic sequence of events' (Medak) that led Croatia's non-institutional cultural scene from independent cultural production to civil action and political activism and ultimately to their engagement with local politics. Our synopsis of these talks introduces how improving the context for Croatia's independent culture since the 1990s provided the conceptual backdrop for socially engaged activist confrontation, which eventually prepared the ground for a new political actor in 2017.

Philipp Dietachmair – You are a member and president of the Multimedia Institute.[1] It is the Multimedia Institute that gave the initial impulse that led to the founding of Clubture Network,[2] which links many different initiatives of independent cultural production from various locations across Croatia, and you are also working on and off with Pravo na Grad[3] (Right to the City) Zagreb. When you think about the situation in Croatia, when the Multimedia Institute started more than 15 years ago, was there a key moment or situation, maybe even some sort of irritation that prompted the establishment of the Institute and all these other organizational structures in motion? Do you see a thematic red thread or overall vision that concerned all of you initiators from the beginning and is maybe still there nowadays?

Tomislav Medak – First of all, all my functions just refer to formal roles because the Multimedia Institute is actually a collective. We have changed roles over time as the new activities, initiatives, and organizations that were emerging from our work required people from the Multimedia Institute to commit more time and effort to these other activities. There is a certain division of labour in all these organizations, but official roles do not necessarily matter that much. Since the very beginning, the defining characteristic of our organization was that it was in equal degree focused on its specific field of activity – technology, culture and theory – as it was on the transformation of the larger context it was operating in. Our interest in critical media culture, commons-based peer production or political cinema doesn't feed directly into our cultural activism or Right to the City activities, but they're attuned, I think. They are a reflection of a specific 'co-gestation' of both the ideas and the understanding of how to intervene in the context.

What defines the broader context of the work of what we in Croatia call independent or non-institutional culture is that in 1991 there was a real caesura, when the cultural system that existed up to that point was reduced to the so-called pillars of national culture that were supposed to implement the ideological programme of the newly elected nationalist government, i.e. to set the Croatian cultural identity as radically apart as possible from other Yugoslav identities along ethnic lines. The rest of the cultural system was either marginalized or totally dismantled. The Yugoslavian cultural system was relatively diversified and it had both a structural place for large bourgeois cultural institutions such as national theatres, museums, et cetera, but also provided material and infrastructural resources or infrastructure that supported alternative and counter-culture. Particularly the Socialist Youth Organization, social and cultural centres, and student centres provided semi-autonomy from the more top-down controlled institutions. This semi-autonomous system allowed artists and cultural workers freedom to experiment, self-define purposes of their work, and express dissent. This was also regarded by the ruling system as a way to sandbox whatever was potentially dangerous or conflicting into a less central part of the cultural system. However, there is sufficient evidence of artistic and cultural production to challenge the prevalent notion that in Yugoslavia there was no freedom to do things that were dissenting and sometimes subversive.

The cultural system was also very much defined by the project of socialist modernization, with the idea that social development and development of culture and artistic expression go hand-in-hand. This was not merely an ideological position. It had an actual socioeconomic foundation. After the Second World War the development of the country was put on course to provide education, work, healthcare, housing, and culture for everyone (or ideally everyone). Accelerated industrialization, urbanization and mass intellectuality obviously required a strong cultural component – be it as architecture, as design, or as diversified cultural institutional field. All of that was part of the socialist cultural system.

Then when the Croatian nationalists came to power they had a very instrumental role in mind for culture. Much more instrumental than the communist party in the previous period. The imperative was that the cultural system should put into practice the idea of national cultural identity cleansed of elements of shared Yugoslavian history and of common identity with other Yugoslavian peoples, particularly Serbs. With the imposition of that mission the institutional system was transformed in such a way that it was purged from its modernist, internationalist and utopian elements. The alternative and counter-cultural segment of the Yugoslav cultural system, which consisted of socialist youth centres, cultural centres in the neighbourhoods of big cities and smaller towns and villages – all of that was either reduced or shut down in the early 1990s. The new national cultural policy had no use for that segment of the cultural system, just as it had no use for high modernism. Its outlook was much more feudal. This meant that people who had been the building blocks of that cultural landscape had to find alternative forms of engagement.

The second defining element of the context of non-institutional culture was that it emerged from the opposition to politics of war and nationalism, resisting the radical transformation of society. The various actors – ethnic and sexual minorities, anti-war and human-rights activists, journalists and public intellectuals, artists and cultural workers, dissenters in general – that found themselves in opposition to the nationalist politics, all converged around the Anti-War Campaign and several media outlets, most prominently *Feral Tribune*.

Within that framework a lot of the modernist themes of cultural production and also some of the figures who were important in the cultural system of the 1980s entered a new type of politically engaged work. It becomes clear when looking at that context of the 1990s that much of what we see nowadays in this much more advanced independent cultural scene dates back to developments of that period. Modernism, internationalism, and emancipatory outlook of the present are in continuity with modernism, internationalism, and utopianism of the period before. There are formative legacies from that period. For instance, the magazine of the Anti-War Campaign *ARKzine*. *ARKzine* started as a fanzine and then it developed into a full-fledged bi-weekly newspaper. It mixed journalism with maverick critical theory and emerging critical digital culture. *Feral Tribune*, the only high-circulation weekly that was adamantly anti-nationalist, merits particular mention. These were the 1990s, the Years of Lead for my generation. Many people who would start doing cultural work in the late 1990s and early 2000s have been informed by this historical context. The Multimedia Institute is only one result of that.

So, to go to back to your question, how come that this segment of culture was so politically oriented? It had to do with the historical circumstances that I just described. Understanding that political activities are not separate from cultural work was important.

Then 2000 was a very important year. We opened our own cultural space called net.culture club MaMa.[4] But also the government changed, the decade-long reign of the nationalist HDZ came to an end and a new social-democrat-led coalition started to transform the cultural system, which resulted in a number of fundamentally new ideas being implemented. The government introduced Cultural Councils at the Ministry that were responsible for the evaluation of cultural projects and responsible for the allocation of finances. These developments also meant that suddenly there was some money for the non-institutional culture. Equally important was that this growing capacity of non-institutional culture carried over into a concern for the development of the cultural system in general.

The problem with the public institutional sector was that in the 1990s it was fully subsumed under the dictum of nationalist politics. After 2000, once the political loyalty to nationalism was no longer the imperative, there was no clear model anymore for appointing the directors and managers of public cultural institutions. So it came down to a narrow managerial principle. If somebody was considered a good manager by political structures, didn't make waves by antagonizing political decision-makers and could guarantee the employees that the public funding was stable, their artistic programme was irrelevant. In this specific context a super-stabilized cultural system emerged in which public institutions received their funding regardless of what they did, of how much that corresponded to their plans or the priorities of cultural strategies. This situation has provided us with the cultural policy model as it mostly continues to this day, with few exceptions. It also created a lot of ossification in terms of what is being produced, how much institutions serve the interests of artists in their respective field, to what degree are they willing to engage with the changing social and political context around them, what new audiences they can reach, whether they can produce internationally relevant work. This is obviously very different in our segment of non-institutional culture, but non-institutional culture had quickly reached its financial ceiling from public funding sources and presently is struggling to survive, let alone continue developing under that ceiling. For us, this was a clear signal that efforts to transform the cultural system in general, making it more open to development, innovation and new actors, were going nowhere. So, we placed emphasis on compensatory mechanisms in the cultural system that could support and provide stability for the activities of non-institutional cultural actors. A first step in this direction of creating policy change bottom-up came through Clubture, a network for cultural programme exchange that would allow organization members from across Croatia to jointly propose and collectively decide how to allocate the money for their collaborations. The purpose of Clubture was to strengthen initiatives and organizations working outside of the large cities, particularly Zagreb – helping them grow and consequently helping independent culture to become more decentralized and diversified. This was initially done with the support of the Open Society Foundation and later from various sources. A second big step was when the collective effort of that scene managed to persuade decision-makers to create the Kultura Nova foundation, whose purpose is to support the development and stability of non-institutional culture.

A crucial moment of importance for this orientation on building capacity and cooperation for collective agency came in 2003, when the nationalists re-assumed power and the cultural minister decided to terminate the Cultural Council for New Media Cultures, which was financing primarily our segment of cultural production. The recently established Clubture network provided the bond of trust and solidarity inside the scene that allowed us to organize overnight some 70 organizations from all over the country to join the protest at the Ministry against that decision. In the end the Cultural Council for New Media Cultures was preserved. This was a moment of practical realization: Clubture's success provided us with a clear sense that instead of focusing on one's own best chances of survival, we needed to explore what could be done collectively to improve the context of our work – for the whole non-institutional cultural sector, but also in more broader terms for the larger social context we were operating in.

PD – How and where did this broader contextual thinking evolve first? Besides the immediate need to build an ad-hoc civil society coalition for protesting against the ministry's decision, what was the deeper reasoning for developing structures that meant to involve so many different cultural actors and initiatives from all over the country and to really start thinking and strategizing about the setup and position of the whole non-institutional scene in a larger group and together?

TM – When I think of it, a point of entry into that form of agency was also our socio-epistemic concern at the time. We were thinking of collective agency more in terms of networks or systems, rather than pursuing ideas of a monolithic organizational form. There was definitely some understanding from the beginning that we do not exist separately from our context. Our social and cultural centre MaMa was not established in order to be a venue for our programme, but to serve as a resource for a broader scene of initiatives, organizations and communities that had no access to infrastructure they needed for their work. From day one it was open to everybody to work there and this had amplificatory effects that we had little control over. For instance, we wanted to have two turntable decks, so that DJs could come and play music. A whole young generation of DJs, who at the time didn't have access to such equipment, started to hang around MaMa, developing their skills and learning from each other. Then suddenly we had a whole scene of young music producers who started doing music on their computers. They started organizing music nights on Fridays, when they would come together, listen to each other's music and share tips and tricks – and then it dawned on us: 'Aha, okay, but then let's start a net label. Let's make that music free. Let's see how we can explore that culture is something that can be collectively produced.' At that time we became interested in free software, with its productive model that rested on the abolition of a private property model. We wanted to see then how that concept could be transferred to the sphere of cultural production. All of these things somehow came together, but they were always done under the premise that we were not developing only our own interests. We were exploring the context and trying to provide resources for the context. We could say that there was an idea of open access there from day one, but that would be claiming prior wisdom with the benefit of hindsight. Nevertheless, all that was somehow already inscribed in the organizational DNA of the Multimedia Institute. But also this had a lot do to with Marcell Mars and Teodor Celakoski, who brought us all together and played a crucial role in the opening of MaMa: how they were thinking personally, how they approached their work, how they immediately opened it up to new people and new initiatives. We were really a numerous and quite heterogeneous community of people in those early days, drawing other communities to our space, which I guess goes to show we were from early on investing in developing the context everybody was operating in, rather than simply focusing only on our own work.

PD – How did your efforts for developing and improving the context of this scene of independent culture and non-institutional initiatives – a quite wide and demanding field of civil action in itself already – then further evolve towards creating coalitions that ultimately tackled so much bigger questions of public space? Like for example the campaign against the monetization of the national highway system that some of the key figures of your cultural scene and partners from various trade unions engineered in 2015, or the many protest actions you carried out earlier in Zagreb already and together with activists from other segments of civil society.

TM – It's a sequence of events that is evolutionary and organic. As I have already indicated, an important need of the independent cultural sector was space to work. In the early 2000s, together with youth and environmentalist organizations we started to petition the City of Zagreb, saying that in the midst of the sudden real estate boom in Zagreb, the municipal government should start thinking about what it wanted to do for the public with the spaces that were owned by the city and were quickly being transformed into commercial-only venues. For instance, the entire cinema network, which consisted of 40 public cinema theatres across various neighbourhoods, was shut down and sold off. Previously, Kinematografi Zagreb had been a self-managed company and now it was privatized, its theatres sold one by one and ultimately the company itself disappeared. A neighbourhood such as the one we are meeting in today – around the Kvatrić square, which is quite central and quite prosperous – had no cultural infrastructure left before the independently operating Booksa[5] opened here. Before the Kinematografi were eviscerated, many neighbourhoods outside of the immediate city centre had more than one cinema theatre, and once it was gone suddenly there was nothing. So, in the early 2000s we were petitioning the City that in the midst of this radical transformation of the urban landscape it should set aside some of the spaces it owned for public use. This was also a chance for the municipal government to address the needs of the entire non-institutional sector, which was highly dynamic and yet had little access to resources. We started an advocacy process, demanding that the City take into consideration these needs, and before the local elections in 2005 we pushed them to sign a declaration in which they committed to ten action points that would have moved forward the position of Zagreb's independent culture and the youth sectors quite significantly.

To demonstrate the need and the potential, on the initiative of BLOK's Urban Festival and Platforma 9.81 we organized a big ten-day occupation of the Badel Gorica complex, which is an abandoned city-owned industrial site east of the centre of Zagreb. The occupation of the factory in the format of a broadest range of cultural programmes on site immediately turned out to be a highly successful public act: The city mayor Milan Bandić was invited for the opening and seeing thousands that have turned out for the opening of this cultural event, he solemnly promised to make Badel-Gorica a cultural and youth centre. In a matter of three months, however, the area transformed into a warehousing and commercial centre. This turncoat behaviour by the city mayor was a trigger that led to the establishment of Zagreb's Right to the City platform – Pravo Na Grad and its activities.

The events around the Badel-Gorica industrial site made us aware that we were dealing with a much broader process of social transformation, initiated by the process of privatization of social property dating back to the 1990s. Many of the formerly worker-managed companies were actually being run into bankruptcy, only in order to seize and monetize their assets. In parallel, at the end of the 1990s the whole banking sector was bailed out and then sold off in the early 2000s to foreign banks. Once the nationalists were voted out of power, these banks then flooded the economy with loans, which in return created a real estate boom and there we were. What we were facing was a continuation of the privatization and hollowing out of the productive segment of the economy in the 1990s which even included outright theft of communal property. Privatization of companies is perceived as criminal primitive accumulation. Privatization of space was a continuation of that processes, a second privatization. We articulated this both in terms of the continuity of the prevailing economic process and emphasizing how this will be transforming the future of our local environment. Zagreb was at the forefront of these developments, but things were no less intense in the coastal areas of Croatia, wherever land could be transformed from a low-value regime of use to a more intensive regime of use. Transforming agricultural land into developable property would return ten times the value of the land. This further drew our attention to the underlying structures of economic and political processes.

Around the time when Right to the City started to do actions against the city mayor, who was personalizing all executive power in the city, our attention was very concretely caught by the shopping mall project for Zagreb's Petar Preradović square, which is commonly known as the Flower Market Square and is Zagreb's favourite square for meeting people and protesting governmental decisions.

The realization of the development project there required an overhaul of the entire building regulation in order to pull it off in such a sensitive urban area and make it profitable to start with. It basically boiled down to the public hand generating profit for a private investor, a friend of the city mayor, by donating public land, by allowing him to construct buildings with a much higher density than originally allowed for that inner-city area, by agreeing to the construction of a privately operated public car park that attracted even more traffic to an already very congested area of the city that should have been pedestrianized instead, etc.

Contestation against this development project would play a significant role in the evolution of our scene: We understood that the process of activist confrontation around that development project allowed us to assume political subjectivity that we didn't have before. Suddenly political structures considered us a counter-subject, not only a subject to their decision making. This was another important development in the self-realization of what it is that can be achieved and how it can be achieved. So, things started to scale up very noticeably from then on. The whole issue around the question of the commons came back into focus. It's particularly there where the original interests of the Multimedia Institute came together and converged with this process of an evolution of cultural activism over the years. From the beginning we were very much interested in issues of the commons and we did work on Free Software, doing localization of Creative Commons licenses, thinking about how these models of property-less collective production can be transferred into broader cultural production. These were all elements of concrete practice. Another more conceptual element was critical social theory, particularly social geography, the work of Henri Lefebvre, David Harvey, and other critical geographers. They were formative for our work because they provided us with some tools to understand these processes from a theoretical point of view. And then, from these starting points, the issue of how do we build political subjectivity became important. Because what the confrontation around the Flower Market project demonstrated was that if we can achieve political subjectivity we can also transform the decision making process. Otherwise one remains just a subject to decision making. Seeing our capacity to mobilize masses and have new forms of agency they cannot control, the political structures developed a form of fear. It's only if you have the collective capacity of action to realistically disrupt the operations of people in institutional power and change the balance of power, that you will really get recognized.

Many people who have experienced this period of the 1990s think of themselves as political beings. To then find yourself in a situation where you suddenly feel that you are not just on the defensive, but that you can interrupt something and maybe shift the political ground, was already a hugely motivating factor on a basic individual level; this feeling that not everything is set, that you are not condemned to a melancholic type of political subjectivation, but that there is an opening of a horizon – no matter how particular or not, how general or not – a prospect that is immediately articulable as universalist in the sense that you can do something to change how things operate.

Our context of collective agency obviously also strongly subscribes to ideals of social justice. Most of us are doing a type of work that doesn't deliver much monetary satisfaction. People are in it for the collectivity, for the society. I would also say that maybe there is something generational which I started to notice now that since 2015 we have once again new nationalist governments to deal with. Most of us have a feeling that we've spent the best years of our life, if not our entire lifetime in a continuous process of dismantling of society. The permanent crisis, which already started in the 1970s, continued throughout the 1980s and extended into the traumatic breakup of Yugoslavia and its wars and nationalisms – this continuous socio-economic and existential crisis has really marked many of us. It's interesting to see that a lot of people of the now younger generations have not gone into cultural work as we did. They decided to work directly with trade unions, or in the field of political analysis, or journalism, so they actually found other fields of engagement. I don't know if it's because the space of independent culture was already taken, that there were organizations and people of my generation doing this work within the cultural field already. Or if these younger generations were politicized around majoritarian issues, whereas we were politicized around minoritarian issues. The younger generation now concerns itself from the get-go with issues of labour, issues of free education, broader issues that directly concern many, in particular the working class and the underclasses. For us, who have gone through our formative years in the 1990s, it was much more issues that concerned those who have found themselves under the existential threat of nationalist politics.

As I have already described, similar societal and political questions as those that have been the concern of this younger generation, have of course also been driving the transition of our independent cultural sector towards establishing broader civil coalitions – particularly in the framework of the Right to the City or in the campaign against the monetization of the highways. The independent cultural sector made a gradual shift from its initial political attention to minority rights towards focusing on the socio-economic and political rights of the majority, including larger questions of class struggle, economic inequalities and social polarization. This shift obviously reflects the changing conditions under which independent culture had to exist during the 1990s and the political and social context the sector operates under nowadays. External circumstances define what new initiatives see as their space of action, where people find what their political flame could be. This is what has encouraged this ecosystem of independent culture to expand towards forms of work that are not simply cultural and to reach out and work together with initiatives in many other fields of social engagement, including the work with refugees, electoral politics and many other forms of engagement. Everybody in our scene is really quite attuned and open to engage in all of these different segments. I think this is really important because high modernism as represented in contemporary culture is too often relevant for only a very small demographic. Although it is an important field, one cannot build a wider claim to achieve larger political effects by solely relying on that segment of society. What is required therefore, is to start thinking structurally in terms of how cultural hegemonies are produced and reproduced.

PD – In the spring of 2017, a number of individuals who have also participated in some of the campaigns at municipal level that we discussed earlier teamed up with other political activists and movements to run for local elections. This new political platform called Zagreb je NAŠ![6] stands close to the work that for instance Right to the City had done, but is a very different endeavour in terms of its collective composition and goals. How would you assess the significance of this new political platform and the municipalist politics in Croatia?

TM – Over the last four years we have been witnessing a deepening instability in Croatia's political system. It started crumbling from within in the sense that it had been structured along a polarizing axis of nationalism versus anti-nationalism for too long. This bi-partisan system of nationalist HDZ and anti-nationalist SDP with their satellite coalition partners has safeguarded the model of socio-economic development that Croatia took in the early 1990s and that resulted in growing inequality and lasting stagnation. The breakdown of the neoliberal consensus in the aftermath of global recession of 2008 only precipitated that instability.

The current volatility in this system was on full display with the coalition government that took office in November of 2015. The nationalist HDZ[7] under the leadership of Tomislav Karamarko and in an alliance with a spectrum of minor radical right-wing political parties formed a government in coalition with a smaller reformist alliance of regional politicians called Most[8] (Bridge). They agreed on a non-partisan prime minister, a Canadian citizen and former manager of an international pharmaceutical company, who effectively held no control over the coalition. It was in particular Zlatko Hasanbegović, the Minister of Culture in this government, who was charged with drumming up a cultural war over the WWII legacy in order to hide from view the deep contradictions and the weaknesses of that government. In his public interventions Hasanbegović, a revisionist historian specializing in the twentieth-century history of Muslims in Croatia, has successfully synthesized the vilification of the anti-fascist resistance along the narrative of two totalitarianisms, the new identitarianism of the European New Right and the neo-conservativism promoted by the Catholic circles that have just recently campaigned against same-sex marriage and abortion. He immediately mounted an attack on independent media and progressivist culture across both institutional and non-institutional domains. But that government collapsed already in June 2016, when Most left the coalition. Before these events, there were huge protests against the government organized by trade unions and civil society organizations, which were sparked by discontent with the fact that the new school curriculum that was under development with broad participation of educators around the country was stopped and undercut by this government. This led to the largest protest rally in two decades with 70,000 people attending in Zagreb and tens of thousands in other cities, which had a delegitimizing effect on this coalition. As a consequence, in November 2016 we had new elections that the social democrats of the SDP managed to lose, to everyone's surprise. The HDZ came back victorious under the leadership of Andrej Plenković, a conservative figure of the political centre with a background in EU affairs, who again formed a coalition with Most. This coalition again collapsed in a matter of months, but Plenković managed to avoid new elections by forming a coalition with a number of smaller parties.

In recent years, several political actors outside the establishment have entered the electoral politics, not only Most – but also Živi Zid,[9] which works both as a political party and an activist group that has been opposing forced evictions over the last five years. Their electoral successes were carried by the rising swell of voter dissatisfaction and are an indication of the failure of the development path Croatia has pursued over the last 25 years and an indication of the more general breakdown of neoliberal consensus. It is clear that there's a need to find new forms of democratic political agency that would allow disenfranchised citizens to make their claims, as well as a need to produce a new vision of development of society that starts from a realistic assessment of where they stand and what they can collectively achieve. Both this collective capacity to act and this change that starts from where people actually stand is in the blind spot of the political establishment. Bound to their political structures and the political system they have built, they cannot even detect this space of agency as a space of transformation. They fear the demos.

This is why a number of individuals, some of whom have previously also been involved in our struggles, have decided to enter the political arena by forming a platform that would bring together other progressives and citizen groups around Zagreb's neighbourhoods that have been actively opposing the way the city was governed over the last fifteen years. By joining forces with already existing smaller parties on the left, they made it their immediate goals to oust the mayor of the City of Zagreb whom we have also been fighting on various occasions. Their ambition is to re-democratize the city and to articulate an alternative vision of development of the city.

Zagreb je NAŠ!'s platform building was following the municipalist methods that we have seen being successfully developed and put in practice in Spain – to build the democratic process from the bottom up where the struggles were unfolding before and in a way that is completely diametrical to the ideological and political framing imposed by the media and the existing parties. The experience of Barcelona en Comú[10] and Ahora Madrid[11] has served as an inspiration and in Zagreb, given the previous mass mobilizations, Zagreb je NAŠ! had a foundation from where it could make its entry into the political system. But there is also the peripheral position in European capitalism, which we share to a large degree with countries like Spain and Greece. What are the peripheral economies of European Union actually able to achieve in terms of economic development and don't we need another vision of international development in general? The overarching issue at this point is that the European Union project has very little to say about this predicament, for example, the models of sustenance and survival that have developed in these peripheral economies. I think there is a lot these political contexts can learn from each other, although concrete situations can be fairly different too and therefore political strategies and political visions are somewhat different as well.

A strong strategic point of Zagreb je NAŠ! is its intent to revive the relevance of politics at the most local level. Zagreb has three levels of political representation in the city. There is the city assembly, but then there are 17 district councils and over 200 neighbourhood councils. And this is where Zagreb je NAŠ! wanted to start from. The wager was unless it managed to connect how people experience and sustain their existence in their immediate social context with how political decisions are taken at the higher representative levels, it would not be able to succeed in bringing in new forms of democratic politics.

Zagreb je NAŠ! started to build the platform relatively late – a mere three months before the local elections.

There were many people from different backgrounds who became involved: neighbourhood initiatives, social justice struggles, labour activism, environmentalism, student occupations, independent media, cultural activism, LGBTIQ activism, education, refugee relief... Individuals from all these different backgrounds started to gather, gradually expanding the political platform to over 500 activists and supporters. A month before the elections the platform had to put on hold this expansion and focus on helping the groups of people in the various neighbourhoods to organize themselves to stand for elections on the lower and most immediate levels of local representation.

Zagreb je NAŠ! thus formed a list for the city assembly and had a mayoral candidate. It was the first time that any electoral list had an equal number of women and men following the zipper-principle. It also agreed a coalition with the four existing political parties on the left. In the end the coalition and neighbourhood groups were able to create together lists for the city assembly, 15 districts and 44 neighbourhoods assemblies. The programme of priorities was opened to public deliberation on an online discussion forum and these proposals were then integrated into the final programme of priorities for the campaign.

Zagreb je NAŠ! campaigned through concrete political actions. Through these actions it tried to bring back to the public's attention the fact that the city mayor has personalized power, that he has ignored the demands of the citizens and has failed to bring meaningful development to the city. It also tried to re-articulate its proposals for the city's development and its values such as social justice, economic democracy and sustainable development in relation to concretely existing problems in the city, which ultimately focused messages in the campaign on five major issues and problem areas. For instance, inefficient operation of public transport, overpriced drinking water as a direct result of a public-private partnership and failure to close down the landfill in Novi Zagreb.

The campaign was ignored by the mainstream media for as long as the coalition didn't announce its mayoral candidate. In Croatia we have direct mayoral elections and they carry more weight than the elections for the city assemblies and lower levels of municipal representation. Up to that moment Zagreb je NAŠ!'s campaign had to rely on Facebook, which turned out to be probably its strongest campaigning instrument. But, once it announced Tomislav Tomašević as its mayoral candidate the coalition around Zagreb je NAŠ! started to appear very prominently in the media and were presented as the only legitimate alternative to all other political parties and candidates who have in a smaller or greater capacity helped reproduce the crony system of government that we have in Zagreb at the moment.

And then on the day of the elections the coalition managed to win almost eight percent of the vote for the city assembly. It also managed to get a number of seats in each of the 15 districts and almost all of the 44 neighbourhoods it was running in. This was obviously a huge success, surpassing the most optimistic expectations. The day before the elections one could still doubt whether the coalition's vision of how to re-democratize the electoral politics and how to shift society's development towards a more just, more sustainable, and more economically democratic society might fall on deaf ears. It might have not passed the 5% electoral threshold, even though it brought a completely fresh perspective, raised concrete new issues and outdid all other political options in the campaign. Had it failed to pass the threshold, that would have been a very clear signal that the issues it proposed to tackle, and that we have also been working on over the last fifteen years through the Multimedia Institute and Right to the City, are only marginal for the future development of this society.

The fact that it nevertheless managed to re-articulate its principles and escape being type-casted, that it managed to put new concerns on the political agenda and that it received a lot of public support in a very short period, gives at least some assurance that entering the electoral political landscape might be transformative in the long run. Especially given the overall trajectory of Croatian society, which has moved to an ever greater inequality and conservativism. In that respect it was also indicative that the coalition prevented the anti-establishment parties on the right from passing the threshold. There is obviously a desire among voters to see something else come into existence rather than perpetuating the same polarizing matrix created by nationalists and their opponents that has dominated the political field in Croatia since the 1990s. There might actually be space now for a different imaginary of social development starting from where we are. Now that Zagreb je NAŠ! has made the jump into the representative bodies, it will have to face new dynamics, new contradictions and new challenges that it will have to embrace and make the best of.

Notes

1 www.mi2.hr.
2 www.clubture.org.
3 www.pravonagrad.org.
4 www.mi2.hr/mama.
5 www.booksa.hr.
6 www.zagrebjenas.hr.
7 www.hdz.hr.
8 www.most-nl.com.
9 www.zivizid.hr.
10 www.barcelonaencomu.cat.
11 www.ahoramadrid.org.

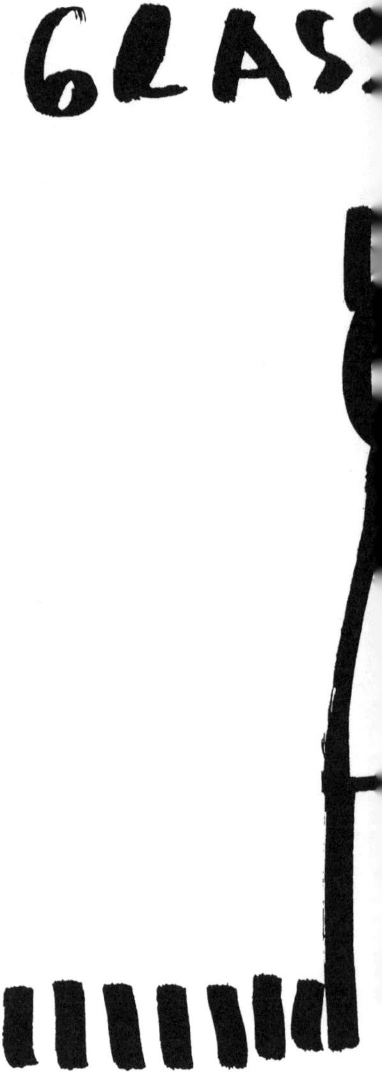

GLASS

ROOTS

On ‘Social Culture’ in Poland

Igor Stokfiszewski

Fundamental re-evaluations have taken place in the realm of culture in recent years. With artistic practices extending beyond the production of artefacts, and underpinned by influential aesthetic theories (such as relational aesthetics in visual arts, raising the status of shaping human relationships rather than producing artworks,[1] and performative aesthetics in theatre, where the event becomes the main means of expression, its prime aim being to affect its participants[2]), the cultural activities of public institutions are being transformed. Artists no longer supply objects: they create situations, build relations, organize events, and strive to have an impact on reality (including both politically and socially).[3] Audiences no longer contemplate works or performances; they become active subjects of happenings, they experience artistic situations and are transformed by them, they are influenced by the course of events. Mainstream institutional culture is being scarified by the subversive approach of artists, reconstructed by disputes surging within the field of culture (including those most publicized concerning labour and democratization[4]), and by research on the mechanisms of cultural production both within institutions[5] and at the point of encounter with the social sphere.[6]

The work of the institutional cultural mainstream also finds itself modified by the achievements of organizers of cultural activities, and by artists influenced by experiences in the fields of cultural education, pedagogy and rehabilitation through art. The latter usually work within a specific subfield of public institutions (in cultural centres, education departments of central and local artistic institutions or in academia). And a final observation: the challenge to mainstream culture as inadequately satisfying the public's cultural needs emerges also from recent research in the fields of anthropology, sociology, economics and cultural studies. The discovery within rural sectors with little access to mainstream culture of 'their own cultural repertoire';[7] the retrieval of folk cultural practices and also models of self-assembly and unofficial institutions of folk culture; unwrapping the processes of adjusting and aestheticizing of urban spaces by their users; releasing the identity-forming potential latent in collective performance (ceremonies and protests), and many other phenomena evident in recent years, indicate the inadequacies of mainstream culture in sustaining, stimulating and organizing cultural expression on the part of social communities.

Seen through the lens of the above processes, cultural and artistic institutions appear to have become the object of a criticism that corrodes their framework and demands reform of their practices. Looking at the network of these institutions from the outside reveals a different picture. In response to the inadequacies in official circulation of culture, an autonomous circuit of cultural practices and institutions has emerged via various forms of social self-organization: a domain of grassroots, organized social production of culture, characterized by a substantially different approach than that of the mainstream to cultural practices and to defining functions of culture and structuring organizations in the field.

This paper endeavours to characterize this field of the social production of culture; the attempt to describe it is rooted in the conviction that it contains a rich reservoir of practices arising from anthropological and philosophical foundations that can direct our thinking about culture (including mainstream institutional culture) towards its deeper social roots, and liberate creative potential for identity, community and development. I refer to the field as 'social culture' for the sake of simplicity; the term's similarity to the category of 'social economy' is not without significance here. In both cases, it concerns autonomous fields creating goods and values, as well as a philosophy of action, a sociology of culture and economy, and an anthropology of the cultural subject distinct from the public and private spheres, since the main focus here is the social aspect.[8]

A Map of 'Social Culture' in Poland

To tackle a characterization of the field of 'social culture', the process of its mapping must be explained first. For Poland, the story behind drawing the map of culture covering areas independent from the 'jurisdiction' of mainstream institutional culture is explored by Edwin Bendyk in his paper 'Metakultura rozwoju' ('Metaculture of development'): 'The Polish Culture Congress 2009 organized under the heading "Culture Counts!" opened up a broad debate concerning the links between culture and dynamic social and economic development', which resulted in the emergence of wide-ranging sociological, anthropological, economic and cultural research that has been pursued continuously over the past six years, searching for an answer to the question about cultural practices shaping the social community and their position in relation to the institutional circulation of culture.[9] These practices currently constitute the resources on the basis of which we can ascertain a widened field of cultural activities in Poland or outline its newly emerging autonomous spheres. I also consider them to be a knowledge resource for notions of 'social culture'.

Bendyk has also contributed to this mapping. He has conducted three research programmes ('Culture and Development', 'Culture Scheme' and 'Fractals: Towards a Metaculture of Development') that aim to provide knowledge about peripheral culture with potential for real transformation and development.[10] These questions are also the subject of extensive anthropological and ethnographic research conducted by Kolektyw Terenowy (Field Collective). *Action research* was carried out in two villages, Broniów and Ostałówek, in the south Mazowsze region (revealing rural communities' 'own cultural repertoire' and indicating practices supporting self-expression, creating community, driving social and cultural activities as well as transforming material manifestations of rural life). This provided a treasury of knowledge about social creativity and production in peripheral areas functioning without access to official cultural circuits and which, according to indicators, ought to be characterized by social collapse.[11] Studies have been carried out of rural environments and small towns in terms of cultural diversity not understood as cultural production but rather as a 'cultural opportunity',[12] and on urban culture in all the richness of its forms and aspects.[13] These explorations demonstrate the variety of cultural circuits that exist with their own particular institutional autonomy, reception habits, patterns of participation and, last but not least, their own aesthetics.

On the subject of aesthetics – research analogical to the Field Collective studies but applied to urban areas has been carried out by a Poznan centre led by Marek Krajewski. It reveals the existence of 'invisible cities', i.e., a self-organized and aestheticized stratum within the urban tissue that expresses the needs and expectations of its users and thus falls outside notions of aesthetics, architecture and urban planning, organization and development of public space.[14] Grassroots cultural production led researchers to take a closer look and analyze probably the most common form of self-expression: mass-produced photography. The 'radical programme of visual sociology' formulated by Marek Krajewski and Rafał Drozdowski enables us to see the advanced universality of the impulse to create cultural representations of reality and at the same time to perceive the complicated nature of the only seemingly banal impulse of 'taking photos'.[15]

Other areas investigated in Poland include cultural production in the digital environment[16] and subcultures such as reconstruction groups.[17] Meanwhile, our knowledge of means of cultural expression according to social differences has been enhanced by studies conducted by sociologists Maciej Gdula, Mikołaj Lewicki and Przemysław Sadura. Their *Praktyki kulturowe klasy ludowej* (Cultural practices of the folk class) reveals cultural stratification along distinctive and economic lines (i.e., according to social codes and symbols and according to economic resources).[18] The idea of competing institutional circuits – an official network of cultural centres versus self-organization and unofficial folk institutions, including fire departments and rural women's associations – also emerges here.

There are studies on cultural institutions and 'non-institutions' in Poland (including squats).[19] A similar search for unusual forms of 'self-organizing and unofficial institutions of culture' inspires the work of researchers who talk about a network of 'social museums'.[20] Particularly noteworthy are performance studies as a research field encompassing the theatricalization of collective actions that have identity-forming capacity and can give meaning to the social experience of reality, while revealing the deep roots of Polish cultural performances in pre-Christian tradition and Romantic messianism.[21]

The catalogue of studies listing examples of cultural activities not limited to the institutional network must include the work of Obserwatorium Żywej Kultury (Observatory of Living Culture): the research network clustered around Professor Barbara Fatyga (University of Warsaw), which aims to develop a complete methodology of description, analysis and evaluation of 'living culture', understood anthropologically and sociologically.[22] Last but not least, the broad framework of Polish research described includes long-standing projects undertaken under the supervision of economist Jerzy Hausner, based on the hypothesis that culture is a collection of practices, initiatives and organizational solutions that can become the flywheel of social and economic development. On the one hand, they emerge from observations concerning the dwindling development potential of previous social and economic ideas and, on the other hand, from a belief in the innovative character of approaches characterizing grassroots initiatives in the area of culture that go beyond the paradigm of culture industries or notions of a creative class.[23] Alongside typical scientific research projects, activities that combine practice and theoretical reflections in different regions of Poland deserve special attention. Particular mention should be made of the Mazowiecki Instytut Kultury (Mazovian Institute of Culture) and its project *Kierunek kultura* (Direction culture), which included the organization of cultural events around the Mazovian region as well as producing three theoretical publications edited by Wojciech Kłosowski.[24] The approach proposed by culture animators engaged in the project, which was characterized by empowerment, enhancing community bonds, participation, individual change and transformation of reality, was reflected in many activities that I would classify as 'social culture'.

These explorations complement the institutional map of cultural activities across the country with 'cultural "hot spots"',[25] creating a multi-layered picture of practices, organizational forms and circuits that constitute the current cultural space of Poland as densely 'populated' with 'cultural subjects': individual practitioners, initiatives, informal groups, NGOs, institutions, etc.[26] It is impossible to enumerate all the subjects that, over the past six years, have attracted the attention of researchers participating in analysis, animation and *action research*. They include social centres, NGOs, rural women's associations, urban movements, social libraries, public cultural institutions, cooperative enterprises, grassroots non-institutional action 'makers', cultural centres, station houses of volunteer fire departments, squats.[27] The list should be complemented with foreign centres linked with Polish establishments and initiatives or overlapping with them by virtue of comparative studies,[28] and many others operating in the field of creating new 'perspectives on culture and the common good'.[29] This list does not even begin to outline the scale of these phenomena. Przemysław Sadura estimated that the NGO sector in Poland includes about ten to twelve thousand organizations involved in culture. As Sadura concludes, the collection of studies 'reveals an image of a cultural sector dominated financially by state and public institutions and in terms of initiatives by formal and informal self-organization'.[30] Obviously, not all these places are 'cultural "hot spots"', but the most distinctive entities from the 'social culture' sphere support the claim that 'this is the ... dimension that is the most innovative and pro-development in character'.[31]

Independent Culture and 'Social Culture'

The Polish Culture Congress organized in 2009 by the Ministry of Culture and National Heritage was a catalyst for studying unofficial cultural circuits. However, the grassroots movement of social production of culture in the country was developing independently from the ministry's involvement, and coincided with the publication of a book proposing a cultural-anthropology perspective that changed the idea of centres and peripheries. *Łowcy, zbieracze, praktycy niemocy: Etnografia człowieka zdegradowanego* (Hunters, gatherers, practitioners of powerlessness) by Tomasz Rakowski analyzed the culture of people digging in Wałbrzych district bootleg mine shafts, farmers from Świętokrzyskie district and hunter-gatherers living by an open-pit mine near Bełchatów. The same year, the Brave New World Cultural Centre in Warsaw opened – a social cultural institution active until 2012, which was one of the most ambitious attempts to establish an institutional model beyond the public circuit.[32] In Kraków, along with the Culture Congress, an ephemeral cooperative, Goldex Poldex, rooted in the situationist movement, hosted an anti-congress of culture initiated by circles associated with the Ha!art Corporation, one of the most dynamically developing publishers in the third sector.

These three events reveal an approach to cultural activities in Poland different from that of the mainstream – while at the same time preserving differences between themselves – and have gained importance over the past few years. Rakowski's book draws particular attention to grassroots cultural production, self-creativity and cultural production rooted in local communities. The opening of the Brave New World Cultural Centre focused on establishing social cultural centres in Poland as key culture-formative subjects. Meanwhile, the anti-congress emphasized the power of non-institutional circulation of independent culture.

In mentioning the anti-congress, it is not my intention to undermine the Ministry's initiative of the Polish Culture Congress as a catalyst for new approaches to culture. The anti-congress contributed to the search for self-definition on the part of that section of the artistic milieu that recognized its values and practices as different and often provided an alternative to mainstream institutional culture. It resulted, for example, in the publication of *Kultura niezależna w Polsce 1989-2009* (Independent culture in Poland 1989-2009).[33] This 'report of the history of enthusiasm', as the volume is described by its editor, Piotr Marecki, shows how eight areas of artistic activity (literature, visual arts, theatre, comic books, music, Net art, cinema and the circulation of zines) were developed during the first two decades after Poland's political and social transformation in the third and 'fourth' sectors, that is, created in NGO working conditions or according to the situationist model, as ephemeral activities based on resistance to dominant cultural, social and economic patterns. Five years after the publication of this volume, it is interesting to note that the 'independence' of the culture described in the report was related particularly to the system of artistic production, but not to the philosophy of creativity. Independent culture, as perceived by the writers of the volume at the time, still remained the domain of artists who produced and exhibited their works. The fact that they, on the other hand, were operating outside mainstream institutional culture allowed them to present content and formulate criticism in ways that could not find legitimization in official culture. Therefore, if 'independent culture' is to result from the transformation of cultural production, then 'social culture' results from a changing approach to the functions of culture, its objectives, its social roots, i.e., approaches to such issues as subjectivity, community, locality, resources, ecological responsibility, democracy.

The foundation for the emergence of 'social culture' in Poland is the 'turn to democracy',[34] and its manifestations are visible in politics (for example, by implementing participatory instruments), in the social sphere (the renaissance of social movements, which in Poland manifested as urban movements or the labour-democracy movement), as well as in culture. Here, it is based on the idea that cultural production is the domain of each and every one of us, and that its functionality depends on the way that the social values and extra-artistic objectives of these practices are implemented. This distinction may seem a sophism designed to multiply discursive entities. However, we are now at the heart of the debate about the future of non-institutional circuits of culture in Poland, but also elsewhere. I want to state clearly that the difference between systems of cultural production (whether art is created in public, private or non-governmental, or even informal institutions) in any context does not guarantee the release of creative potential and says nothing about the social impact of culture. The fundamental issue is a change of approach towards who actually creates culture, how and by what means, within which organizational and institutional framework and, most importantly, for what purpose. If culture created outside institutional circulation is to have the right to demand recognition and legitimization, it must be a form of counterculture, i.e., it must present an alternative anthropology of the artist, attribute different qualities, skills and functions to the artist, build bridges between the creative activities of the artist and social space, demand approaches to art other than the mainstream ones.

The sphere of 'social culture' I am interested in encompasses organized forms of activities (within the boundaries of the wider field of independent culture) that aim at practices that go beyond artistic production or works. The 'social culture' circuit includes independent movements, organizations and institutions oriented towards democratic, pro-subject, pro-community and pro-development social impact by means of cultural instruments.

Polish Manifestations of 'Social Culture'

Mapping manifestations of 'social culture' in Poland and elsewhere is a risky undertaking, since its parameters are unclear. This can be ascribed to the inner dynamic of its development as an autonomous area of social and cultural activity or to cognitive limitations (a meta-culture of research that still creates analytical barriers). The fact remains that cultural activity in my area of interest is not that easily distinguishable from other types of social activity. It would not be easy to explain why an urban movement aiming at neighbourhood integration that objected to its opinions being ignored in making decisions concerning the repurposing of an old preschool building and adjoining area on a particular housing estate in Warsaw should call itself Kultura na Sielcach (Culture in Sielce). There was, indeed, a neighbourhood appeal that included a call for 'more culture in Sielce' (in the sense of community cultural centres), and fewer new blocks and apartment buildings, but hardly any practices carried out by the collective (protests, legal interventions, meetings) are rooted in the sphere of culture.

Why do we include the activities of the Łódź Cohabitat Foundation in the sphere of culture? Most distinctive among its operations is creating and providing access to green building prototypes. In this sense, it is a proposal for an alternative lifestyle and, therefore, indirectly for a different culture. These practices could be successfully analyzed as stemming from architecture or even digital culture, if the main resource of the foundation is their community of Internet platform users.

Alternative lifestyle cultures can also be found in squats and autonomous social centres across Poland, and happening-type events staged by urban movements (such as the parade of wooden houses organized by Otwarty Jazdów (Open Jazdów) collective activists in Warsaw's city centre) are to some extent a legitimized methodology of social resistance in both social-movement theory and art theory.[35]

Moreover, these 'cultural "hot spots"' in Poland cannot be differentiated according to their organization type. They include public establishments, NGO institutions and informal groups. Arguably, one could claim that most of them emerge from grass-roots activities. For example, the Łaźnia Nowa Theatre from Kraków Nowa Huta was an association before it became a municipal institution. Nevertheless, it seems that today the area of 'social culture' falls outside this type of classification and its parameters are more like vast land tracts than borderlines or border posts. Therefore, any attempt to identify an autonomous area of 'social culture' has to be based on designing a catalogue of approaches, values, operating philosophies, going on to include institutional forms or organizational structures.

The catalogue below of approaches, values and philosophies of action in Poland is composed of practices and aims reflected, to varying degrees, in the initiatives, organizations and institutions of the country's cultural sphere. Nonetheless, in my opinion it forms the foundation of the activities of every initiative, organization and institution recognized in recent years as a 'cultural "hot spot"'.

I consider the following list of characteristics (based on practices observed in Poland) to include the most essential features of 'social culture':

– Expression of subjectivity. Initiatives within 'social culture' are directed at creating platforms for individual expression on the part of its participants. The relation of a given practice to an individual's manner and content of expression becomes the measure of its openness. Limiting mechanisms are eliminated and mechanisms of absorption and inclusion are developed instead. The form and content of individual expression are not evaluated nor are they described according to artistic criteria. Enablement is taken to be axiomatic.

- Individual creativity. Practices within 'social culture' are oriented towards creativity rather than imitation or performing according to a score or repetition of a previously proposed scenario. (In the case of theatre performance, the result is collaborative work on content proposed by participants.)
- Individual resources. A key role here is the ability to extract and employ the individual resources of participants. I have in mind mostly non-material resources: skills, knowledge, cultural competence, but also material ones: objects (which become props or costumes), spaces (becoming the space of collective work), devices (to create stage design, props, etc.).
- Interaction. In the area of 'social culture', individual creativity is only a component (or starting point) for collective expression. The effect (event, activity, work) is the result of collective creativity. This collective creation is possible due to the richness of interactive practices, from being together to the exchange of experiences and collaboration.
- Communication. Initiatives in the area of 'social culture' generate rich means of communication, information exchange and maintaining contacts. It is not necessarily related to digital communication, though in some areas this is highly developed. Nevertheless, constant communication, irrespective of its form, is characteristic of all 'social culture' groups, organizations and institutions.
- Collaboration. The effect of a given practice does not result so much from the composition of individual expression but rather from co-creation, cooperation, collaboration.
- Trust. Achieving results in common creation requires building trust within an initiative. It is a question of developing strategies of interaction that rule out (or minimize) mutual distance and prejudice, and that base cooperation on belief in candid motivation. The interactive practices mentioned above also contribute to building mutual trust: spending time together, exchange of experiences, etc.

- Conciliatory approach. Initiatives, organizations and institutions have developed their own mechanisms of reaching consensus related to the activities undertaken, reconciling differences, antagonisms and conflicts.
- Mutual practices. One such mechanism, which also performs other functions, is practising mutuality: exchange of goods and services between individuals, reciprocation, offering gifts, barter, disinterested sharing, passing on individual skills or knowledge.
- Respect for individuality. Initiatives in the area of 'social culture' have developed their own mechanisms of respecting individual qualities, desires, preferences and interests. The mechanism of recognition is not related here to authority, skill or achievements; recognition comes a priori from being a person (or a non-human actor, an animal or plant[36]).
- Focus on diversity. Such practice is by definition focused on the diversity of its participants in terms of age, nationality, gender and other identity parameters.
- Common resources. 'Social culture' has developed mechanisms of sharing individual resources (for example, through mutual practices, interaction, collaborative activities) and, therefore, defining common resources: skills, knowledge, competence, identity and memory shared by all participants.
- Communal ownership. This leads to redefining the issue of ownership. A given initiative, organization or institution in the area of 'social culture' belongs to all its participants. The ownership is a result of identification with the initiative, cooperation and consensus.
- Participation. 'Social culture' is focused on participation. It is not addressed to consumers, but rather to participants and (co)creators of culture.
- Shared decision-making. Participation leads to shared decision-making in all aspects of activities of an initiative, organization or institution of 'social culture'. These have developed decision-making chains enabling a common adoption of decisions, which can take into account many participating subjects. This also permits the avoidance of situations in which decisions are made by some and implemented by others who do not identify with the decisions in question.

- Co-management. Participation and shared decision-making are reflected at a formal level in co-management. The legal foundation for co-management in the area of 'social culture' remains an open issue. Nevertheless, the internal regulations governing initiatives, organizations and institutions are moving unambiguously in this direction.
- Inclusiveness. As with mechanisms of interactivity, initiatives in the field of 'social culture' have developed a rich set of instruments enabling the inclusion of new subjects (participants, performers).
- Accessibility. Widespread accessibility is one of the most important parameters of activities within the area of 'social culture'. It can be achieved through various methods of communication and with different results, but a characteristic feature of planning activities within projects is to aim at the widest possible level of accessibility, based on a belief in the necessity of inclusiveness.
- Openness. Understood as the mechanism of various levels of engagement. Simply put, initiatives, organizations and institutions in the area of 'social culture' plan their activities so as to facilitate participation by undertaking supporting functions, attending events, being a 'spectator' or casual viewer, according to individual preferences and capabilities.
- Responsibility towards stakeholders and respecting their position. 'Social culture' operates in an environment packed with many stakeholders. Cultural activities in public spaces, in social areas, at the point of contact between various circuits, require precise identification of stakeholders and mediation between them.
- Diversification of funding and remuneration. One of the most complex aspects of operating within 'social culture' is the issue of stability and sustainability. Financial resources (as far as they are necessary) come from public and private sources, membership fees, other fees, crowdfunding. In practice, there are resources that are treated as financial (for example, equipment). Remuneration for participation is a separate issue. There is an observable tendency towards an expectation of financial reward, which would also include other (immaterial) benefits of participation.

- Institutionalization. In the area of 'social culture', there is a noticeable tendency towards institutionalization, enabling further development of activities but at the same time retaining the organic, separate nature of initiatives within 'social culture'. Although this area has been institutionalized, the model pursued is set by institutions for the common good – co-managed by their participants, open and inclusive, with mediatory approaches and common ownership.
- Social mechanisms of sustainability. Where there is loose organizational structure or lack of institutionalization of an area of 'social culture', it is common to see the development of social mechanisms of sustainability such as continuous communication and frequent meetings; the realization of short-term objectives to integrate the group and sustain the vitality of collaboration.
- Self-sufficiency. Aiming at self-sufficiency or treating self-sufficiency as a guiding principle of activities is a noticeable tendency within 'social culture'. I have in mind both resources at the disposal of a group or community allowing it to operate without external support, as well as social and ecological responsibility.
- Social and ecological responsibility. 'Social culture' takes into consideration such parameters as the quality of life, the social security of its participants and a high quality of relations between them. It also takes into account their well-being, dignity, sense of fair treatment, appreciation of effort and contribution. It also considers impact on the environment and sustainable development. Natural resources, energy and pollution are used reflectively. Recycling – reusing materials used in a given project – is a very important practice. There is a preference for local resources and locally available products, skills, etc.
- Multigenerational horizon. 'Social culture' attempts to extend the temporal horizon of its practices. The ambition is to take into consideration long-term consequences and the quality of life of future generations.
- Critical attitude. The guiding ideal within 'social culture' is a critical attitude towards one's own practice and surrounding reality. The ambition is also to develop tools to correct the direction of activities in accordance with

the organic development of an initiative and its changing external – social – parameters.

Philosophy of 'Social Culture'

Approaching culture within the 'social culture' framework is fundamentally based on a belief in the transformative power of everyone's self-expression. It is transformative in the sense of enabling inner change in a human being and also bringing about change in reality. 'Social culture' is based on the anthropology of a powerful subjectivity and the instrument of its implementation is the empowerment of others. These three elements make up the fundamental practice within the sphere of 'social culture'; its organizations and institutions establish a platform of expression for non-professional creators, establishing a framework (and supplying basic material resources) for the self-expression of others. Aiming for self-sufficiency, achieved through self-organization and establishing one's own institutions, is also a manifestation of the anthropology of a strong subjectivity.

Strong subjects establish strong communities. The sociology of 'social culture' enables recognition of the idea that a grounded subjectivity does not result in the weakening of community bonds due to conflict between individuals. On the contrary, it is uncertain and weak individuals who are more inclined to conquer territories of recognition by means of conflict. A strong subject is open to collective experiences. Being deeply grounded in oneself allows one to see others as separate, authentic entities rather than as some kind of threat. The community created by such subjects through interaction within the framework of 'social culture' is integrated, dense, emphatic.

This does not happen naturally. The sphere of 'social culture' has worked to develop protocols that strengthen tendencies towards creating collective bonds. They are based on co-management and democratization of decision-making processes. Participation is not understood here as simply including 'members of their audiences' in activities in the field of culture, but is more a question of co-determination with regard to forms of processes within 'social culture' overall.

These approaches translate into questions of agency. The transformative principle – the idea that culture can transform individuals and reality – leads to a growth in potential of collective agency in communities bound by 'social culture'. This is why cultural groups in Poland and anywhere else can also function as social or urban movements that attempt to achieve political goals.

'Social culture' attaches importance to sustainability processes – innovative approaches to funding, but also to triggering mechanisms of sustainability based on the conscious shaping of group relations: by rotating leadership, for example, or by including new subjects in practices or intertwining various areas of activities (from creating culture to social activism, towards producing knowledge and coming back to creating culture).

Thus 'social culture' is heading towards production of the common good, i.e., non-material values shared by all people, values essential for living, which cannot be appropriated by anyone. I have in mind both natural resources and cultural heritage, language and human relationships. The creation of the common good is achieved by institutions of 'social culture' that should reflect the idea of a common good: they should belong to all participants, shared, democratic, adjusted to expanding resources of common wealth.

How to Develop 'Social Culture'?

I am convinced that 'social culture' in the form of mentioned initiatives, organizations and institutions in Poland (which have been the object of analyses, studies, animation and action research in recent years) is at present the most valuable manifestation of culture as a process of collective creation of social reality that exists thanks to negotiating values and meanings that reflect the objectives of social community. 'Social culture' can definitely become a model for other cultural circuits (institutional and independent). The autonomous area of 'social culture', however, needs to be allowed to grow further as an original domain of cultural practices, not only with regard to initiatives and movements in Poland, but in many other European countries and beyond.

Prevailing discussions concerning the de-hermeticization of cultural institutions, pluralizing the system of cultural production and the organizational diversification of the field of culture in Europe seem to be dominated by the idea that building bridges between various approaches to culture is the right direction. This is true, but given the advantage held by the public sector and the operating potential of the private sector, 'social culture' should be allowed to enhance its own power as an autonomous area of activity before we decide to introduce it into a relationship of interaction with these other sectors. Only then can it develop its own practices and strengthen its approaches, and only then can it have an impact on the shape of culture in general. Therefore, in conclusion, I would like to express my strong belief that today in Poland, and in Europe in general, we can develop 'social culture' most effectively by creating frameworks that support its self-development: enabling grassroots cultural production, organization and working to promote practising 'social culture' and, last but not least, by establishing social institutions of culture.

The Polish version of this paper, which has been published in the book Kultura i rozwój. Analizy, rekomendacje, studia przypadków, ed. Jerzy Hausner, Izabela Jasi ska, Mikołaj Lewicki (Warszawa-Kraków: Instytut Studiów Zaawansowanych, Fundacja Gospodarki i Administracji Publicznej, 2016) was translated by Monika Bokiniec and edited by Anna Zaranko.

Notes

1 Nicolas Bourriaud, *Relational Aesthetics*, trans. Simon Pleasance and Fronza Woods (Dijon: Les presses du réel, 2002).

2 Erica Fischer-Lichte, *The Transformative Power of Performance*, trans. Saskya Iris Jain (London and New York: Routledge, 2008).

3 Artur Żmijewski, 'Stosowane sztuki społeczne', *Krytyka Polityczna* no. 11–12, 2007, pp. 14–24; 'To nie sen awangardy: Z Arturem Żmijewskim rozmawia Piotr Kosiewski', *Didaskalia* 112 (2012), pp. 47–80; 'Sztuka działa: O tym, jak sztuka staje się faktem politycznym opowiada Artur Żmijewski – kurator niedawno zakończonego w Berlinie Biennale – w rozmowie z Igorem Stokfiszewskim z Krytyki Politycznej', *Przekrój* no. 28/29 (3497/8), 2012, pp. 70–71; effectiveness of contemporary art was a subject of *Nie lękajcie się,* special issue of *Krytyka Polityczna* 30 (2012).

4 Katarzyna Górna et al., eds., *Czarna księga polskich artystów* (Warsaw: Obywatelskie Forum Sztuki Współczesnej, 2015); Iwo Zmyślony, 'System nas wykorzystuje: Rozmowa z Winter Holiday Camp', Dwutygodnik.com, 2014, 1, p. 124, www.dwutygodnik.com/artykul/4992-system-nas-wykorzystuje.html (accessed 6 November 2015); *Krytyka Polityczna* 2015, pp. 40–41.

5 Michał Kozłowski, Jan Sowa and Kuba Szreder, eds., *Fabryka Sztuki: Podział pracy oraz dystrybucja kapitałów społecznych w polu sztuk wizualnych we współczesnej Polsce* (Warsaw: Fundacja Nowej Kultury Bęc Zmiana, 2014) (accessed 6 November 2015).

6 Teresa Wilk, *Rewitalizacja społeczna poprzez współczesną sztukę teatralną w ocenie reprezentantów (twórców i odbiorców) sztuki dramatycznej Legnicy, Nowej Huty i Wałbrzycha* (Katowice: Wydawnictwo Uniwersytetu Śląskiego, 2010); Maciej Gdula and Przemysław Sadura, *Klasowe zróżnicowanie stylów życia a stosunek do teatru* (Warszawa: Instytut Studiów Zaawansowanych, commissioned by the Zbigniew Raszewski Theatre Institute, 2013) (accessed 6 November 2015); Wojciech Józef Burszta et al., *Badanie publiczności teatrów w stolicy* (Warsaw: Fundacja Generacja, Fundacja Obserwatorium, Instytut Teatralny im. Zbigniewa Raszewskiego, TR Warszawa, 2013) (accessed 6 November 2015).

7 Tomasz Rakowski, 'Etnografia/Animacja/Sztuka: Wprowadzenie', in *Etnografia/Animacja/Sztuka: Nierozpoznane wymiary rozwoju kulturalnego*, ed. Tomasz Rakowski (Warsaw: Narodowe Centrum Kultury, 2013), p. 29.

8 The expression 'social culture' appears in the title 'Artistic Culture – "Social Culture"', in *No Culture, No Europe: On the Foundation of Politics* (Antennae), ed. by Pascal Gielen (Amsterdam: Valiz, 2015). The authors of the volume do not explain this notion but their observations suggest that their understanding of 'social culture' is close to the one I propose in this paper.

9 Edwin Bendyk, 'Metakultura rozwoju', in *Kultura i rozwój: Analizy, rekomendacje, studia przypadków*, ed. Jerzy Hausner et al. (Warsaw: Instytut Studiów Zaawansowanych; Kraków: Fundacja Gospodarki i Administracji Publicznej, 2016), pp. 27–45.

10 Detailed descriptions and results of the programmes 'Kultura i rozwój', 'Spisek kultury' and 'Fraktale. W stronę metakultury rozwoju' conducted by Edwin Bendyk can be found on https://spisekkultury.wordpress.com/ (accessed 6 November 2015).

11 Rakowski, 'Etnografia/Animacja/Sztuka'.

12 *Stan i zróżnicowanie kultury wsi i małych miast w Polsce: Kanon i rozproszenie*, ed. Izabella Bukraby-Rylska and Wojciech Józef Burszta (Warsaw: Narodowe Centrum Kultury, 2011).

13 Wojciech Józef Burszta et al., *Kultura miejska w Polsce z perspektywy interdyscyplinarnych badań jakościowych* (Warsaw: Narodowe Centrum Kultury, 2010).

14 Marek Krajewski, ed., *Niewidzialne miasto* (Warsaw: Fundacja Nowej Kultury Bęc Zmiana, 2012).

15 Rafał Drozdowski and Marek Krajewski, *Za fotografię! W stronę radykalnego programu socjologii wizualnej* (Warsaw: Fundacja Nowej Kultury Bęc Zmiana, 2010).

16 Mirosław Filiciak and Alek Tarkowski, *Dwa zero: Alfabet nowej kultury i inne teksty* (Gdańsk: słowo/obraz terytoria, 2015).

17 Tomasz Szlendak et al., *Dziedzictwo w akcji: Rekonstrukcja historyczna jako sposób uczestnictwa w kulturze* (Warsaw: Narodowe Centrum Kultury, 2012).

18 Maciej Gdula, Mikołaj Lewicki and Przemysław Sadura, *Praktyki kulturowe klasy ludowej* (Warsaw: Instytut Studiów Zaawansowanych, 2014) (accessed 6 November 2015).

19 'JASKÓŁKI: nowe zjawiska w warszawskich instytucjach i nieinstytucjach kultury' was implemented by the Association of Creative Initiatives 'ę' in 2014 (accessed 6 November 2015).

20 'Social Museums, Local Collections: Dynamics of Changes in the Cultural Landscape' was implemented by the Ari Ari Foundation in 2013 (accessed 6 November 2015); 'Social Museums, Local Collections: Report from the Research', ed. Monika Maciejewska, Longin Graczyk and Ari Ari Foundation (accessed 6 November 2015); Krzysztof Żwirblis, *Muzeum Społeczne/Social Museum* (Zielona Góra: BWA Zielona Góra, Galeria Arsenał Białystok, 2014).

21 Dariusz Kosiński, *Teatra Polskie: Historie* (Warsaw: Wydawnictwo Naukowe PWN, Instytut Teatralny im. Zbigniewa Raszewskiego, 2010); Dariusz Kosiński, *Teatra polskie: Rok katastrofy* (Warsaw: Instytut Teatralny im. Zbigniewa Raszewskiego; Kraków: Wydawnictwo Znak, 2013).

22 Information on the activities of Obserwatorium Żywej Kultury is available at http://ozkultura.pl/ (accessed 6 November 2015).

23 Jerzy Hausner, Anna Karwińska and Jacek Purchla, eds., *Kultura a rozwój* (Warsaw: Narodowe Centrum Kultury, 2013).

24 Wojciech Kłosowski, ed., *Kierunek kultura: Promocja regionu poprzez kulturę* (Warsaw: Mazowieckie Centrum Kultury i Sztuki, 2009); Wojciech Kłosowski, ed., *Kierunek kultura: W stronę żywego uczestnictwa w kulturze* (Warsaw: Mazowieckie Centrum Kultury i Sztuki, 2011); Wojciech Kłosowski, ed., *Kierunek kultura. Uwaga na podmioty!* (Warsaw: Mazowieckie Centrum Kultury i Sztuki, 2012).

25 Rakowski, 'Etnografia/Animacja/Sztuka', p. 12.

26 Kłosowski, *Kierunek kultura*, p. 51.

27 Initiatives worth mentioning include: Autonomiczne Centrum Społeczne Cicha4 (Lublin), Hackerspace (Warsaw), Cohabitat Foundation (Łódź), Stowarzyszenie De-novo (Dynów), Stowarzyszenie Kulturotwórcze Nie z Tej Bajki (Ostrowiec Świętokrzyski), Stowarzyszenie ToTu – Akademia Twórczych Umiejętności (Czaplinek), Stowarzyszenie Terra Artis (Lanckorona), Raft Association (Olsztyn), Village Theatre 'Węgajty' (Węgajty), Political Critique (Warsaw) with its network of community centres and clubs organizing, for example, grassroots celebrations of the anniversary of 1905 Revolution in Łódź, forums of culture in Cieszyn and conducting long-term work on preserving the heritage of industrial culture in Ursus, a Warsaw district, in the Gdańsk shipyards, in Ostrowiec Świętokrzyski and Gniezno, the Rural Women's Association (Lesznowola), the social movements Kultura na Sielcach (Warsaw) and Otwarty Jazdów (Warsaw), Praska Biblioteka Sąsiedzka (Warsaw), Łaźnia Nowa Theatre (Nowa Huta, in Kraków) and Zamek Cieszyn (Cieszyn), 'The Districts' studio of socially engaged art (Lublin) and collectives gathered on the Off Piotrkowska premises and in other places around Łódź.

28 Including Teatro Valle Occupato (Rome), culture commissions of the 15-M Movement (Spain), autonomous social centres such as ESC Atelier and Cinema Palazzo in Rome, cultural centres deriving from the domain of social economy such as Les têtes de l'art (Marseille) or Platonique (Spain), social movements such as Culture2Commons (Zagreb), hybrid establishments, for example the cultural centre Pogon in Zagreb (social-public) and Subtopia in Stockholm (social-public-private).

29 From the title of the book describing these organizations and institutions, Charles Beckett et al., eds., *Build the City: Perspectives on Commons and Culture* (Warsaw-Amsterdam: Krytyka Polityczna, European Cultural Foundation, 2015).

30 Przemysław Sadura, 'Inicjatywy nieformalne, NGO-sy, hybrydy:

zróżnicowanie poszerzonego pola kultury', in *Kultura i rozwój: Analizy, rekomendacje, studia przypadków*, ed. Jerzy Hausner et al. (Warsaw: Instytut Studiów Zaawansowanych; Kraków: Fundacja Gospodarki i Administracji Publicznej, 2016), pp. 157-175.

31 Sadura, 'Inicjatywy nieformalne, NGO-sy, hybrydy'.

32 Tomasz Rakowski, *Łowcy, zbieracze, praktycy niemocy: Etnografia człowieka zdegradowanego* (Gda sk: słowo/obraz terytoria, 2009).

33 Piotr Marecki, ed., *Kultura niezależna w Polsce 1989-2009* (Kraków: Korporacja Ha!art, 2010).

34 Christina Flesher Fominaya, *Social Movements and Globalization: How Protests, Occupations and Uprisings are Changing the World* (New York: Palgrave Macmillan, 2014), p. 187.

35 See 'Cultural Resistance in a Globalized World', in Fominaya, *Social Movements and Globalization*, pp. 81-104.

36 Bruno Latour, *Politics of Nature: How to Bring the Sciences into Democracy*, trans. Catherine Porter (Cambridge, MA, and London: Harvard University Press, 2004).

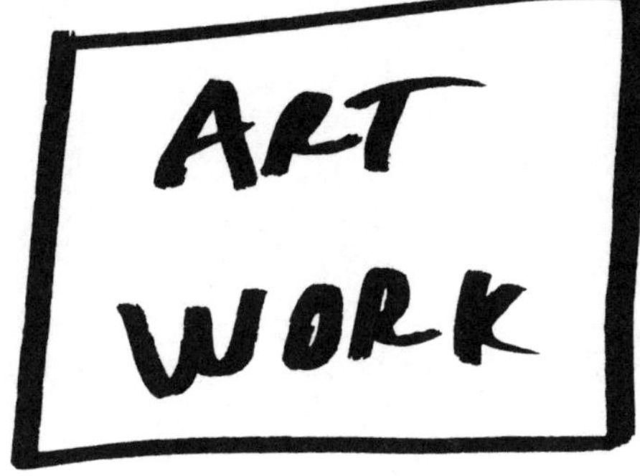

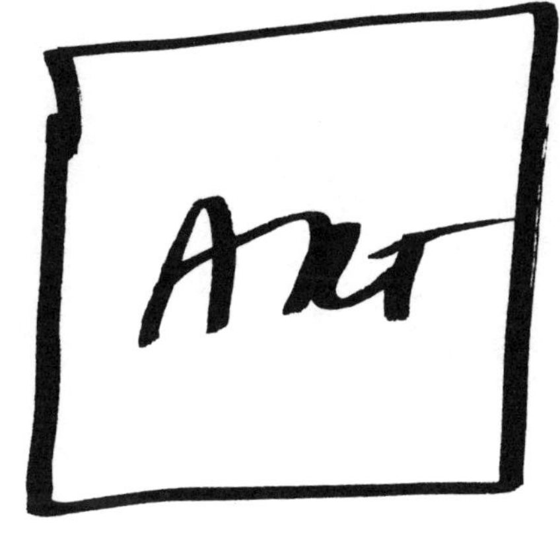

WORK

Rethinking Relationships
The Civic Role of Arts Organizations in England

Andrew Barnett

Patterns of arts production and consumption have changed dramatically over the last three decades as a result of new technology, shifts in public attitudes and expectations, and changing demographics. New technology has transformed the ways in which the arts are presented, consumed and created by both professional artists and amateurs dedicated in their practice. Arts organizations have also had to respond to an expectation that they should be more engaged with and engaging of their audiences and communities; and to the expectation that the diversity of these communities should be reflected in the work produced. These trends are only likely to become more marked.

Since May 2016, the Calouste Gulbenkian Foundation (UK Branch) therefore has been conducting an Inquiry into the civic role of arts organizations in England, the sort of arts organizations we have been supporting as a foundation for over sixty years. Preliminary findings from the first phase of this work – research, consultation and analysis – are clearly relevant to this book of essays. The impetus for the Inquiry was a view that the relationship between arts organizations and the public is changing and is likely to change even more because of social, political, economic and cultural trends. Our hypothesis was that this relationship needs re-examination and re-negotiation. Our aspiration was to help arts organizations become 'future proof' by encouraging them with, and supporting them in, the task: to turn the dial.

At the heart of our Inquiry lies a question: how can arts organizations better fulfil their civic role? This was not born from mere curiosity but from ambition. This is an ambition consistent with the work of the Foundation over six decades and with our international role as a small part of a bigger European organization. It comes from a belief in the benefit that participation in the arts confers on all of us – validating our stories and creating new ones – and their potential in a changing world to bridge diverse communities and renew the bonds between us. And from a belief that the inherent creativity in all of us offers rewards all around. François Matarasso says it best in his book *Mirror Images*:

> Art's ability to ferry us between different shores of understanding is vital in a public space dominated by communications that are reductively simple ... or simply deceptive. When political divisions are daily widened by

words of fear and hatred, the complexity of artistic statements are necessary firebreaks.

Throughout the Inquiry, we have been inspired by engagement, and the insights, from practitioners across England and several organizations we looked at abroad. Visiting them has, for me, been important. Our work has produced a bank of forty case studies identified by experts as demonstrating inspiring practice. The number will grow as we progress. Some of these organizations operate at a local or 'hyper local' neighbourhood level, but nevertheless have strong international connections. Interviewees who had participated in international study trips and exchanges stressed the inspiration these had provided. However, our case study organizations often appear not to be networked with organizations with the same or similar concerns or ways of working based in the UK, let alone abroad. There is clearly opportunity to benefit this work by encouraging better national and international connections.

Contested Language: Civic vs Civil

There is a subtle difference between the title of our Inquiry and the intended focus of this book. Our inquiry is into the *civic* role of arts organizations. This book is about the scope these organizations have for *civil* action. 'Civic' and 'civil' are similar words, but they are not the same.

For us, civic role was preferable to the alternative suggestions because:

- it suggests the importance of place and place making, to which the arts and culture are vitally important;
- of its association with 'civic virtues' (discussion of which dates to ancient Greece and Rome) and their vital link to education;
- of its association with great philanthropists and pioneers of the nineteenth century who sought to make the arts available to all during the Victorian era;
- it suggests the importance of active engagement in the public sphere perhaps most particularly, and most now under challenge, democratic processes.

When we use the term 'civic' we are not seeking to privilege the urban over the rural, state over independent action, or established forms over new. We are seeking simply to emphasize the importance of arts organizations acting as public as opposed to private organizations with responsibilities for their communities and to society more generally. In using the term 'civic role', we will stress the positives from its past and re-invent it as appropriate to arts organizations in the twenty-first century.

During the consultation with arts organizations some asked why we had decided to use the term civic as opposed to civil, in the sense of 'civil society'. In Britain definitions of 'civil society' are yet more contested than definitions of 'civic role'. The term 'civil society' tends to be synonymous with associational life, divorced from the profit motive and independent from government. We preferred the term 'civic' because it can encompass partnership working that blurs the boundaries between the voluntary, private and public sectors.

Words carry resonances of history and social context that are more textured than dictionary definitions. Our use of 'civic' feels right for us but I do not believe it limits us to an Anglo-Saxon enclave.

Geography Makes a Difference

The review of the literature suggests that geography makes a marked difference in how the civic role of arts organizations is conceptualized.

The US literature is more substantial than that in Europe. It sometimes uses the term 'civic role' which is absent elsewhere. On occasion, it refers to 'the place of art in the world' making a link between it and education in civics. Over recent years in the US, some arts practitioners have also placed an emphasis on 'communities not audiences'. This points to issues of strategy and mission. The implication is that an arts organization might re-consider its mission, build partnerships with other local organizations and focus on the needs of its community and how it can meet them, while at the same time pursuing its artistic ambitions. Obviously, this is a governance issue and a matter for trustees who are community aware and engaged.

Recent continental European literature tends to emphasize the role of arts and cultural organizations as political activists or supporters of activism, leading campaigns on social, economic and environmental issues. Its roots are perhaps partly in central and eastern Europe where, once the socialist regimes and the Soviet Union fell apart, there was a flowering of new politically engaged artistic activity and entrepreneurialism. Many organizations with a bias towards the civic in continental Europe are deemed to have common features. These include a hybrid nature with commercial and subsidized and community activity rubbing shoulders within the same organization. They are also characterized as 'alternative', not necessarily concerned with national culture or the artistic canon and as adopting new organizational structures and ways of working. That has its place. I am pluralist.

The UK relevant literature does not emphasize political activism and the power of the arts to mobilize campaigns and achieve political change (a common feature in continental European and the US literature). Rather, the civic is framed as concerned with individual self-realization and the relationship between the individual and their community and wider society.

Our consultation suggested that there was resistance amongst arts organizations to the notion that having a civic role might mean engagement with politics. Perhaps this is because of a feeling that art plus politics equals propaganda which equals inferior art. To quote François Matarasso again, he argues that: 'Art is an antidote to political slogans and dangerous simplicities. It makes things more complex, not less. It helps us see things from other points of view.' He suggests that, instead, it helps us to consider things in all their complexity from different angles. It allows us to come to our own view. It is the opposite of propaganda.

While the literature is nuanced in its conceptualization of civic role, one common feature spans the different geographies: the belief that in turbulent times, there is an urgency about arts organizations being supported and encouraged to think and act civically. That remains the case whatever your emphasis: it is about community (a feature of practice in the UK), activism, inclusion, or social justice (a framing we observe in the US).

Our Own Focus

The lens through which we see the civic role of arts organizations is that of organizational mission and strategy in part because we want to move beyond definition. It is about the ethos of organizations and how they see their role in the world and whether they think and act in way that emphasizes community and society generally.

Much of the feedback we received during the consultation stressed the importance of individual artists and arts practitioners. There is a point there but one we've decided for reasons of manageability to revisit at another time. Some suggested in the consultation that our project should extend beyond the arts and encompass culture more broadly and cover, for example, food and horticulture. While our focus continues to be arts organizations, we are interested in how the communities they engage with choose to frame this engagement and this may be through broader culture. This seems crucially important given that one of our themes is listening to people and putting them first: The former artistic director of the London International Festival of Culture intentionally elevates cultural democracy over a previous concern with democratizing culture:

> I passionately believe in cultural democracy... Going into somewhere like Tottenham, the idea that there's no culture there is bollocks: it's full of culture, it's just not culture like our culture. It's culture around food, it's culture around music, it's culture around block parties, it's culture around carnival. Those things are really exciting; they allow us to think about things in different ways, rather than just make another theatre show.

It has been challenging to encourage people to think beyond individual projects to the 'civic stance' of an organization. When we initially canvassed for inspiring examples of arts organizations re-imagining their civic role and at the cutting edge of practice, most suggestions received were individual projects. Few were examples of arts organizations taking a strategic approach, on which we place an emphasis.

One final caveat: our starting point is that arts production by itself, divorced from civic intent, is a public good deserving of support. Not all arts organizations will want to engage with an agenda that extends beyond the arts and nor should they be forced to do so. But, we have been so impressed by the civic practice of our case studies that we want to examine, celebrate it and facilitate its development at a crucial time of change.

Change Will Never Be This Slow Again

In the seventy years since the establishment of the Arts Council(s) in the UK, there has been significant debate about both the rationale for and the extent and focus of public funding for the arts. Comment has regularly surfaced that more should be spent outside London, on smaller and emerging as opposed to established arts organizations, on BAME (Black, Asian & Minority Ethnic) arts and on amateur arts. Within the context of harsh public spending costs, fiscal restraint and a crisis in local authority funding, the debate becomes ever more intense. This is a debate that has largely passed arts organizations in Europe by as support for established arts practice generally holds up and is divorced from what happens on the radical fringe.

With sometimes dramatic cuts in funding for arts organizations in England, this has stimulated interest in, and debate about, the responsibilities of organizations that receive public funding. They can better justify their role and, with support, can do so. In some areas, arts organizations are deploying their creativity to help local authorities achieve better outcomes such as health and social care outcomes, with stagnant or reduced budgets (perhaps not just social prescribing but cultural prescribing).

Arts organizations are not the only ones under pressure. There is growing disillusionment with conventional political processes although the recent General Election of 2017 saw much higher turnouts and a failure for any one political party to secure a majority (further suggesting social and political division if we didn't already know that and a need for a different settlement). A striking aspect of our first consultation was belief in 'people-powered' local action. The suggestion was that an emphasis should be placed on inspiring and supporting local people to recognize and build on their assets, including skills and capabilities. Arts organizations have the creative processes and people with the skills to enable and facilitate this.

A further spur for action is the need to stimulate children's participation in the arts. Major studies in the US have demonstrated that when the arts are an integral part of education children learn more and achieve better qualifications. Yet the Warwick Commission (2015) concluded that the arts and creativity are being squeezed out of schools. The Social Mobility Commission (2016) concludes that in Great Britain 'for this generation of young people, it [social mobility] is getting worse not better'. It also says that it isn't just the poorest in society that face barriers to progress. Other research demonstrates that children's life chances are significantly affected by the quality of cultural education they receive.

One role of arts education – delivered formally through the education system or less formally though participation in the activities of arts organizations – is to foster creativity. Looking ahead, technological developments are likely to mean that only the most creative of us will be able to gain and keep employment. Some suggest that developments in artificial intelligence may mean that up to 30 per cent of job roles can be mechanized. The NESTA report (2015) *Creativity vs Robots* found that 87 per cent of highly creative workers are at low or no risk of automation, compared with 40 per cent of all workers. Other social trends that highlight some vacuum arts organizations can fill include:

- the shrinking of public space in city centres where people can congregate free from pressure to consume and move on;
- the chronic problem of loneliness among older people;
- a massive decline in engagement with organized religion.

Five Metaphors for Understanding What's Happening

During our work, and with the guidance of our advisory panel, we found it useful to develop five metaphors to describe different aspects of the civic role of arts organizations. Any individual organization may display several aspects, but it is not necessary to cover all these bases to achieve an exemplary civic performance.

Colleges – Arts Organizations as Places of Learning

Education is about skills and creativity and about knowledge and experiences too; it is in part based on experience of the world and its complexities, knowledge that acquaints us with our history and culture and that of others. Emphasis has rightly been placed on creative education and what happens in schools. However, we also learn outside formal educational settings, and throughout our lives. The arts are integral to this. Arts organizations have a role as places of life-long learning, enabling everyone to reach their potential.

Town Halls – Arts Organizations as Places of Debate

Art has always stimulated and reflected current debates about issues as diverse as human rights and strife between different generations based on wealth inequalities. Pressing issues today include climate change, increasing inequality and the implications of Britain's withdrawal from Europe. Trust in organizations is waning and there is scepticism about experts. There is a risk that some issues are regarded as too big and therefore insoluble. Arts organizations provide safe places for considering and debating difficult issues. They can present issues in their full complexity and give them a human texture. They can go further and mobilize campaigns.

Parks – Arts Organizations as Shared Spaces Open to All

Having shared public space is important. In some cities there is a sense that there is very little non-commercial public space left. People feel crowded out. Public parks are perhaps the best example of an open community resource in which all can gather. They help to maintain and develop a sense of community. Parks offer people choice: to quietly read, to play football, to have a picnic, to mix or remain solitary. Similarly, arts organizations can help to create a sense of community by providing open and non-judgemental public space.

Temples – Arts Organizations as Places of Enlightenment and Solace

Roger Scruton suggests that during the Enlightenment, as religion started to lose its central position in our society, art and literature took its place. For some: 'arts organizations are temples of culture, regularly visited on days of rest'. In a secular society arts organizations provide us with an opportunity to contemplate moral questions about how we live and how we relate to others. They provide us with an opportunity to reflect on what is important, for example kindness and love. They generate empathy. They provide solace in difficult times and encourage hope.

Home – Art Organizations as Home

In the Victorian era the new city museums and galleries were regarded as a new kind of 'domesticated public space' (alongside parks). The idea was that they provided a sphere separate from industrial capitalism and offered refuge, beauty and morality. Early supporters of the Sunday opening of these museums and galleries contrasted the 'public house' with the 'public home'.

Today, they provide diverse groups of people with the opportunity to create work based on their experiences and aspirations. They provide them with a place in which their experiences are legitimized and valued. They provide them with 'a home'.

Another Lens: Back To the Future

Alongside metaphor, there is practice in our past that may serve as a useful guide for the future: versions 1, 2 and 3.

The Arts as a Means of Education and Control (Version 1)

In the 1800s, Mechanics Institutes provided lectures in the arts, sciences and technical subjects and acted as libraries for working people. Public museums, arts galleries, libraries and parks, 'new forms of public space', were established in the Victorian era. Museums and galleries were regarded as a means of education and control of the 'working classes'. More positively, they were viewed as an idealized 'domestic sphere: separate from industrial capitalism and offering refuge, beauty, and morality... [While] the beauty of nature (and nature through art) was a necessary counterpoint to cities, particularly industrial cities'.[1] In 1903 the Workers Educational Association (WEA) was founded. It was committed to widening participation in learning and education with a social purpose. It continues today and is one of the largest voluntary sector providers of adult education in the country. The Pitmen Painters and Whitechapel Art Gallery provide good examples of initiatives established to educate the 'working classes' which drew wider interest and public acclaim.

A New Emphasis on Access and Participation (Version 2)

Throughout the twentieth century the major preoccupation was access and participation but largely in support of a 'high art agenda': 'if only you come to see what I do you will love it'.

The Second World War created a sense of solidarity and a desire to raise public morale which led to the creation of the Council for the Encouragement of Music and the Arts. This gave money to ballet, opera and drama companies to perform in military camps and before civilians. Performances in the UK took place often in community or church halls and overseas in makeshift theatres in camps – sometimes very close to the frontline. Approximately 2.6 million shows were staged; for some audiences, this was the first time they ever saw ballet or opera.

Based on the success of the Council for the Encouragement of Music and the Arts, The Arts Council of Great Britain was created by Royal Charter in 1946 to provide 'great art for all' (nearly seventy years on we question if that has been achieved) although the balance between 'great art' and 'for all' has often been called into question.

The next major landmark is the White Paper for the Arts produced in 1964 by the first Minister for the Arts, Jennie Lee. She argued that the arts should be part of everyday life for children and adults. Her vision remains a rallying cry for many artists and arts organizations today. The 1960s were a progressive decade in which authority was questioned and there was a demand for rights for women and minority groups. In the arts, this manifested itself in 'community arts', marking a departure from traditional practice because it was rooted in community collaboration and a concern with social justice, including some of the 'protest' seen in countries outside the UK. The movement grew gradually during the 1960s and 1970s. By 1974, the Association of Community Artists counted 149 different groups; some still in existence today.

Co-production and Everyday Creativity (Version 3)

In recent years, arts organizations have shown a renewed interest in facilitating and enabling creativity in their community and in the individual 'non-professional' as artist or curator. As Alistair Hudson from mima says the focus has shifted to 'user-generated' content.

The case studies that we have compiled of arts organizations re-imagining their civic role, discussed in detail in the next chapter, provide many inspiring examples of co-production with local communities or communities of interest. For these organizations, creative practice is part of their DNA and they demonstrate it by exploring the issues and concerns of the people they work with and for. These issues and concerns are broad ranging and include: housing, immigration, loneliness and isolation, health and social care. Creative processes and techniques are being used to find imaginative solutions.

Arguably, as opposed to 'place making' being synonymous with economic regeneration, there is greater interest in how the arts can make areas better places to live, for example by building social capital and contributing to community cohesion (ACE's Creative People and Places programme does this as do other initiatives).

There is also a more general trend towards recognizing and encouraging the artist in all of us or 'everyday creativity'. This is perhaps best exemplified in two relatively recent initiatives: Fun Palaces and the BBC's Get Creative Campaign. In 2014 a reimagining of the late great Joan Littlewood's Fun Palaces was staged to mark her centenary. It was so successful that Fun Palaces have been held internationally every year since. The guidelines for local groups seeking to host one is that it is free, local, innovative, transformative and engaging.

In late 2015, 64 Million Artists was commissioned by Arts Council England to deliver a nationwide consultation looking at the value of everyday creativity within arts and culture in England. This work was part of what led to the formation of BBC Get Creative, a campaign run by a group of cultural organizations to celebrate and support activities such as crafts, taking photographs and cooking. Get Creative is trying to inspire people to try something new. It has, for example, produced a series of videos showing tips and tricks in activities as diverse as nail art and woodwork.

Case Studies – The Same But Different

All the organizations in our case studies have common features. First and foremost, they are organizations dedicated to excellence in artistic practice and the fostering of individual creativity. They have inspiring leadership committed to the civic role of their organization and generous in demeanour. People are central to their practice, meaning that their aesthetic is based on working with and in their local communities, facilitating and enabling them to pursue their interests and needs. Place is important to them including in some instances 'place making' being a core concern. Finally, fostering relationships and developing strong human connections is a key aspect of their approach.

Place and Place Making

All arts organizations have some commitment to the place or location in which they work. Some are formed in response to a specific local issue; for instance, the Ministry of Stories was set up in Hoxton to reach four boroughs, including three of London's poorest ones.

Many are connected to a place by the people that create or work in the organization. For instance, a group of local volunteers spent ten years trying to establish a local gallery space, creating Lightbox in Woking. The gallery continues to focus on its local audience, including ensuring that its board of trustees is formed of local community members, helping to deepen its roots in the local area.

At mima in Middlesbrough, Director Alistair Hudson has an active philosophy of localism, as 'the antidote to the international blockbuster', endeavouring to 'shake off' the historical idea of a museum as detached, not relevant or not accessible to local communities. Taking this theme literally, mima curated an exhibition entitled 'Localism', telling the story of Middlesbrough through contributions made by locals.

The ambition to improve access to the arts and, importantly, the spaces of arts organizations, either or both where art is created or performed, has a notable effect on the physical spaces of the communities where art organizations operate.

All the organizations interviewed said they had social objectives that went beyond the delivery of arts activities though differed as to how central to their mission these lie (with a myriad of different practices). Some interviewees described their concern as being less about applying creativity in a cultural context and more about the application of creativity to life. For example, Battersea Arts Centre is using creative processes and techniques to help young people develop new social as well as creative enterprises. Another dimension of difference in the case studies is the extent to which the organizations operate at the local or hyper local level or have a national or even international remit. One feature though is that some of the organizations that are most rooted in a place tend to have quite strong international connections.

International Inspiration

Many of the arts organizations we interviewed cited international inspiration for their work. Ministry of Stories is modelled on not-for-profit organizations in the USA. Situations is part of a 15-year long network of ten to fifteen international organizations. Entelechy Arts, Streetwise Opera and Battersea Arts Centre were all influenced by the inspiring projects they visited on a study trip to Brazil. Star and Shadow cite as an inspiration 'similar radical cinema models throughout Europe'. The Freedom Festival is part of European networks in order 'to open up progression routes for local artists' and to share resources. It particularly admires the

French system's focus on residency. We were struck by examples from Portugal where the Foundation is headquartered. Two things are striking: work with individuals facing great disadvantage such as prisoners (prisoners and people with disabilities in the case of PELE based in Portugal); and how, in Porto's Casa da Musica its leaders are working with the homeless and supporting its choir Som da Rua showing the mainstream reaching out to the periphery.

Some of our case study organizations have a focus on the transformation of individuals. for example supporting and nurturing young people or supporting older people though the transitions that middle and later life can bring. Others spoke about their work in terms of building a sense of community and community cohesion. Some took this one stage further and, while they do not describe it as such, are engaged in community development. By this we mean that they are facilitating and developing community organizations and businesses. The objective is to leave a legacy in the community beyond the life of any one project or event.

Moving from the individual to a concern with community and social cohesion the Sage Gateshead has recently changed its mission:

> ...from enriching life through music to making change though community, culture and place. So from something that we felt ... [was concerned with the] individual to more of a focus on a) the collective and b) the wider sense of culture.

Situations has also recently been considering its approach:

> ... one of the things she [Nina Simon] talks about is that in the past we've thought about targeting or reaching particular communities ... [so you] tailor the work to that targeted community. And increasingly what's far more interesting ... [given the post Brexit landscape] is how you create connections between people who have different interests, and you create a community around a project that creates those connections.

Most of our case study organizations are dependent on project funding. In some cases, this means that they work with different groups over time or that projects may vary in their emphasis. For example, while the focus of the organization may be older people, it may at certain points in time concentrate on work in care homes while at others, it may work with people with dementia. This is funder-driven. Other organizations are committed to specific local communities or to working over the long term with defined groups of people. One case study interviewee for example, referred to working with the same individuals over the course of a twenty or thirty year period.

Working with one or two vulnerable or under-served groups is the focus for some of our case study organizations: young people living on estates on which drugs and gangs are a prominent feature; migrants living in refugee camps or working class people living in areas. Other organizations are committed to working with the public and providing them with opportunities to engage with art forms or otherwise develop their creativity. Notably two interviewees referred to the fact that they would like to use processes that they reserve for groups traditionally regarded as underserved to engage with the wider public.

Barriers and Levers For Change

We asked our case study organizations about the challenges they are experiencing in re-imagining their civic role and the opportunities they identify to develop this. The following emerged:

Leadership

While our case study organizations have excellent leadership, our impression is that many are over-stretched and under-supported. One refers to lack of time and space to think strategically and aspires to create opportunities for herself and for others.

People and Skills

Co-production with communities requires a different skill set. This means that producers, curators and artists may require training and support to enable them to deliver this work well.

Partnership Working

The case studies identify many examples of different sorts of partnership working with other arts organizations, with universities, with social sector organizations and with local authorities. However, with a few notable exceptions, the impression given is that our cohort want deeper partnerships that last for longer periods of time.

Funding

These organizations are not pre-occupied by funding but they do point to difficulties: co-production means not knowing where the work might go at the start, whereas funders often want certainty. With sustained national funding privileging a few, the more common project funding makes it difficult to sustain valuable work in the community. Conventional evaluation techniques often sit uncomfortably with the nature of the work and its ethos.

Growth and Replication

Some smaller, newer organizations are seeking to grow or replicate their models. A few are doing this successfully despite a harsh funding environment. A few of these speak of concerns including losing their community roots and a dilution of quality in their engagement activity and artistic product. Rather than being concerned about organizational growth, for some the main emphasis is on building social capital locally. Funding is usually targeted at a privileged few for core costs or small, one-off projects; it is rarely available for work that could be spread or grown.

Business Models

One case study organization refers to how an emphasis on the civic means working in new ways with different sorts of people. It potentially opens access to a wider range of different funding sources, local or health authority contracts, for example.

Diversity

A few organizations refer to the challenge of ensuring their participants and staff are sufficiently diverse to reflect the communities in which they are based or work. Success factors appear to be a willingness to go to communities as opposed to expecting them to come to you and working with their definition of what constitutes the arts and culture. Peer support and networking may be valuable here.

Language and Communication

One theme that emerges strongly from the interviews is problems of language and communication. The view is that we lack a common language and a classification system. This makes it difficult to describe this work well, in all its variety. This is important because the implication is that we lack the tools for analyzing and understanding it better. Some also refer to its lack of profile and the need to promote it and its value more effectively. We have developed some principles to be tested alongside our metaphors.

The Arts Offer Something Truly Unique

The arts provide a window through which we can collectively understand our place in this changing world. They possess unique potential to inspire, challenge and connect (between each other and, inside, between our own hearts and minds). Culture affords us an expansive idea of who we are and invites us to step into others' shoes. The arts are a medium for information, help equip us with the ability to think critically, and enable us to empathize and imagine. Our community coheres only within the bounds of that imagination and we need to push that as broad as our community is diverse.

Funding constraints have stimulated a debate about the responsibilities those organizations supported by public funding have and who they perceive to be their beneficiaries. Questions are asked about the role of arts organizations – particularly national companies and building-based ones – in the wider ecology of the arts, and their communities. Emphasis is rightly placed on how arts organizations engage the least served.

Yet the argument that art just needs more money feels wanting. And the old discourse that pits the intrinsic versus the instrumental is a dead end. Arts organizations, like others in the public or social domain, need to think through why they exist, and for whom, and what that means for them going forward. Often sitting at the heart of communities, seeking out renewed relevance will mean having an awareness of the changing nature of those communities and the balance in them of different age groups and those with different cultural heritage.

Those that rise to the challenge can realize their full potential. Transitioning from old ways of doing things to new models – journeying from version 1 to version 2 or 3 – has huge potential for new connections to be forged including directly with people and communities. These are communities that feel more divided and deserving of love and care than ever.

Bringing It All Together

When we established the Inquiry, we said our goal was to have catalysed a strong and growing movement of arts organizations that fully embrace their civic role by 2025. Our aspiration is that these organizations would make a significant positive difference to the lives of large numbers of people living across the English regions and have ripple effects elsewhere. I hope my colleagues in the Foundation headquartered in Lisbon will take and interest and interpret this to their own context.

But to achieve this, change is needed in: organizational governance and support for leaders; partnership working and the extent to which arts leaders act as local 'connectors'; networking and support including access to international inspiration. Changes are needed in policy and funding, too.

This ambition is too big, and the issues identified too complex, the potential programme of work too large, for one organization by itself. Our Inquiry is an invitation to all born of curiosity, generosity and ambition to do something different that befits the twenty-first century: the arts can heal our wounds and bring communities together.

This Is More Than Theory For Me

I've seen first-hand the civic role arts organizations can play and none stands out more to me than our work alongside With One Voice.

It began as London was preparing for the 2012 Olympics. Matt Peacock of StreetWise Opera and Ruth Mackenzie, charged by the London Olympic Games Organising Committee to curate the Cultural Festival, with myself and others, came together to respond to the simple challenge: how could we find a place in the great Olympic celebration for the homeless and the marginalized?

The answer was London's own Royal Opera House. Three hundred people with experience of homelessness came in from the cold and were welcomed to that iconic venue as equals. We were treated to more than a dozen performances and the most moving rendition of *O Sole mio* by a single elderly homeless man positioned in the gallery and whose voice echoed around the space. This one-off event turned out to be anything but. Two years later, we were back; this time taking the main stage of the Royal Opera House.

With the next Olympics approaching, this time in Rio de Janeiro, we continued to support exchanges and learning. There proved to be appetite for a global arts and homelessness movement. For the 2016 Cultural Olympiad, there was not one performance but nearly forty. With choirs popping up in iconic venues such as the steps of the Teatro Municipal (Rio's equivalent to the Opera House) and the Museum of Tomorrow, a jaw-droppingly contemporary space which echoed to the sounds of homeless people singing and playing instruments. And as they sang, twenty homeless people wandered around the crowd on stilts a couple of metres high.

In cities like Rio de Janeiro and London the number of homeless people is growing. To see some of the most vulnerable people in society take centre stage and be applauded for their talents was one of the most profoundly moving cultural experiences of my life. It left me knowing that there is so much more to be done.

Notes

1 Amy Woodson-Boulton, 'The City Art Museum Movement and the Social Role of Art', www.branchcollective.org/?ps_articles=amy-woodson-boulton-the-city-art-museum-movement-and-the-social-role-of-art.

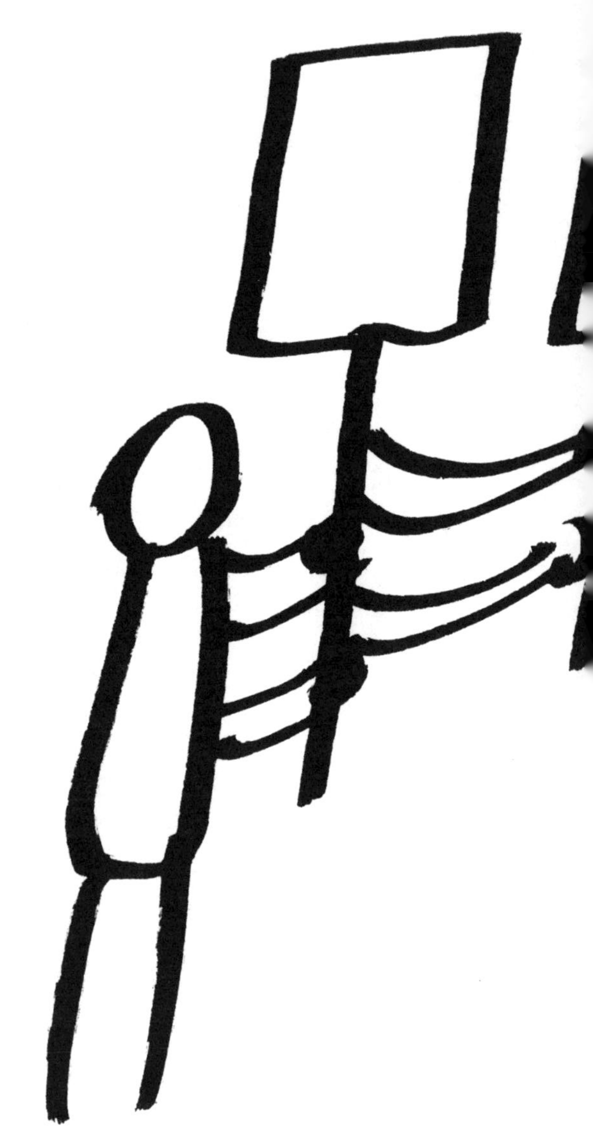

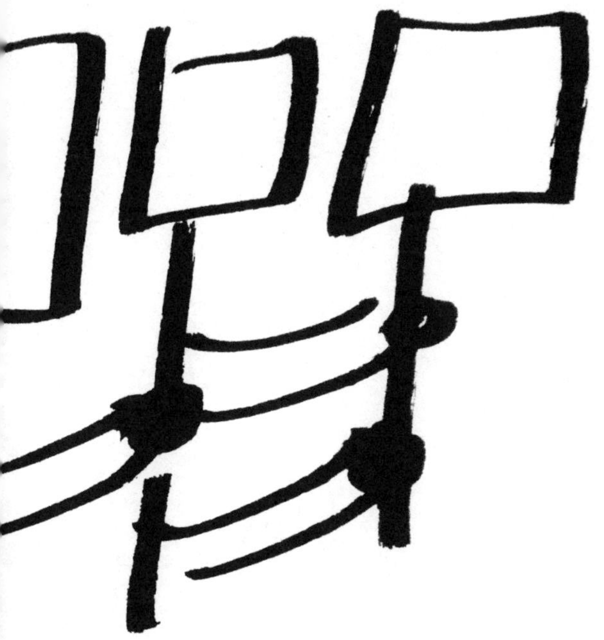

Performance of Dissent
From Cultural Resilience to Catharsis and Reconciliation in the Former Yugoslavia

Milena Dragićević Šešić
in Conversation
with Borka Pavićević

Paradoxically, the state and its institutions were freed from assuming their responsibilities of statehood, while we, the artists and civil society, began to believe that in fact we were in charge for providing catharsis and reconciliation. So we started to assume responsibility ourselves, for peace-building, for exploring historical facts.

This is how Borka Pavićević describes the political environment for her cultural work and civil engagement in 1995, when she established the Centre for Cultural Decontamination.

The CKZD is one of the most established centres of politically engaged cultural work in the former Yugoslavia and defines itself as a 'toponym of politics, art and civil society, a point of education and production, a public forum, a community'.[1] The public cultural role the Centre plays for Serbian society and the region today grew out of Borka Pavićević's long-standing work as a dissident theatre maker and anti-war activist, which dates back to the Yugoslavia of the 1960s. For this publication Borka Pavićević has met with university professor Milena Dragićević Šešić, a cultural researcher at Belgrade's Faculty of Drama Arts, whose academic work and teaching has influenced many of today's critically engaged cultural workers in the region and beyond. During their talk at the CKZD in late spring 2017, they revisited some of the forgotten struggles and successes of politically engaged theatre in Yugoslavia, discussed the necessity of and limits to civil resistance and art activism in times of war and explored the role of culture in re-shaping collective memory afterwards. At the end of their conversation they ask what civil society and new forms of cultural activism across Europe could learn from the collapse of the Yugoslav idea of a cosmopolitan, modernist and multi-cultural political space.

Milena Dragićević Šešić – I have been following your work since the first years of the *Belgrade International Theatre Festival* – BITEF[2] in the early 1970s, when you where one of the festival's jury members and moderated round-table discussions there. Your role in Serbian society resembles one that Miroslav Krleža assumes in his book *Moj obračun s njima* (My Confrontation with them), an active yet contrary position.[3] Your theatre work at the Atelier 212[4] as an activist was provocative, even within the so-called self-management system of socialist Yugoslavia. The concept and the activities of the 'self-managed communities of interest' (known by their acronym as SIZes) in the field of arts and culture as well as all the actions taken by the so-called temporary or permanent working associations of artists and cultural workers were important areas of liberty and self-organization. This is an unjustly neglected episode of our history that has not been addressed by a single analytic text yet. The negative aspects of socialist cultural policy, the censorships, bans and pressures usually get most of the attention. Nonetheless, with Atelier 212 and the BITEF festival, theatre director Mira Trailović succeeded in creating spaces of freedom where you, then a young theatre maker, or Biljana Tomić, a visual-arts curator, were given a great deal of leeway in your work. How do you see that period today? How do you remember your struggle for developing a new form of theatre that would assume artistic freedoms, open new possibilities and promote civil liberation within a more or less typical institutional repertoire theatre like the Atelier 212?

Borka Pavićević – I still hope Milena, that one day you will write a book about the period of self-management and that time of transition. It started in Slovenia, I was working in Ljubljana at that time, and it made room for these new forms of association, which was a great inspiration for me. In 1976–1977, when I was at the drama section of the Slovenian National Theatre, the changes had already begun in the Youth Theatre there. All this allowed for a greater involvement of the artists and for shrinking the administrative staff. A new principle existed in these associations that regulated and evaluated our work in terms of relevance and reach, but foremost in terms of artistic or cultural impact. It is important that we are talking about this, because nowadays, with all the re-writing of history in our countries, more is said about the restrictions of socialism and much less about its emancipatory policies, in education, or also towards women. It is often surprising how fragmented school education is today compared to the overall humanist and cultural education back then, when there was a certain grasp of a larger whole in the curriculum. Krleža was a writer who truly inspired me too. Today there is nothing comparable left in the educational curricula that could serve as a source of critical thinking, regardless of whether it is from Croatian or Serbian literature. In Yugoslavia, it was also normal that the faculties of philosophy in Zagreb, Sarajevo and Belgrade taught sociology of religion, because in a secular state understanding the impact of religion was important. The lack of a serious university department for the sociology of religion is one of the key reasons for today's religious occupation of public space, and it also comes with some sort of prostituting of religion in the absence of a real knowledge about it.

Another issue I see in our region now is the lack of internationalism, which actually became one of the underpinnings for the damaging de-solidarization effects of today's globalism. Think about 1968, which was a big year internationally but also for Yugoslavia. That year made an essential impact on us because it had an international reach. Now that we have comparable cultural movements in our countries again, from the *Šarena revolucija*, the Coloured Revolution in Skopje, to the *Ne da(vi)mo Beograd* (We Won't Let Belgrade D[r]own) campaign here in our city, to the protests of the *Kulturnjaci*, the cultural workers in Zagreb, and I have a look at how our authorities try to constrain them, I get the feeling that they try to impede any form of rebellious thoughts, and want to establish a form of protectionism that spares them from whatever internationally oriented or universal cultural uprising of similar nature. Yugoslavia hovers over everything like a spectre. In 1968, I was sitting on the editorial boards of the *Susret* and *Student* youth magazines, which heavily relied on information from Berlin, Paris, and so on. Rudi Dutschke and Daniel Cohn-Bendit, their ideas were known here. We all recognized what was under discussion at the Odeon, we were all reading Sartre.

MDŠ – To us, secondary-school kids back then, *Susret* magazine looked amazing. All of a sudden we had this innovative and well-designed publication in our hands. Bogdan Tirnanić, its editor-in-chief, came to my high school to promote it and we all had the feeling that we were citizens of the world. He presented the newspaper in his very charming way, encouraging us to be both readers and contributors. We suddenly got our own magazine and we saw ourselves as part of something that was not only generational, but widely interconnected, a worldwide counter-culture movement.

BP – *Susret* was another emancipatory idea of that time. Belgrade found itself in the middle of the cold war between the two superpowers, in very practical terms. Belgrade's privileged role was its ability to translate. The BITEF festival, for example, was a place where theatre people from the East and West really learned about each other.

MDŠ – The city was indeed a space for exchange, cultural acquaintance and translation. Zygmunt Bauman and Leszek Kołakowski were translated here at a time when they still lived in Poland. At the same time, a lot from the West that was banned or totally unknown in the East was available here then, from Roland Barthes and Foucault to Freud and Marcuse.

BP – Fashion, nightclubs, discos, even the famous erotic magazine *ČIK*, all manifested liberal tendencies within the space of culture at that time. This intertwining of politics, revolution and art made a big impression on me. There was no atmosphere of fear at that moment in Belgrade. Of course officials wagged their finger at us, especially in 1968: Children, they said, watch out what you're up to or the Russians will invade here, just like they invaded Czechoslovakia! But this liberalization genuinely came out of our position in the cold war. Heiner Müller or Roberto Ciulli came to the BITEF not just to attend a theatre festival. They were essentially interested in seeing whether a third way was possible within socialism.

One of the first real civil actions happened right there at the BITEF in 1968. It was an artistic protest against the Soviet occupation of Czechoslovakia. Film director Želimir Žilnik, producer and composer Bojana Makavejev and scriptwriter Branko Vučićević circled around Atelier 212 in their Deux Chevaux just before a performance of the Gorki theatre from Moscow. The car was equipped with a stove pipe and done up like a tank. They handed out leaflets to the people of Belgrade, I still have them here. One of them read: 'To the bourgeoisie attending BITEF in Belgrade, we hereby inform you that troops of the Warsaw Pact marched into Prague on 22nd of August. Citizens, do return to your homes!' We stood at the door to our stage and informed everyone on their way in that they were actually *Cominformists*.[5] The Deux Chevaux was the same Žilnik had used in his film *Rani radovi*. The police recognized its licence plate and the car was listed as evidence when they pressed charges against him afterwards. Someone at Atelier 212 must have connected the dots and everything erupted.

The police visited us also at the *Susret* magazine, because they suspected Marija Čudina, the famous poet who worked as our proof-reader and was a descendant of Russian anti-communist immigrants, to be the link between the public protests in Moscow and our dissident scene here in Belgrade. There was a whole investigation of *Susret* and they combed through everything. A process that would later be repeated when there were demonstrations in solidarity with the Polish Solidarnošć in the 1980s. So, at the time there were possibilities, but we also experienced many bans. There was also a powerful wave of repression against the Yugoslav '68ers and some of the leading activists of my generation, such as Vladimir Mijanović, actually did end up in jail.

MDŠ – The leading theme of our conversation is the role of culture in past and present civil actions and movements in our region, and how civil engagement, cultural issues and artistic actions relate to our culture of memory today. Why have the events we just discussed been erased from our history? How did these cultural developments disappear from our collective memory?

BP – They were erased by the institutionalized nationalist systems, in combination with a lack of capacities to analyse their previous contexts. There are no self-reflexive texts which would be simultaneously critical and illuminating for the social and political context within which theatre functioned here. As our cultural analysts Jovan Ćirilov and Dragan Klaić would say, the history of theatre isn't just the history of what was staged, but also what was not staged. Our society actually has always been characterized by cultural circles that run in parallel: the establishment is always against whatever the opposition proposes, and experiences it as a destructive force, as subversion. Consequently, there is no analysis of how Atelier 212 alongside introducing an international repertoire also took its position as a public place for scepticism, a place of criticism that also worked with a lot of sarcasm and irony. It was the first institution that dared to use offensive words on stage and display nudity, as we did in *Hair*. What for example was the actual significance and relevance of these artistic moves as they represented a clear breach with the legacy of the Socialist Realism?

Atelier 212 was known for its knowledge of international developments and for sharing the insights it gained from the world stages. This was the benefit of Yugoslavia's position in the international context and allowed us to refer to all these political processes and events around the world, the war in Vietnam, for example. But we were at all times sharing these ideas and learnings through our distinctive institutional repertoire. However, until around 1978–1979 this repertoire always served as a critical analysis of the system, which also became very manifest in occasional repressions such as plays being taken off our agenda.

MDŠ – Nevertheless, it seems that the whole political dimension of the repertoire of the Atelier 212 was swept aside and what people still remember today is more the freedom of the acting, the artistic virtuosity. The Atelier's engagement and political nature, the questioning of social values left less of a trace in our collective memory than Zoran Radmilović's acting, his famous lines and anecdotes.

In 1981, you founded your new company named New Sensibility. At that time several other theatre companies already tried to create room for doing theatre outside the institutions. I am thinking of groups such as Pod razno or Dvorište for example. Thus new, self-managed, permanent working associations of artists that had started operating in Serbia opened some room for a different type of acting, for a more direct contact with the audience. But it seems that with New Sensibility you were after something very different, something much more ambitious. What was your reasoning behind your departure from Atelier 212?

BP – My kind of value-driven neo-Romanticism was essential. In other words, I felt that a new sensibility was required to go along with the scepticism at Atelier 212. We had staged a play by Alexander Vampilov, directed by Egon Savin and then a whole generation of young artists arrived, Enver Petrovci, Tanja Bošković and others. This is when the clashes began within the Atelier collective. There was strong opposition to a different approach, to a different way of speaking. And then the BITEF festival pulled out too. BITEF's rootedness in Atelier 212 was a big institutional privilege that also encouraged me to make yet another different kind of theatre.

Bogdan Bogdanović, the renowned architect and urbanist was mayor of Belgrade at the time, which is vastly important. He supported a proposal of the architect of the *RTV Serbia* television and *Politika* newspaper buildings, the great Uglješa Bogunović, to give us the former brewery for the first performances of *New Sensibility*. The second floor of the brewery had this incredible six-thousand square meters of space where IRWIN, the famous art group from Slovenia, and so many others put on their first shows in Belgrade.

MDŠ – We have to underline how cutting-edge thinking this was at the time. Worldwide, using post-industrial architecture for cultural purposes became a more widespread phenomenon only by the mid-1980s. The early 1980s thus were a time when in Yugoslavia we were still completely in line with international cultural innovation trends.

BP – Indeed, this was of central importance and people find it hard to understand today, in this age of post-colonial culture. We were always proclaiming that there can be no imitation in theatre. A crucial prerequisite to achieve this is to have people who have an open ear for their time, for the moment, who feel the essence of a situation, of their age and embrace creativity in alternative ways. The ability to develop such 'new sensibilities' is connected to a certain intellectual depth and a broad horizon which, I have to repeat, was possible in the Yugoslav milieu and its connectedness to the world.

For the BITEF festival we spontaneously discovered many other new places as venues, the *Barutana* armoury, the *Izlog* shopping window on Maršala Tolbuhina street, the *Avala* film studio in Košutnjak, the catacombs under Tašmajdan park, the church that is now the BITEF theatre and the local municipality building just across from Atelier 212. We put on performances wherever the setting was best suited to their artistic content and soon began to understand that there was no such thing as set design anymore. Getting access to all these spaces was a huge battle of course, but we had a mayor who understood this struggle and took a strong stand in converting all these different places into centres of culture, at least temporarily. Many performances were on just for one summer and in different places across that whole part of Belgrade we might call downtown today. As an urbanist and mayor, Bogdan Bogdanović felt this was what Belgrade should become. Instead of all those 'furniture salons', as he said, which could remain along Knez Mihajlova street in the inner city, there should be a cultural vitality through small organizations, with their own productions, in informal locations. All this does not exist anymore and it is a shame to see how many of these spaces have been entirely commercialized today.

MDŠ – We could describe these new groups of artists, most of them from the theatre and film world, as the embryonic state of the independent cultural scene in Belgrade.

BP – Indeed! And this is how things stood in 1984, when the police arrested the members of the so-called Free University, which had for several years already organized informal lectures and debates outside the official state university structures. For the Godot Fest of 1984, we played *Viđenje Isusa Hrista u kasarni V.P. 2507* (Spotting Jesus

Christ in the army barracks V.P. 2507), by Ivo Brešan. The army officials were watching us closely and their highest ranks warned us: 'You will not put that on, absolutely not!' We were called in for a lot of fierce meetings with the Belgrade City Committee. But we just told them, it was their job to oversee what went on in the army, while what Shakespeare and Brešan did was just our business. And of course we managed to put on that play without a trace of censorship or self-censorship. However, this was when we heard of somebody named Slobodan Milošević for the first time. He was the Secretary of the City Committee then and had only just appeared. It was he who demanded that the entire Free University group, intellectuals who had been gathering for discussing dissident views on social development and other questions, would be arrested immediately.

MDŠ – And the repression began. The period of the 1970s, but particularly the early 1980s were a remarkable time for Yugoslavia. Various new things were underway in the capital cites of all our republics, and it has hardly been analysed how these different circles interconnected. We had an engaged urban, cosmopolitan, Yugoslav, dissident and activist scene, but on the other hand there was already this nationalism. We were aware of it, but somehow we did not quite see it yet. It was an ongoing struggle between one and the other and there were still pockets of freedom until 1987. The magazine *Potkulture* (Subcultures), which we had started in 1984 appeared for the last time in 1987. By then it had all become clear, when in Slovenia for instance the new right-wing *Nova Revija*, which featured many national writers and thinkers, was already being published.

BP – In 1987, we were in Slovenia for a collaboration with the Croatian dramaturg Vjeran Zuppa to stage *Tosca* in Celje. I remember very well how he predicted that the new nationalist elites would always find agreements among themselves sooner than we do. And indeed, when Milošević and Tuđman met in Karađorđevo in 1991 to carve up the country, all our nationalist writers and historians from all the different republics rubbed elbows with each other and all got along just very well. The ideological separation was working highly effectively. I always have to think of that when nowadays Air Serbia lands at the Franjo Tuđman Airport in Zagreb.

MDŠ – This efficiency continues to this day when you think about how in 2016 Zlatko Hasanbegović, Croatia's extreme right-wing Minister of Culture invited our nationalist historian Bojan Dimitrijević for a discussion of their radical revisionist views on our histories. This encounter showed how much these divergent nationalist movements are in fact mutually complementary. There is a sort of paradoxical harmony among them as they are fighting for their goals side by side, while we as civil society, although we have always remained in dialogue in the region, continue to criticize and blame each other for mistakes, because we think this is part of our identity as good democrats.

The events of 1991 brings us to the core of our conversation and the period when all your work in the framework of the peace protests began: Your participation in the so-called *Belgrade Circle* and the Druga Srbija (Other Serbia) movement including its seminal publication, and your engagement in a series of anti-war actions in Belgrade from Crni flor (Black ribbon) to Poslednje zvono (Last bell) and the Igman Initiative, your risky visit of the besieged Sarajevo, in April 1995.

BP – In 1991, we first formed a group of writers, antiwar activists, intellectuals and other public voices that we called a civil movement of resistance, which went by the name of Association for a Yugoslav Democratic Initiative – UJDI. We thought at the time that we would still be able to do something. There was a precise description for forming a board for this civil movement that was still pan-Yugoslav. And there was a manifesto published in the name of the group that called for the possibility of multi-citizenship across all the republics of Yugoslavia. We believed there would be no war, if multi-citizenship would be recognized and that Bosnia could be saved in this way. Nikola Barović, who was a lawyer, and the Slovenian theatre director Primož Bebler prepared a manifesto for this idea. Our assumption was that this forthcoming war was a war over passports. It matters very much that this proposal existed. It still resonates in our heads today as the only normal way of thinking about saving the country. All this was laid down in the unforgettable, but nowadays little known book *Vjetar ide na jug i obrće se na sever* (The wind goes to the south and veers to the north), which included the anti-war correspondence of the Slovenian, Serbian and Croatian writers Maruša Krese, Biljana Jovanović, Rada Iveković, and Radmila Lazić. It was published in the *Apatrid* books series, which you co-edited for Radio B92, at that time the main independent cultural media institution that showed clear resistance.

The civil resistance movement was very important because numerous initiatives came out of it 1991–1992. With the Belgrade Circle and its public debates another civil option was created, an association of independent intellectuals as well as journalists and media professionals. At that moment being part of the Belgrade Circle most essentially represented a public distancing from the rah-rah propaganda politics of Slobodan Milošević, the official newspapers, the state television, the agitating interviews, the infamous Memorandum of the Serbian Academy of Science and Arts, in short, the entire nationalist occupation of the public political and cultural space.

MDŠ – In 1991-1992, we were all still living in the same country, but it began to slide and disappear in the cracks that started to show in the other republics. Many of the civil protests in Serbia, such as the March 9 demonstrations against media manipulation and the 'TV Bastille', the opposition's nick-name for RTV Serbia, were not supported in the other republics, because it did not suit anybody there to recognize that another Serbia existed in Belgrade too, a civil Serbia that did not accept state television propaganda or a regime that had by then already completely asserted itself as a populist autocracy. And then of course all the memories of civil resistance were buried by the horrors of the wars that followed.

BP – When war broke out in Bosnia, the writer Biljana Jovanović came up with a new proposal, which remains unforgettable: Biljana sent an official and open letter, saying that for the purpose of an exchange of lives three hundred of us would move to Sarajevo, if they allowed three hundred citizens of Sarajevo to come to Belgrade. Out of this spirit many important civil actions grew, such as the Black Ribbon initiative in 1992, when thousands of people in the streets of Belgrade, in solidarity with the first victims in Sarajevo, were wearing black ribbons, as if they were out for a funeral. We were lighting candles in the park around the building of the Presidency and other civil society organizations joined us in this action, even the Srpski pokret obnove (the Serbian Renewal Movement). Those were the most massive anti-war demonstrations in Belgrade of the time, which later on continued with actions like The Last Bell.

MDŠ – What is also very little known today are the student protests of 1992. They began in Belgrade, in May, as a sign of resistance to the siege of Sarajevo and as a public voice for peace in Bosnia. Nobody, including the world press, reported about them and they were ignored until the university departments closed in August and the protests started to dwindle naturally as students had to go back home for summer. There is a whole generation that led these protests and left the country without graduating at the end, among them for example Branislav Jakovljević, who edited the protest bulletin *Dosta!* and is now a theatre scholar at Stanford University. He has recently published a book on our subject of discussion, titled *Alienation Effects*.[6]

Around 1994 then, you realized that straightforward civil activism in the streets, which increasingly took place outside public perception, was no longer sufficient. What was needed, you concluded, was to create a more powerful formation, a more cohesive organization that would provide a platform and a space where various civil initiatives could convene.

BP – Exactly! The Belgrade Circle had published the book *The Other Serbia* in 1992. It was edited by the anthropologist and human rights activist Ivan Čolović and the sociologist Aljoša Mimica and included some thirty texts by members of the Circle who all opposed the nationalist ideology and wanted to show that another Serbia existed. Looking at the fierce reactions this publication received it obviously had a huge public impact and its legacy seems to remain important, with the attacks continuing even today. The book illustrated the Circle's cultural discourse, it raised questions, like the many public sessions we held did too and of course there were differences and disputes inside the Circle itself. The whole situation was not easy and we should not forget that Bosnia provided such a huge trauma. It was really humiliating, painful, and unbearable for us to speak about Bosnia and to tell them about everything we were doing here in Belgrade, while they were sitting there in isolation. We no longer knew what we could still do to make it stop, to stand up to the xenophobia, the nationalist hatred, the madness, this enormous pull towards provinciality and the fragmentation, while witnessing the carve-up of the entire Yugoslav territory.

And then, at a certain moment we found new courage and conviction that if these nationalists cooked up this chaos, we in culture and with the help of art had to turn things around and show opposition again. Come on, we said, let's make a new cultural centre that will be more tangible, have more impact, be more emotional and empathic. I have to admit there was quite a lot of encouragement and also great capacity for support from inside the Belgrade Circle; all these theatre directors, artists, writers, architects, former mayors like Bogdan Bogdanović and so on. Hence the idea for a new cultural space emerged, a place that would be more sensitive, vibrant and assertive, and through 'cultural catharsis' and by using art, performances, exhibitions and public actions would most firmly transmit our civil resistance against the appalling nationalism. Our cultural sign of life was of course a highly political gesture and we therefore called it the Centre for Cultural Decontamination.

This politicization in a cultural sense was meant to function as a tool of catharsis against the ongoing crimes, against the war. At that moment, however, culture did not play a crucial role yet in the wider political context of Europe. It did not enjoy the place it has today when it is clear that human rights cannot function without culture. During the breakup of Yugoslavia, there was no understanding of this connection and human rights questions, cultural issues and the struggle against the war existed as separate spheres. This is why culture at first did not have that many options for support and contacts in Europe. Which led to certain extremes in the other direction and a situation where the state and its institutions were paradoxically freed from assuming their actual responsibilities of statehood, while we, the artists and civil society, began to believe that in fact we were in charge for providing catharsis and reconciliation. So we started to assume responsibility ourselves, for conflict resolution, for peace-building, for exploring historical facts.

In our work for forming the Centre for Cultural Decontamination we followed an initially twofold process. First, there were these dreadful wartime traumas we had to come to terms with. Croatia, especially Vukovar at the beginning and then Bosnia. But at the same time we also wanted to remember the country that was, and we felt a fierce need for it not to be entirely lost. We all represent citizens of a former country, a territory, with four million dislocated people. Some of us live inside this territory, many outside, which is grimly but accurately described as 'brain drain' today. When I see how the successor states of Yugoslavia continue to abuse civil rights, maintain irregular voting lists and so on, I believe the idea of the ethnic cleansing of territories in a way strongly prevails to this day. Each of these new national states clearly still assumes the existence of communities of 'undesirably citizenry' in their territory. We have recently experienced this again with our regional initiative for a Declaration for a Common Language, which has been signed by a few hundred linguists, writers, scientists, activists and other public figures from Bosnia, Croatia, Montenegro and Serbia.

MDŠ – 'Undesirable citizens' also seems to live on as a populist label for all those who cultivate critical thinking in our new nationalist contexts. *Hrvatski Tjednik*, a right-wing weekly from Zagreb just today has published something like a Wanted poster with photographs of all the Croatian writers – mostly women – who signed the Declaration and put this under the agitating title 'Stop the Vampires Rising from the Rubbish Heap of History'.

Let's briefly go back to the time of the beginning of the wars, when the drama in Vukovar started to unfold, when Sarajevo was besieged and the embargo on Serbia cut off all intellectual and physical communication channels. How did the civil movements in Serbia maintain contacts with other pro-peace and anti-war groups in the region and maybe even elsewhere in Europe? And why did the Centre for Cultural Decontamination open its first programme with *The Possessed*, Albert Camus' adaptation of Dostoevsky?

BP – Well, we had to start with Camus because of his premise that terror does not rely on the strength of the terrorists and autocrats, but on the weakness of us liberals. At the very beginning, we tried to somehow describe all that was going on in the region, to present it in images. Along with this first performance, the work of Ana Miljanić, an exhibit called 'Živeti u Sarajevu' (Living in Sarajevo) was put up at the Centre in 1995. I am not sure when precisely the Centre developed this role as a space to which people from all the other republics could come to speak and show how things were there. But it must have been around that time that we started to develop into a platform that could increasingly convene all those activists in one place.

We still keep the *Sarajevo Survival Map* of Suada Kapić, which she drew from memory and which always stirs great interest among all our visitors at the Centre. Suada's book *Živeti u Sarajevu* (Living in Sarajevo) was part of the 1995 exhibition of the same name and people's reactions were more than dramatic when they saw the map of occupied Sarajevo. The exhibit was supposed to be up for ten days, but it remained open for more than two months. This indicates how little people knew of Sarajevo and the huge need for information they had. Many came to the Centre for Cultural Decontamination to see and hear who of their friends was dead and who was still alive. They thought we knew something more. They often would find someone on the posters, especially the theatre posters from the famous besieged Sarajevo War Theatre SARTR, and, thrilled, they would say, 'He's alive!' Many asked us questions, people came who had been helped by someone to get out of besieged Sarajevo. Two women, Muslim, who had been allowed to pass through enemy lines by the Serbian guards, came to express their gratitude and to ask us to help them find those who had let them through. Those conversations during this project, it was something incredible.

From the beginning, the Centre was working in a way that allowed every discussion, every event to result in a next idea and production. People were always asking us about who actually curated and decided on our programme. But anyone who had an inspiration, a good suggestion for another civil action or an art project that stood for a particular social issue or an important value that promised to push a button of general interest in the profoundly restrictive political and social context we lived in, could start doing something here. Systems of knowledge and insights intersected and everyone was a teacher and student at the same time. But as a Centre for Cultural Decontamination it was also very important that action met with emotion, that we empowered each other and experienced that we were not alone in our thoughts, because many of us felt very alone in these times.

Work was not separated from life at the Centre. The foundations of our cultural work rested on many important figures who had been thrown out of their jobs during the Milošević time. People were fired from various positions in the public institutions, universities, television, radio, even schools. Slobodanka Božović, for example, ran her Škola ljudskih vrednosti (School of human values) here at the Centre. This was a totally authentic self-educational programme for school children. Žo and Prota from the experimental art and design collective ŠKART lived in a room here in the annex that still leaked when they started renovating and designing it. We learned that there must be infrastructure if there is to be resistance. So, design was absolutely a part of our critical thinking, of protest, rebellion, subversiveness, and of defining an alternative cultural lifestyle.

Despite the embargo and the public prejudices towards a place called Centre for Cultural Decontamination many people came to us from the region and also from elsewhere in Europe. I remember the night in the summer of 1995, when some amateur radio operators who were at the Centre transmitted the news that Ratko Mladić had marched into Srebrenica. Or when *B92* journalist Julija Bogoeva, who reported from the War Crimes Tribunal in The Hague, brought us *A Cry from the Grave*, the film documentary about the Srebrenica massacres that happened under Mladić.[7] The Centre was the first place to show the film in Serbia and it took years before it was aired on public television and a larger public in the country started to realize the extent of the crime.

MDŠ – When it comes to your role as a cultural platform for civil dissent, I will never forget the Human Rights Day of 1996. There was a plan to suspend all shows scheduled in the Belgrade theatres for that occasion on December 10. And then all the actors and directors gathered for a discussion right here, at the Centre and not in their own theatre venues, at the actual sites of the boycott. Different voices and opinions were expressed and even among the most progressively thinking theatre people present here, there were strong pleas for the show to go on, under all conditions and at any cost. Some just could not understand how the silence of the theatre for that day was a significant means for the political struggle. That evening most of us came to understand a great deal: That there is a big responsibility for those who have acknowledgement in public space and thus the social power and obligation to raise their voices. This is what we were expressing very clearly to those politically in power back then. And it seems to me that to this day, our governments have not understood this power of civil action yet. Unfortunately, even among those whom we had recognized as democrats at that time, the significance of civil society and civil action was never really taken into consideration. Civil society was seen as an anti-patriotic, anti-national and traitorous element, despite the fact that it did represent a firm core of resistance against the war politics of the Serbian institutions and authorities. Even when colleagues agreed with our critical stand, they often felt it was disgraceful to voice it in public, because this shamed the country. Nationalism justifies every lie, it seems.

In this context, the vast relevance of your programming at the Centre for Cultural Decontaminations for the Serbian public is really crucially related to the possibilities that you offer people to understand and acknowledge the crimes that were committed in their name. Despite the documentary films and the trials at the Tribunal in The Hague, the subject of war crimes in Bosnia, committed by people who came from Serbia is still taboo in our society. Many in Serbia are still irritated when this subject is mentioned and do not find that public acknowledgement of these crimes is necessary, because the other sides have committed crimes too. There is also little interest in more collective knowledge about the crimes that were committed inside Serbia, the mass graves, the refrigerator trucks. What dominates in Serbia today are politics of what I would call 'shameful forgetting', a deliberate erasure of all the historic facts that we find disgraceful. It is interesting that social anthropologist Paul Connerton, who distinguishes between seven types of forgetting, does not mention this dimension.[8] For our region we would also have to add yet another notion of memory which I would describe as 'confused silence'. We do not really know how to think and feel about all these disturbing facts, so we quickly slur over them and immediately forget them.

In this context, I found your *Transitional Justice* programme in the early 2000s very essential. The Centre put together a number of conversations, seminars, publications and translations of entire literature editions on the topic. From my point of view, this greatly supported a wider public understanding of the very concept of transitional justice in the region. The programme was delivered through debates, films, research projects and other activities, which were considering how transitional justice might actually be implemented and to what extent our societies and politics were prepared for it or not. The public role of the Centre for Decontamination was huge here because it demonstrated what an important contribution culture can make to the transformation of Serbian society, a society which one day I hope will manifest itself again as a progressive and open one, which builds on justice and solidarity.

BP – I initially was of the opinion that we do not need the Tribunal in The Hague. I thought that after all the divisions we would just ensure that all these displaced people and their families could return to the country they originally came from and then we would see how that would really look like in terms of citizenry. These were the questions we tried to address with the *Transitional Justice* programme. It was very much related to the ideas of Étienne Balibar, his reflections on transnational citizenship and a Europe of citizens versus a Europe of nations.[9]

The topic of displaced citizens has always remained an important element in our exhibitions too. In 2010, we did the really important project *Ko je tebi Reihl-Kir* (Who was Reihl-Kir to you?) Josip Reihl-Kir was the Chief of Police in Osijek in Croatia who saved the lives of many people who are residing in Serbia today. We tried to find these displaced persons and documented how many of them there really were. In the opening stages of the war, in his function as a high-ranking police officer, he personally tried to mediate between Serbs and Croats in Tenja and Osijek. He tried to keep them apart to prevent the upcoming bloodshed, he literally went from one to the other. Reihl-Kir was a peace activist *par excellence* and, of course, he was assassinated already in July 1991. A peace activist in the ranks of the state police and inside an apparatus that wanted war was something deeply troubling for many at that time. Numerous visitors of the exhibition asked questions at the Centre and expressed how strongly they felt about his murder. We showed the project in Zagreb too, just across the street from the party headquarters of the still nationalist HDZ. And although it was such a simple presentation – his office, his coat and a file cabinet containing information about his assassination – many people who visited the exhibition there experienced it as a cathartic moment.

Slobodan Šnajder, our Croatian colleague and author of the play *Hrvatski Faust* (Croatian Faust) from the early 1980s, once famously predicted that our greatest patriots will turn out as the greatest traitors at one point. And indeed, the new nation states have started taking shape through a profound process of cultural disintegration that we have witnessed since then. They all have to distance themselves from the shared past, otherwise their flimsy narratives won't work. Hence this horrific return of turncoats as heroes, hence the tearing down of monuments to de-legitimize the socialist legacy, so they can reinforce the new national order and its new class. Everything is fragmented today. The past is fragmented. The Centre for Cultural Decontamination represents an effort of working against this and towards re-creating a larger cultural whole.

In that sense, our *Moderna* cycle in 2001 was incredibly important, a contribution to establishing a new culture of remembering historical events from before the 1990s, which had been largely pushed aside and started to be forgotten. Among its many activities, which started at the Avala film studios, *Moderna* for instance published a newspaper series designed by graphic artist Branko Pavić that was typeset both in Latin and Cyrillic script again. The whole programme ended with the performance *Bordel ratnika* (Warriors whorehouse), directed by Ana Miljanić and based on a book by Ivan Čolović. It included a lot of turbo-folk songs and the sentimental musings of some wiseguy nationalist thinkers who were acting as if in some school of philosophers. All this was pretty hilarious! Quoting the flyer, 'it addressed the vanishing of a Yugoslav identity and the emergence of others and how they relate to each other'. The presentation took place at the Yugoslavia Museum, the former Museum of the 25th of May, which marks Tito's birthday. But the beginning of the whole plot of the performance with Tito and the brothel and the brigands was actually staged just outside the walls of the famous Villa Mir, from where Slobodan Milošević earlier that year had to depart for the Tribunal in The Hague. This whole performance was really a process of cultural decontamination.

MDŠ – ...and you thought that the catharsis was complete at last.

BP – But after his death in 2006, the Serbian authorities ordered his coffin to be displayed in the very same Yugoslavia Museum. It was an attempt for a public installation, a staged political re-engagement with a toponym and it became crystal clear that nothing had actually been completed yet.

MDŠ – Our conversation is a contribution to a collection of texts that examine the potential of civil initiatives in the cultural field for influencing public and political space. What is really a troubling question in this context is to what extent the current right-wing movements such Dveri, 1389 and Naši in Serbia, the Sixty-four Counties movement in Hungary or Pegida in Germany do perhaps represent a natural evolution of our civil societies, which would mean the emergence of a much darker side of the engaged citizen idea that is promoted by people like us. Also, many new party projects and governments in Central and Eastern Europe clearly use cultural agendas for their attempts to transform societies, but in a regressive glorifying sense and by referring to an imagined heroic past. Looking at these developments in the civil and governmental sphere in our region many of these new agendas represent very conservative and repressive political projects whose cultural arguments nevertheless often seem to reach citizens more effectively than we from the progressive social forces do. Since the outset of the dramatic transitions in our region in the 1990s, we have tried to positively influence change in our societies with alternative ways of producing public knowledge through artistic projects and cultural initiatives. Today, I wonder, if our nationalist opponents are not about to become much more effective in using this civil role of culture than we have ever been. This is deeply disturbing and requires a fundamental rethinking of the modalities for our socially-engaged cultural struggle as well as finding new forms of political processes that help us to protect a certain standard of social and public values. The most essential question here is how can we create, perhaps through culture again, a civil space that allows all players in a society to equally act together?

In this context an important question arises at the end of our talk: What can we learn from the break-up of Yugoslavia and the fact that this idea of a cosmopolitan, modernist, multi-cultural and international political space did not succeed in opposing the nationalist, retrograde and populist forces? What can Europe, when we think about the many challenges the European Union is currently facing, learn from our experiences?

BP – Our region has indeed sent many messages to Europe about what happens when modern history is taken hostage by authoritarian rationales and their devastating forces. But it seems we have not succeeded in articulating this clearly enough yet. The break-up of Yugoslavia is not easy to understand and it was even harder to experience. We were all real-time witnesses of the 'collapse of the notion of utopia', to quote Agnes Heller.[10] The whole process has still not been entirely clarified, but the media machine had been working savagely already in the 1980s to prepare the ground for the collapse of a political idea that was built on social progress, under the recessive blows of nationalist and ethnic movements. No one in Europe can take it for granted today that they will be spared such developments. In Yugoslavia we started with internationalism, continued with multi-ethnicity within borders and with multiculturalism, only to find ourselves in a region today which is obsessively talking about cultural differences. The effects of these enforced distinctions not only destroy the culture of the 'other' but also what is genuinely 'own' culture. Look at Macedonia today, the myth of Alexander the Great is supposed to reconstruct a country that has 360 monasteries from the twelfth and thirteenth centuries. In fact, all these efforts to culturally stand out among the neighbours destroy all public perceptions of what really would be their own culture. Because of the narrow-mindedness of nationalist party politics and their petty power games we have lost sight of what we have lived through in this region and what we have survived. Including the fact that we are the ones that would have quite something to say about the burning cultural and political issues in Europe today.

However, when witnessing all these demonstrations in many countries in our region and elsewhere in Europe, I have the impression that people are increasingly sick of this narrowmindedness and self-centredness of their national elites. These struggles represent genuine cultural resistance. In that sense, the *Šarena revolucija* in Skopje, the *Protest protiv diktature*, the teachers and cultural workers' fights against privatizations in Croatia, all these movements represent the most European momentum we have in our countries today. Not what politicians are doing, but this Europe of scepticism, doubt, critical thinking, inquiring truth and cultural resistance is what matters most now.

Original in Serbian transcribed by Ognjenka Đorđević and translated by Ellen Elias Bursać; summarized and edited by Philipp Dietachmair.

Notes

1 www.czkd.org.
2 www.bitef.rs.
3 Miroslav Krleža, *Moj obračun s njima* (Sarajevo: Oslobođenje etc., 1988).
4 www.atelje212.rs.
5 The so-called Cominform was a Soviet-dominated information bureau that was founded in 1947 to coordinate international communication efforts among Communist parties in Europe. Its office was initially located in Belgrade before the expulsion of Yugoslavia from the group in 1948. During the process of de-Stalinization the Cominform was dissolved in 1956.
6 Branislav Jakovljević, *Alienation Effects: Performance and Self-Management in Yugoslavia, 1945-91* (Ann Arbor, MI: University of Michigan Press, 2016).
7 *A Cry from the Grave*, directed by Leslie Woodhead. Antelope Productions, 1999. TV Documentary.
8 Paul Connerton, *Seven Types of Forgetting* (Cambridge, MA: Cambridge University Press, 2008).
9 Étienne Balibar, *We, the People of Europe?: Reflections on Transnational Citizenship* (Princeton, NJ: Princeton University Press, 2003).
10 Agnes Heller, 'From Utopia to Dystopia: A Story of Historical Imagination', *Graduate Faculty Philosophy Journal* 37, no. 2 (2016), pp. 289-304.

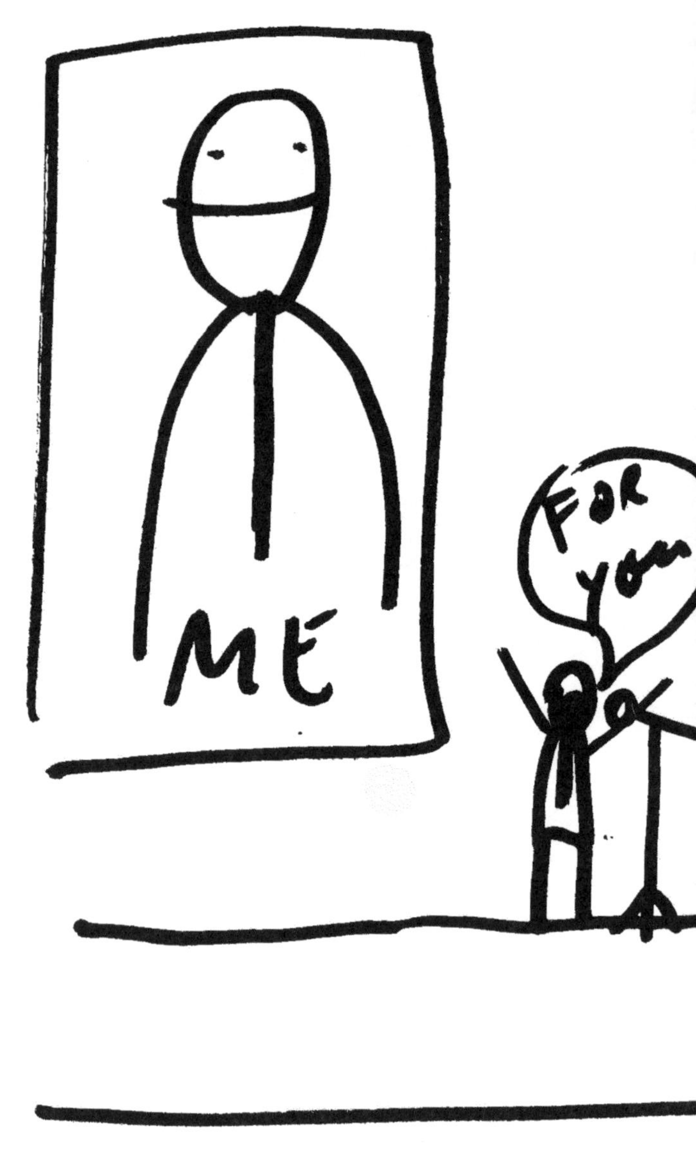
ME
FOR you

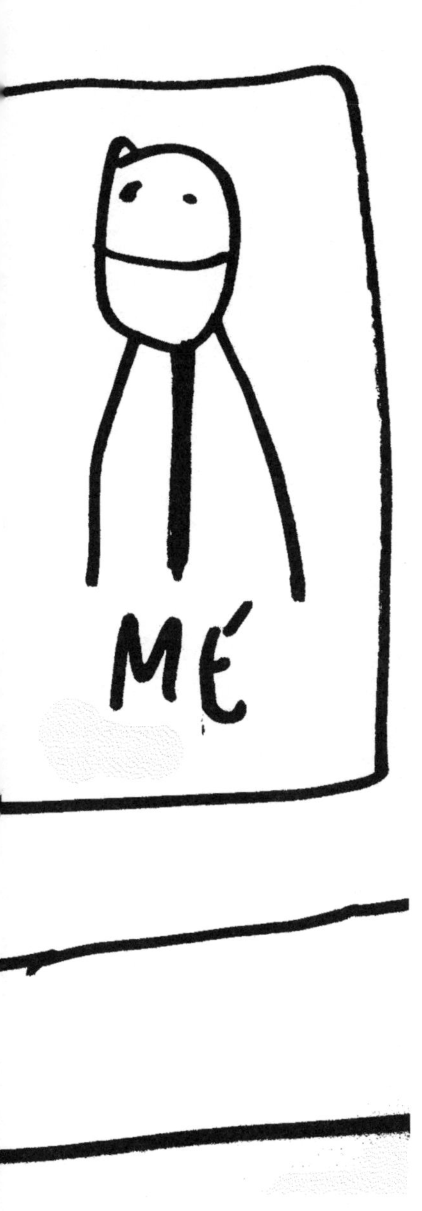
MÉ

A Stage for Resistance
The Cultural Scene in Turkey

Hakan Topal

Introduction

Turkey is going through an especially depressing political period. The Erdoğan regime's Sunni-Turkish supremacy is suffocating every aspect of life and undermining the secular foundations of the Turkish constitution. Minorities, including Kurds, Alevis, non-Muslims, women and LGBTQ are suffering under the crushing sectarian oppression. Democratic rights are eroding as thousands of journalists, academics and artists are being prosecuted on account of their opposing opinions. Since the July 15, 2016 failed coup attempt, tens of thousands of state employees have been fired with no judiciary due diligence. This coup was alleged to be orchestrated by Islamist cleric Fethullah Gülen, who lives in the United States and has controlled a large international network of schools, universities and businesses all over the world. In the post-coup crackdown, many Gülen-affiliated universities were closed, and his businesses were taken over by the state.[1] Beyond the Gülenist networks, Erdoğan opportunistically used the coup attempt as an opening to undermine the opposition in general. Many critical scholars, including those who signed a peace statement, were fired; hundreds of journalists were and are still being detained, waiting for an excruciatingly slow justice system to operate. In other words, intellectuals who had nothing to do with the Islamist/Gülenist conspiracy find themselves immobilized, with their passports confiscated and unemployed. Thousands of educated young professionals, academics, and artists are trying to escape the country to the European Union and the United States, resulting in a large-scale brain drain. Those cultural producers who are able to keep their jobs in public institutions are forced to work in constricted conditions; censorship and/or self-censorship (to preserve livelihood) has become common practice.

These relentless Islamist assaults depict a gruesome cultural-political context; however, the tyranny is met with steadfast resistance; the vitality, creativity, and solidarity of secular democratic forces constantly injects new energy into the political domain. The diversity of the opposition reminds us that Turkey, a country of 80 million citizens with a long history of democratic involvement, cannot be ruled by an autocratic regime. Although at times many feel desperate, we remind ourselves that there are millions of like-minded Turkish people who have the potential to change the direction of the country. We have seen it before; the Gezi Uprising was a turning point for Turkey. Although the current political parties do not offer much-needed alternative(s), many are rather optimistic that a new breed of political leaders, cultural producers and social theorists who are inspired by the Gezi solidarity and its aftermath will define the upcoming era. With this hopeful note in mind, I would like to scrutinize the possibility and limitations of the Turkey's cultural-political scene in relation to its institutions. Focusing on academic and cultural contexts, I will consider culture as a territory where new possibilities of poetic resistance can emerge and be sustained. As an artist, activist, and a Gezi Platform organizer in New York City between 2013–2015, I mostly rely on my personal and rather passionate observations.[2] Over the years, I conducted interviews and organized Gezi talks, panel discussions and symposia, which defines the backbone of this essay.

Circumstantial Realities

As I write this article, the Turkish people went to the polls on April 16, 2017 to vote on new amendments to the constitution. After an awfully unfair referendum process characterized by state coercion and tight media control, Erdoğan received the votes needed to obtain new presidential powers by a mere 51%, giving him unprecedented authority while effectively annihilating the 'separation of powers'.[3] The results are highly contested by the opposition as well as by the Organization for Security and Cooperation in Europe Office for Democratic Institutions and Human Rights (ODIHR) which identifies the possibility of a vast election scam with millions of fraudulent votes, particularly in the South-East region, where Kurdish feudal landlords are still in control in most of the cities.[4] No matter what the results will be after the legal disputes, this referendum puts Erdoğan's long-lasting reign and his legitimacy in question while raising serious doubts about Turkey's democratic future.

Since the moment Erdoğan took public office as Istanbul's mayor in 1994, he has been a skilful manipulator. Coming from fundamentalist/Islamist political roots, he and his close allies have increasingly used versions of Sunni-Islam and Turkish Nationalism to create new social assemblages by amplifying cultural-social fault lines in society. With the help of the (neo)liberal pundits, he portrayed secular people as well as religious minority Alevis as the guardians of the old regime, while offering his dystopic neo-Ottomanist vision as the new template for his oppressive regime. From the beginning of his tenure, he used duplicitous techniques to eliminate his political opponents. Media organizations have been seized or fined, he empowered Gülenist-Islamist religious fanatics to eliminate the secular constituents within the military, academia and other state institutions. Through fraudulent application of law, he restructured the state apparatus and provided unprecedented economic powers to businessmen close to him. Regrettably, up until the 2013 Gezi Uprising many (neo-) liberal pundits aligned themselves with the Islamists. These pundits were ignorant about Turkey's violent neoliberal transformation and systematic depoliticization and bluntly supported his policies despite the fact that there were clear indications about the degrading democracy.[5] These pundits, including some of the leftists, understood Erdoğan's capitalist policies as part of the democratization process[6]. For instance, a prominent socialist writer and editor of the Birikim Journal Ömer Laçiner called his rise to the power and handling of secular institutions an 'authentic bourgeois revolution'.[7] In contrast to these bogus assumptions, the neoliberal transformation was justified through the absolute domination of the Sunni majority. Clearly the rule of the majority did not bring much needed democratic transformation for Turkey; on the contrary, any demand for justice was met with extreme violent measures.[8]

The end of the peace process between the Turkish State and PKK was one of the biggest setbacks for Turkish democracy.[9] Erdogan's response to his June 2015 general election defeat was sinister; to secure his far-right votes in a re-election, he ended the peace process by denying it even existed in the first place. PKK mindlessly played into his hands, escalating the tension by bombing largely civilian targets in Ankara and Istanbul, effectively compromising the role of HDP – the new, mainly Kurdish, leftist party.

Following a calculated military escalation, characterized by assassinations and public bombings, at the end of 2015 a curfew was declared in many Kurdish cities, hundreds of civilians – mostly women or children – were killed in cross-fires. Thousands of people were detained and HDP's co-chairs, as well as many mayors of major Kurdish cities and parliamentarians were arrested or suspended from their duty. Neighbourhoods were bulldozed to 'clean up' the terrorists; cities looked like war zones. Over the last two years, Erdoğan intensified his bloody war against the Kurdish people, resulting in the deaths of hundreds of civilians; entire neighbourhoods have been erased from the map, and nearly half a million people were forced to evacuate their homes. While Kurdish cities are being reimagined through large-scale gentrification characterized by military operation and social engineering, to pressure the Kurds, AKP's officials made direct comparisons with the great massacre, the 1915 Armenian Genocide.

The Aftermath of the Peace Process: The Cultural Resistance

Amid escalating violence, many artists, academics, and writers including some unions and associations demanded that the government should immediately return to the peace process. At the end of 2015, artists Pınar Öğrenci, İz Öztat, Evrim Kavcar and others joined together for a march called 'I Am Walking For Peace'. They travelled from Bodrum in the west towards Diyarbakır, the largest Kurdish city in eastern Turkey. Along the way, the peace marchers stopped in various cities and distributed press releases. With the slogan 'Not death, but life', they intended to remind Turkish society about the real cost of the civil war.[10] When they reached Diyarbakir on New Year's Eve, they met the mayor of the city Gültan Kışanak – who is now is in prison – and they gathered around 70 people to read their peace declaration and march towards the historical neighbourhood Sur, which was largely demolished by the Turkish state during the clashes with PKK's youth arm HPG at the same times. Before the peace declaration could even be read, the police arrested Pınar Ercan, Pınar Öğrenci, Arzu Erdemir, Atalay Yeni and Aziz Kılınç in addition to 24 local protestors. In court, the artists were accused of supporting the terror organization, PKK. Although there is absolutely no evidence, this is an accusation that the government often uses to undermine the opposition; many prominent figures are illegally kept in prison for years before they face justice. Fortunately, the artists were released, their ongoing court case is a reminder how the government uses 'lawfare' as a tactic to grind the will of the opposition.

Following the footsteps of the peace marchers and responding to an 'Urgent Call for Solidarity' by T.C. Union of Southeastern Anatolia Region Municipalities,[11] a group of artists, curators and critics, initiated by myself and curator Didem Yazici, decided to call upon art organizations to open their windows to display artworks that promote peace. We wrote the following open call:

> The war in Eastern Turkey escalates with increased brutality. The Turkish State applies indiscriminate cruelty against its population within the whole blockaded Kurdish region. Peace protests in Turkey are shut down with sheer force. The mainstream media are silenced, and mute. Every day starts with news alerts of increased state violence and civilian losses. At this moment, we believe it's time for art institutions step up their support for peace through art, and assist artists who firmly demand peace. We urge you to consider opening your street windows and vitrines for art. Even though this may be regarded as a humble gesture, we hope you will consider artworks including installations, poetry, video, and text that question the ongoing war, discrimination, and nationalism. We hope that this peace initiative will resonate with you.[12]

This small but meaningful gesture was met with enthusiasm; many prominent artists and curators signed the petition, yet only a handful of art institutions responded to the call. As the political situation intensified, none of the organizations followed through and organized a peace event or an exhibition.

The institutional landscape in Turkey presents many complications as almost all major art organizations in Istanbul belong to either large banks or corporations controlled by major families. For instance, Arter Contemporary Art Space and Pera Museum are run by the Koç Family, who owns the Koç Holdings, the largest conglomerate and weapons manufacturer in Turkey. SALT is owned by Garanti Bank, the second largest private bank in Turkey, which recently changed ownership to a Spanish investor. Istanbul Modern and the Istanbul Biennial are operated by the Eczacıbaşı family, and finally the Sabancı Museum and Akbank Sanat are run by the Sabancı family. These families and corporations have close ties to Erdoğan's regime and they benefited from ruthless neoliberal transformation that took place since the early 2000s.

In times of political uncertainties, alongside universities, cultural organizations are one of the few institutions that can provide a platform for alternative knowledge production. However, the bourgeois elite have too much to lose; due to their funding structures and patrimonial connections, Turkish cultural institutions stay mute or tackle projects that do not have any political urgency.

Within this deteriorating political context, Russian curator Katia Krupennikova's 'Post-Peace' exhibition proposal for Akbank Sanat was a timely intervention. It was selected by an international jury via a competitive process and dealt with the idea of war and peace as defined by state policies. However, in February 2016, Akbank Sanat abruptly cancelled the exhibition which was set to open in March 2016. Following the outrage from the art community, Akbank Sanat's director issued a short statement citing 'the delicate situation in Turkey'.[13] Both the artists and curator, as well as the jury, clearly understood the cancelation as an act of censorship and they issued various public statements documenting the clear violation of their intellectual work in this last-minute blunder.[14]

As an artist and researcher, much of my work has focused on the Turkish context since the late 1990s. I have travelled to high-alert zones, realized numerous political art projects about the Kurdish issue, Iraq war, Syrian and Iraqi borders, and relentless neoliberal urban transformation and ecological devastation, and presented my work in many of the aforementioned art spaces. These institutions supported these endeavours on different occasions. However, since 2012, the situation changed and I understand that I can no longer present most of my openly political work in these institutions. Art projects especially concerning the Kurds and the South East of Turkey became no-go-zones for most institutions.[15] As a person who grew up after the 1980 coup context, I recognize this self-censorship.

Obviously, my goal here is in no way to undermine the dedicated work of art administrators, as they are fully aware of their own institutional limitations, and they struggle to provide a critical space for interdisciplinary knowledge production. For instance, in his recent job departure talk, SALT's former director Vasıf Kortun identifies many of these institutional issues while critically engaging the transformation of art institutions specifically focusing on the case of SALT.[16] Kortun criticizes the distinction between the public/private claiming that they are defined by a similar 'feudal rule set', and he argues that one should not try to protect the institutions at all costs. While cultural producers are understandably afraid of their jobs and well-being, at times of crises they are forced to keep a low profile or be pushed out. This reluctance of engagement presents a dilemma for curators because as they preserve their silence, they risk becoming 'irrelevant'. One needs to recognize the fact that within the current political climate, anything that is slightly controversial is met with hesitation due to institutional power dynamics, but how should these cultural institutions behave? As Kortun states; 'in this situation to be able to survive should not be a big deal; we should not praise the act of surviving; the thing is how to be relevant.'[17]

How can we achieve an inclusive form of publicness (commons) that enables alternative knowledge production, when everything is subsumed under neoliberal logic? While Kortun points out the blurred line between the public and the private, he does undermine the importance of public institutions and disregards how privatized models played an integral role in reshaping the current neoliberal cultural sphere. In order to create an inclusive democratic model, one has to defend and reimagine the public institutions, and communize the private ones.

The erosion of alternative spaces, and the consolidation of art and culture into private enterprises fundamentally affects the nature of art and culture. In recent years, many alternative art organizations and journals have already closed. Ahmet Öğüt's 2016 installation *Six Months* (*Altı Aylık*) at SALT Bomonti presented the street signs of former alternative art spaces that once constituted a lively art scene in Istanbul. As alternative art spaces vanish, some cultural producers are living in exile to circumnavigate censorship and political pressure. Small non-profit spaces, such as IMC 5533, run by committed individuals try to fill the gap by mobilizing their already limited resources and providing much needed solidarity among artists. Istanbul's Beyoğlu area, once a lively arts and culture centre, currently looks like a devastated neighbourhood characterized by philistinism and mass tourism. The city's energetic youth can only find refuge in secular neighbourhoods such as Kadiköy and Beşiktaş. As the site for Gezi Park, what happened to Beyoğlu is representative for Turkey; the government has been strategically evacuating the city centre through destructive gentrification, as these centres represent the possibility of social hybridization and the site of resistance. An allegorical connection to devastated Kurdish cities is inevitable; the streets currently look awful, filled with aggressive police presence. This forced withdrawal from the centre has long-term cultural and economic implications for the city.

As Turkish cultural institutions become sites of quarantine; artists and academics are forced to work outside the institutional context. This repressive milieu generates its by-product;

a militant-intellectual subject whose primary mission is to tell the truth no matter what the consequences are. This extra-institutional 'parrhesiastic' mission is legitimized by active social processes, the street protests. Public intellectuals are burdened with a debt of public responsibility; they must speak against the tyranny and argue for a new publicness – the true 'commonization'.

Parrhesiatic Mission

While thinking about the politics of withdrawal, as well as short-term tactics and long-term strategies, it is essential to consider the connection between risk-taking, discourse and establishing new 'truth-sets'. In this case, the concept of 'parrhesia' is particularly useful. It is borrowed from ancient Greek, via Michel Foucault, and can be roughly translated as speaking freely, frankly and openly no matter what the outcome.[18] While the speaker chooses directness as a method of communication, the parrhesiastic act carries the dangers of prosecution and highlights the importance of a public intellectual's commitment the idea of freedom of expression and the truth. Parrhesiastic action is not a solitary endeavour; on the contrary, the militancy is defined by its collective nature.

Although conventional cultural outlets are becoming more restricted and exceedingly regulated by the administrative class, intellectual agents are finding new ways of expressions outside of institutional boundaries, even if the ramifications are real. The art community asked art organizations to be a platform for peace in times of war, and over a thousand scholars petitioned the Turkish government to stop its aggression and return to the peace process immediately.[19] Erdoğan responded to this simple but vital request with animosity: four academics were prosecuted and put into solitary confinement only months after they were released from prison.[20] Especially after the July 15 coup attempt, through 'emergency executive orders [KHK]' hundreds of Academics for Peace scholars were fired from their posts or forced to retire. Many of them are currently under investigation, their passports were confiscated and they can no longer find jobs elsewhere, including at newspapers as executive orders prohibit them working in any kind of editorial capacity.[21]

The Erdoğan regime's swift move against peace supporters was to undermine the secular-leftist contingencies and had two interconnected objectives: first and foremost, it was to weaken

HDP's consequential democratic representation of Kurdish people and the left, especially in the South East of Turkey. Secondly, to squash the rising support for the Kurdish autonomous region (aka Rojava Cantons) in Northern Syria, a direct contradiction to AKP's sectarian neo-Ottomanist policies in the Middle East.[22] Almost all the Kurdish newspapers and televisions were closed, their editorial boards were arrested, including many of the guest editors of Özgür Gündem daily. A much-celebrated Turkish writer Aslı Erdoğan's case is particularly telling. She spent '132 days of pre-trial detention' only because she wrote in the newspaper. In a BBC interview, she reflects on the absurdity of the accusations:

> I think the main scandal is this; before, there were no court cases against a journalist based on article 302 [Turkish Penal Code 302 defines the crimes against the Turkish State]. We are the first. Özgür Gündem [newspaper] is a legal entity operating under the permission of the state. It was not founded yesterday. And, [editorial] advisors who had no input into editorial decisions are being prosecuted. What I am saying is that they are seriously bullshitting. This is probably to maximize fear and demoralize [people]. They are currently prosecuting me with a death penalty. What did I do? I was an advisor for a literature section of a newspaper. Cases based on article 302 are usually against the crimes that threaten the state's unity and integrity, for instance establishing an [illegal] army. Abdullah Ocalan [the leader of the PKK] was prosecuted based on this.
> ...How did I destroy the unity and the integrity of the state? I have no single sentence on PKK. I have never touched that. I have never mentioned federation / confederation etc. I knew my place. I saw the Kurdish problem according to the perspective of human rights violations and tragedy. That is why I was surprised. I really think that they wanted to give a message to white Turks, intellectuals and those of the people who supported Kurds by using myself and Necmiye Alpay. You see, what they meant is that 'we are punishing you more than we are punishing the Kurds'. That means 'behave yourself'. That is the only justification I have.[23]

As I illustrated by this handful of examples, the political situation is headed for the worst, yet, there is a silver lining in all this. As

Erdoğan attacks Turkish democracy, he is at the same time delegitimizing his power – even his stoutest propagandists are failing to justify his actions.[24] When there is relentless repression, there is steadfast resistance, therefore hope. While traditional solidarity networks, including political parties, unions and associations are becoming inadequate to respond to the regime's attack, people are inventing new ways of developing solidarities. This grassroots activism emerging from streets puts pressure on political parties to respond and change their tactics. In other words, many of these peace initiatives are effective as they generate a form of knowledge situated in practice and vital for future large-scale solidarities. The new militant-subject has the capacity to resist while producing an alternative life. Resourceful and engaged, intellectual outcasts have the potential to bring various segments of society together in novel ways.

In my recent interview in Istanbul conducted in March 2017 and follow-up correspondence through email, artist Burak Delier identifies the importance of this alternative production, specifically talking about the 'street lectures' that were organized by Academics for Peace.

> I really value street and park lectures by dismissed Academics for Peace, not because they are simply acts of protests, but they radically create a certain publicity; without being in the confines of academia, they are opening the difference between 'true' and 'false' knowledge by producing and distributing beyond official channels. ... Of course, Academics for Peace needs serious organizational [union] support; beyond that we need to have a serious reform and discussion regarding the structures of Turkish universities. While we should not romanticize the street lectures, we need to identify the potential within these crises, and propose veneration and relevancy with respect to knowledge production.[25]

Delier suggests that Academics for Peace and other grassroots engagements offer a new form of militancy that bypasses established confinements and has serious consequences with respect to unorthodox knowledge production. Similarly, in *Commonwealth*, Antonio Negri and Michael Hardt underline the significance of 'co-research' beyond the boundaries of academia.

> Another route has been forged by professors and students who take their work outside the universities both to put their expertise at the service of social movements and to enrich their research by learning from the movements and participating in the production of knowledge developed there. Such militant research is conceived not as community service – as a sacrifice of scholarly value to meet a moral obligation – but as superior in scholarly terms because it opens a greater power of knowledge production. A third route, which has developed primarily among the globalization movements in recent years, adopts the methods of 'co-research' developed experimentally in the factories and applies them to the entire terrain of biopolitical production. In social centers and nomad universities, on Web sites and in movement journals, extraordinarily advanced forms of militant knowledge production have developed that are completely embedded in the circuits of social practice.[26]

While intellectual and artistic activity may have a privileged position, it has a fundamental role in society especially when rooted in practice. As Negri and Hardt state, social movements are not simply demanding real democracy, but at the same time are the sites of a new type of knowledge production through which new revolutionary subjectivities can emerge. This biopolitical struggle underlines the social dimension of alternative truth regimes. Burak Delier emphasizes direct action:

> Discussing the idea of telling of the truth, or considering the kind of subject who can enunciate the true knowledge, illuminates the situation of those dismissed academics. Let's ask this question: at this point in time in Turkey, which kind of knowledge is truer? [uttered] in universities, or in the streets? Can those dismissed [academics] articulate the truth by illegally giving lectures in parks or streets? Or, those who have 'prof' title in front of their names and teach 'constitution 101' course tomorrow?[27]

In this case, the collective is a by-product of social processes that is activated through the radical pursuit of 'activism'. In many aspects, the Gezi Uprising provides the blueprints for a 'temporary autonomous zone', where engaged cultural producers can get together, and transform each other. Tahrir Square, Zuccotti and Gezi Parks, Umbrella Revolution in Hong Kong, are events that should not be evaluated by their immediate political outcomes, but rather by their ability to activate new subjectivities and inspirations for novel solidarity networks.

The Gezi uprising was indeed a defining moment for Turkish political history, because hundreds of thousands of people from Ankara to New York, from Izmir to Diyarbakir gathered around parks to speak up for 'real democracy'. From poetry to dancing, from public lectures to praying, the park became a site of extreme hybridization, where new truth-sets could emerge through the activist 'biopolitical becoming'.[28] In that sense, seemingly incompatible social actors form new bonds through a variety of basic artistic/expressive activities. That is precisely the reason that we need to take artistic production seriously, to appreciate the diversity of voices that escape the hierarchical conventional forms.

Epilogue: Art After Politics, Again.

If art is an act of utterance to an imagined audience, does speaking the truth matter if no one will ever hear you? Artists have a self-defined role in society, which encourages them to speak out – sometimes in silence – to deliberately reflect on their lived experiences as well as the human/non-human condition. The outcome of artistic expression may not be immediately shared by a community, nevertheless every artwork inherits a negotiation; there is a contract between the object of art, its subjects, and its possible spectator. This open relationship is a political one – defined by its inevitable collective nature, situated in its thingness – the very reality of the artwork. Its value comes from looking, reading, listening and/or touching the work together, yet it resists a solidified meaning. The truth of a work of art is defined by a web of relationships, which are always in flux, oscillating – compressing and decompressing. A live community is assembled by an artwork while it is mobilized by it. Art is social as a recursive algorithm, as it defines its own social character, forms its own community. In this regard, understanding is not a transcendent event, rather it is a by-product of a chain of social events of engagement. Artistic expression is inevitably a parrhesiastic act, and the synergetic relationship between an artwork and its possible community compels artists to utter the truth in a precise, direct and honest manner. A person can only be an artist when they accept the responsibility to speak the truth with frankness and openness; and to produce work according to a laborious ethical attitude. Only then, can their work survive through historical scrutiny, become part of the resistance against the tyranny, whatever form it takes.

Artists, writers and academics have always taken risks to face the Turkish state apparatus, its crimes and injustices, even if they face prosecution, pressure, and censorship, yet their fight goes on in most creative ways, inspiring publics, establishing new grounds for contemplation. I am hopeful because of the fact that the right-wing political machinery does not have the necessary cultural toolkit to counter the diverse and engaged voices of the multitude. The Right tries to overcompensate its poverty by enlisting fundamentalists, neoliberals, and shameless capitalists who try to extract any value from rotten conservative values. While (neo)liberal disgraced subjects such as film director Kutlug Ataman and the like may be ready to support, negotiate and shake hands with the fascist regime, a long-term strategic collective can be formulated when cultural producers stay true to their values, uncompromised and steadfastly establishing new spaces for exchange, developing new solidarity networks and creating a better future for all.

Notes

1 Dexter Filkins, 'Turkey's Thirty-Year Coup: Did an Exiled Cleric Try to Overthrow Erdoğan's Government?', *The New Yorker*, 17 October 2016.

2 Gezi Platform NYC was initiated by a group of artists, students and scholars just days after the Gezi Uprising, and organized various demonstrations at Zuccotti Park, Union Square Park and in front of the Turkish Embassy, while most of the talks and seminars were held at the New School for Social Research (http://facebook.com/GeziPlatformNYC).

3 'Questions and Answers: Turkey's Constitutional Referendum', 4 April 2017, www.hrw.org/news/2017/04/04/questions-and-answers-turkeys-constitutional-referendum.

4 Michael George Link, 'Erdoğan's Criticism of Election Observers is Deeply Troubling', 19 April 2017, http://edition.cnn.com/2017/04/19/opinions/turkey-referendum-georg-link-opinion/index.html (accessed 21 April 2016).

5 Cihan Tugal, 'In Turkey, the Regime Slides from Soft to Hard Totalitarianism', 17 February 2016, https://www.opendemocracy.net/cihan-tugal/turkey-hard-totalitarianism-erdogan-authoritarian (accessed 9 April 2016).

6 I recognize the fact that Liberal is a very problematic term. In Turkey liberals are off-shoots of the right wing; they emerged during the era of neoliberal transformation of the 1980s. For the sake of distinguishing them from their Western counterparts, the term Islamo-liberals could fit better as it highlights their complicit relationship with Islamo-fascism.

7 'Ömer Laçiner ile Söyleşi: Sosyalizmin Tarifine Çalışacağız', 18 September 2007, www.birikimdergisi.com/guncel-yazilar/167/omer-laciner-ile-soylesi-sosyalizmin-tarifine-calisacagiz.

8 Today, only a handful of intellectuals support Erdoğan's regime, for instance, popular 'art star' Kutlug Ataman shamelessly attacks the opposition via his twitter feed and makes frequent appearances in the government-controlled media.

9 PKK (Kurdistan Worker's Party) is a Kurdish guerilla group who fought the Turkish state since the late 1970s. Over the last four decades almost 40,000 people died in the civil war. PKK's leadership is currently located in Qandil Mountains in Northern Iraq, and since 2012 PKK's Syrian arm YPG took over the Northern Syria and created an autonomous region, known as Rojava Cantons.

10 Özlem Akarsu Çelik, 'Bodrum'dan Diyarbakır'a Barış Yürüyüşü', 26 December 2015, http://bianet.org/bianet/siyaset/170549-bodrum-dan-diyarbakir-a-baris-yuruyusu.

11 Gültan Kışanak, 'Urgent Call for Solidarity and Action', 23 December 2015, https://hdpenglish.wordpress.com/2015/12/23/urgent-call-for-solidarity-and-action/.

12 'Open Your Windows for Peace', February 2016, http://barisapencereac.tumblr.com.

13 Dorian Batycka, 'Istanbul Gallery Cancels War-Themed Exhibition, Citing "the Delicate Situation in Turkey"', 26 February 2016, https://hyperallergic.com/278987/istanbul-gallery-cancels-war-themed-exhibition-citing-the-delicate-situation-in-turkey/. One has to note that Akbank Sanat organized Kenan Evren's painting exhibit in 1993. Evren was a military general and president of Turkey, who staged the military coup in 1980. He was responsible for mass torture and extrajudicial killings. His paintings are in the collections of the Sabancı and Koç Families.

14 Open letter by Belit Sağ: 'Artist Belit Sağ on Further Censorship at Akbank Sanat', 11 May 2016, http://conversations.e-flux.com/t/artist-belit-sag-on-further-censorship-at-akbank-sanat/3628 (accessed 16 May 2016); Katia Krupennikova, '"Post-Peace" Exhibition Cancelled in Istanbul', 29 February 2016, https://art-leaks.org/2016/02/29/post-peace-exhibition-cancelled-in-istanbul/; 'Anonymous Stateless Immigrants Statement on "Post-Peace" Exhibition Censorship', 6 February 2016, https://art-leaks.org/2016/03/09/anonymous-stateless-immigrants-statement-on-post-peace-exhibition-censorship/ (accessed 9 March 2016); Bassam El Baroni et al.,'Statement by the Jury for the Akbank Sanat International Curator

Competition 2015', 8 March 2016, https://art-leaks.org/2016/03/08/statement-by-the-jury-for-the-akbank-sanat-international-curator-competition-2015/.

15 An organizer from the Ankara Film Festival clearly told me that they cannot present my Roboski Massacre project which deals with the December 2012 incident where Turkish planes bombed and killed 34 innocent villagers and declared it as collateral damage. There is a lot of pressure from the government and sponsors to not support controversial projects.

16 Vasıf Kortun, 'Kurum Soruları', 4 April 2017, http://blog.saltonline.org/post/159221781774/kurum-sorular?

17 Ibid.

18 Michel Foucault, 'Discourse and Truth: the Problematization of Parrhesia', six lectures given by Foucault at the University at Berkeley, October-November 1983, https://foucault.info/doc/documents/parrhesia/index-html.

19 'Academics: We will Not Be a Party to This Crime', 11 January 2016, http://m.bianet.org/english/human-rights/170978-academics-we-will-not-be-a-party-to-this-crime (accessed 16 January 2016).

20 'Turkey: Academics Jailed For Signing Petition: Hundreds Investigated for "Terrorism"', 16 March 2016, www.hrw.org/news/2016/03/16/turkey-academics-jailed-signing-petition.

21 Because of the pressure from their university administration, many academics pulled their signatures to protect themselves and their families. To protest 'arbitrary and unlawful dismissal through decree law and demand their reinstatement', academic Nuriye Gülmen and primary school teacher Semih Özakça have been holding a sit-in in front of the Human Rights Statue in Ankara for over six months and recently they went on a hunger strike and were hospitalized. As I was finalizing this article, they were arrested and their health was deteriorating. Activists have been waging a campaign to save them. 'Nuriye and Semih are on hunger strike! Reinstate them to their jobs!', 7 May 2017, www.change.org/p/government-of-turkey-reinstate-nuriye-and-semih-to-their-jobs.

22 Hakan Topal, 'The Overlooked Besieged Alternative in the Middle East: The Rojava Cantons', 13 October 2014, www.publicseminar.org/2014/10/the-overlooked-beseiged-alternative-in-the-middle-east/.

23 Selin Girit, 'Aslı Erdoğan: Polis ve bomba korkuları arasında sıkıştırıldık', 2 February 2017, www.bbc.com/turkce/haberler-turkiye-38816383.

24 For instance, an Armenian-Turkish 'liberal' writer, Etyen Mahcupyam, who has been a foremost blunt supporter of Erdoğan has recently started to criticize Erdoğan for his repressive attitude. His writings can be reached at www.karar.com/yazarlar/etyen-mahcupyan.

25 Email interview with Burak Delier by Hakan Topal, 5 April 2017.

26 Antonio Negri and Michael Hardt, *Commonwealth* (Cambridge, MA: Harvard University Press, 2009), p. 127.

27 Email interview with Burak Delier by Hakan Topal, 5 April 2017.

28 Antonio Negri, 'The Labor of the Multitude and the Fabric of Biopolitics', *Mediations: Journal of the Marxist Literary Group* 23, no. 2 (2008), pp. 9–24, here p. 12, www.mediationsjournal.org/articles/the-labor-of-the-multitude-and-the-fabric-of-biopolitics.

Contributors

Andrew Barnett (1968) is the director of the UK Branch of the Calouste Gulbenkian Foundation. In the ten years since he took up the role he has introduced a more strategic and 'enquiry-based' approach to the work of the UK Branch with a tighter focus on specific issues. Current priorities are transitions in ageing, valuing the oceans, and participatory performing arts. As a strong believer in the value of collaboration he has played a major role in the establishment of the Making Every Adult Matter (MEAM) Coalition, the Campaign to End Loneliness, and is a founder/director of Social Innovation Exchange (SIX) and founding council member of Collaborate CIC. Andrew lives and works in London.

Llorenç Bonet (1976) is the founder and director of Tenov Books. Established in 2007, Tenov is an independent publishing house with a global outlook. Llorenç is interested in the intersection of architecture with contemporary art and political militancy. As an editor with Tenov he has sought to draw attention to forgotten figures of the Russian avant-garde, such as Aleksei Gan or Georgii Krutikov, and has also edited books by the artist David Bestué and the militant architect Santiago Cirugeda. Bonet lives and works in Barcelona and has taught classes at the ELISAVA School of Design and Engineering and the University of Illinois at Urbana-Champaign.

Ilya Budraitskis (1981) is a curator, writer in art, politics and social theory. He is a current member of the editorial boards of *Moscow Art Magazine* and the LeftEast website. Budraitskis is a visiting lecturer at the Moscow School for Social and Economic Sciences and at the Institute of Contemporary Art (ICA) Moscow. With Ekaterina Degot and Marta Dziewanska, Budraitskis co-edited and authored the book *Post-Post-Soviet? Art, Politics and Society in Russia at the Turn of the Decade* (2013). He also was the co-editor and author, with Arseniy Zhilyaev, of the book *Pedagogical Poem* (2014). His texts have been published in web publications such as Colta.ru, e-flux, Krytyka Polityczna, openDemocracy and WdW Review.

Giuliana Ciancio (1973) is a cultural manager and lecturer in the field of live performing arts. Author and curator of a variety of transnational cultural projects, she is presently the co-curator and project manager of *Be SpectACTive!*, a large-scale EU-funded project focused on active spectatorship and audience development in the performing arts. Since October 2016 Giuliana is a researcher at the CCQO (Culture Commons Quest Office, Antwerp Research Institute for the Arts, University of Antwerp, Belgium). Her research focuses on the relation between top-down policies and bottom-up movements in four European cities in the context of performing arts and cultural policies. Giuliana lives and works both in Belgium and Italy.

Philipp Dietachmair (1973) is a cultural worker and Programme Manager for the European Cultural Foundation (ECF) in Amsterdam. He has studied History and Art History at the University of Vienna and European Arts Management at the Utrecht School of the Arts. Before moving to the Netherlands, Philipp Dietachmair coordinated higher education projects in Bosnia and Herzegovina and organized cultural events in post-war Sarajevo. Since joining the ECF, he has developed and managed the foundation's many collaboration programmes with new cultural initiatives in the EU Neighbourhood regions (Ex-Yugoslavia, Russia, Ukraine, Moldova, Belarus, Turkey and the Arab Mediterranean countries). He has also been involved in a number of field studies and publication projects that analyze the role of the arts and autonomous cultural initiatives in civil society development and transnational collaboration.

Milena Dragićević Šešić (1954) is the Head of UNESCO Chair in Interculturalism, Art Management and Mediation, professor of Cultural Policy & Cultural Management, former President of University of Arts, Belgrade. She has been a guest lecturer at many universities throughout the world. She is a Cultural Policy expert and trainer (UNESCO, British Council, Al Mawred al Thakafy, Council of Europe, European Cultural Fondation, Association Marcel Hicter). In 2002 she was named Commandeur dans l'Ordre des Palmes Academiques from the French Government. Her research interests include cultural policy, cultural management (strategic management, cultural tourism); art activism, alternative art and public space; intercultural dialogue. She has published 16 books, more than 150 essays and her work has been translated into 17 languages. Recent publications include: 'Cultural Rights and Their Contribution to Sustainable Development: Implications for Cultural Policy', *International Journal of Cultural*

Policy (co-authored with Jordi Baltà Portolés) (2017); *Vers les nouvelles politiques culturelles* (2015); *Cultural Sustainability in European Cities: Imagining Europolis* (co-edited with Svetlana Hristova and Nancy Duxbury) (2015). Dragićević Šešić lives and works in Belgrade.

Pascal Gielen (1970) is full professor of Sociology of Art and Politics at the Antwerp Research Institute for the Arts (Antwerp University, Belgium) where he leads the Culture Commons Quest Office (CCQO). Gielen is editor in-chief of the international book series Arts in Society. In 2016 he became laureate of the Odysseus grant for excellent international scientific research of the Fund for Scientific Research Flanders in Belgium. His research focuses on creative labour, the institutional context of the arts and cultural politics. Gielen has published many books, which have been translated in English, Korean, Polish, Portuguese, Russian, Spanish and Turkish.

Max Haiven (1981) is Canada Research Chair in Culture, Media and Social Justice at Lakehead University in Northwest Ontario and director of the Re-Imagining Value Action Lab (RiVAL). He writes articles for both academic and general audiences and is the author of the books *Crises of Imagination, Crises of Power: Capitalism, Creativity and the Commons* (2014), *The Radical Imagination: Social Movement Research in the Age of Austerity* (with Alex Khasnabish) (2014) and *Cultures of Financialization: Fictitious Capital in Popular Culture and Everyday Life* (2014). He is currently working on a book titled *Art after Money, Money after Art: Radical Creative Strategies Against Financialization*.
www.maxhaiven.com

Yudhishthir Raj Isar (1948) straddles various worlds of cultural theory and practice. Currently, he is professor of Cultural Policy Studies at The American University of Paris and Education Director of the Aga Khan Trust for Culture. He is also co-founder and editor of the *Cultures and Globalization Series* (SAGE) and author of numerous journal articles and book contributions. He has been a trustee of several cultural organizations and consultant to international organizations and foundations. From 2004 to 2008 he was President of the association Culture Action Europe and from 1973 to 2002 he served as notably Executive

Secretary of the World Commission on Culture and Development at UNESCO.

Stefan Kaegi (1972) is based in Berlin, produces documentary theatre plays and works in public space in a variety of collaborative partnerships. Kaegi has toured all over Europe and Asia with two Bulgarian lorry drivers and a truck that was converted into a mobile audience room (*Cargo Sofia*). He developed *Radio Muezzin* in Cairo – a project about the call to prayer in this age of technical reproduction. At the moment he adapts *Remote X*, an audiotour for 50 headphones, to Cities such as Taipei and Tunis, and he tours the interactive installation *Nachlass*, which portrays people who don't have long to live anymore. Kaegi co-produces works with Helgard Haug and Daniel Wetzel under the label 'Rimini Protokoll'. Using research, public auditions and conceptual processes, they give voice to 'experts' who are not trained actors but have something to tell. Recent works include the multi-player-video-piece *Situation Rooms, 100% São Paulo* with 100 local citizens on stage and the *World Climate Conference* – a simulation of the UN-conference for 650 spectators in Schauspielhaus Hamburg. Currently they perform *Homevisit Europe* as an interactive performance game in hundreds of households across the globe.
www.rimini-protokoll.de

Ivan Krastev (1965) is the chairman of the Centre for Liberal Strategies in Sofia and permanent fellow at the Institute for Human Sciences, Vienna. He is a founding board member of the European Council on Foreign Relations, a member of the Board of Trustees of The International Crisis Group and is a contributing opinion writer for the International New York Times. His latest books in English are *After Europe* (2017); *Democracy Disrupted: The Global Politics on Protest* (2014); *In Mistrust We Trust: Can Democracy Survive When We Don't Trust Our Leaders?* (2013). He is a co-author, with Stephen Holmes, of a forthcoming book on Russian politics.

Thijs Lijster (1981) studied philosophy at the University of Groningen and the New School for Social Research in New York. In 2012 he received his PhD in philosophy (*cum laude*) at the University of Groningen. Currently, he is assistant professor in the Philosophy of Art and Culture at the University of Groningen, and researcher at the Culture Commons Quest Office of the University of Antwerp. He received the ABG/VN Essay prize in 2009, the Dutch/Flemish Prize for Young Art Critics in 2010, and the NWO/Boekman dissertation award in 2015. He wrote *De grote vlucht inwaarts* (The Great Leap Inward) (2016); *Benjamin and Adorno on Art and Art Criticism* (2017); and co-edited *Spaces for Criticism: Shifts in Contemporary Art Discourses* (2015).

Tomislav Medak (1973) is part of the theory and publishing team of the Multimedia Institute/MAMA in Zagreb. He is a free software advocate, shadow librarian for Memory of the World project and erstwhile militant for the urban activist initiative Right to the City Zagreb. His recent scholarship has focused on structural unevenness of technological development and post-capitalist transition. He is the author of *The Hard Matter of Abstracion: A Guidebook to Domination by Abstraction* (2016) and *Shit Tech for A Shitty World* (2015). He has co-edited, with Marcell Mars, *Public Library* (2015), with Petar Milat *The Idea of Radical Media* (2014) and with Sergej Pristaš *Time and (In)Completion: Images and Performances of Time in Late Capitalism* (2014). In addition to his scholarship, Tomislav also works with the Zagreb-based experimental theatre collective BADco. He lives in Zagreb.

Borka Pavićević (1947) is a dramaturge, columnist and activist from Serbia. She graduated from the Academy for Theatre, Film, Radio and Television, Belgrade with a Master's degree in 1976. As a dramaturge she has worked extensively throughout Serbia and other former Yugoslavian countries. She was the founder of the 'New Sensibility' theatre in the old Belgrade brewery in 1981 and from 1984 to 1991 participated in the artistic movement known as KPGT. In 1993, her time as artistic director of the Belgrade Drama Theatre came to an end, as she was removed from her position due to controversial political statements made in public. In 1994 she founded the Center for Cultural Decontamination, of which she is still the director. She is the recipient of the Otto Rene Castillo Award for Political Theater, New York (2000); the Hiroshima Foundation Prize for Peace and Culture (2004); the Osvajanje slobode prize, awarded by the Maja Maršićević Tasić Fund (2005); Routes Award given by ECF, Amsterdam (2009/2010), and, from the Government of the Republic of France, the Legion d'Honneur (2001). She has published regular columns in such publications as *Susret*, *Vreme* and, most recently, *Danas.*

Dan Perjovschi (1961) is an artist and journalist from Romania. He lives and works in Bucharest and Sibiu. He first introduced his unique critical drawings as commentaries on contemporary politics in weekly magazines in Romania. Later he transformed the walls of many international museums and galleries into spaces for criticism with his humorous but critical comments on the political, social and art world. His solo exhibitions include 'Unframed', Kiasma, Helsinki (2013); 'Not over', MACRO, Rome (2011); 'What Happened to US?', Museum of Modern Art, New York (2007); 'I Am Not Exotic – I Am Exhausted', Kunsthalle, Basel (2007); 'The Room Drawing', Tate Modern, London (2006); and 'Naked Drawings', Museum Ludwig, Cologne (2005). He has exhibited in such group shows as the Jakarta Biennial 2005, Paris Triennial 2012, Sydney Biennial 2008; The Magellanic Cloud, Centre Georges Pompidou, Paris (2007); and the 52nd Venice Biennial (2007). Since 2011 he has been involved in supporting various protests and civil causes in Romania and abroad with his drawings. He was awarded the George Maciunas Prize in 2004 and Rosa Shapire/Kunsthalle Hamburg Prize in 2016.

Igor Stokfiszewski (1979) is a researcher, activist, journalist and artist of socially engaged theatre, community and political arts. He is a member of the Krytyka Polityczna (Political Critique) team, of the European Alternatives board of trustees and of the DiEM25 political movement. His recent publications include: *Culture and Development: Beyond Neoliberal Reason* (editor, 2017); *Kultura i rozwój: Analizy rekomendacje, studia przypadków* (Culture and Development: Analysis, Recommendations, Case Studies) (co-edited with Jerzy Hausner, Izabela Jasińska, and Mikołaj Lewicki) (2016); *Built the City: Perspectives on Commons and Culture* (co-edited with Charles Beckett, Lore Gablier, Vivian Paulissen, Joanna Tokarz-Haertig) (2015); *Zwrot polityczny* (Political Turn) (2009). His recent artistic works include: *Ursus – spacer w czasie* (Ursus – a Stroll in Time) (together with Jaśmina Wójcik, 2015); *Zakłady. Ursus 2014* (Factory. Ursus 2014) (together with Jaśmina Wójcik and Izabela Jasińska, 2014). Stokfiszewski lives and works in Warsaw.

Hakan Topal (1972) is an artist living and working in Brooklyn, New York. He is currently an Assistant Professor of New Media and Art + Design at Purchase College, State University New York. Trained as a civil engineer (B.S. at METU, Ankara), he continued his studies in Gender and Women's Studies (M.S. at METU) and Sociology (M.A. at NSSR, New York). He obtained his Ph.D. in Sociology from the New School for Social Research with a focus on urban sociology and sociology of arts. He was the co-founder of the international art collective xurban_collective (2000–2012) and exhibited his collective and individual art works and research projects extensively, in institutions such as the 8th and 9th Istanbul Biennials; apexart, New York; Thyssen-Bornemisza Art Contemporary (TBA21), Vienna; Kunst-Werke, Berlin; ZKM Center for Art and Media, Karlsruhe; MoMA PS1; Platform, Istanbul, the 9th Gwangju Bienniale, and ICP Museum, New York. Topal represented Turkey in various international exhibitions including the 49th Venice Biennial Turkish Pavilion. His texts and projects have been featured in various international journals, books, and catalogs.
www.hakantopal.info

Antennae-
Arts in Society
Book Series

Antennae-Arts in Society Series

Antennae-Arts in Society is a peer-reviewed book series that validates artistic, critical, speculative and essayistic writing as a full academic publishing method. Contributions to the series look upon the arts as 'antennae', feelers for the cultural interpretation and articulation of topical political, economic, social, technological or environmental issues.

The books in this series bring together audiences of diverse backgrounds: artists and other creative makers, academics and researchers from various disciplines, critics, writers, journalists, politicians, curators, and institutional parties, who wish to broaden their view in different political, social and other contexts.

Proposals for book concepts in all artistic and scientific disciplines that take culture as the base of interpretation for the social fabric of our contemporary lives are welcomed and will be considered for publication by the academic board.

Index

R

S

T

Colophon

Colophon

The Art of Civil Action
Political Space and Cultural Dissent

Editors
Philipp Dietachmair & Pascal Gielen

Contributors
Andrew Barnett
Llorenç Bonet
Ilya Budraitskis
Giuliana Ciancio
Philipp Dietachmair
Milena Dragićević Šešić
Pascal Gielen
Max Haiven
Yudhishthir Raj Isar
Stefan Kaegi
Ivan Krastev
Thijs Lijster
Tomislav Medak
Borka Pavićević
Dan Perjovschi
Igor Stokfiszewski
Hakan Topal

Drawings
Dan Perjovschi

Antennae-Arts in Society Series N°24
by Valiz, Amsterdam

Translation
Esther Banev–ReadyWriters (text Ilya Budraitskis, Russian-English; text Milena Dragićević Šešić, Serbian-English); Monika Bokiniec (text Igor Stokfiszewski, Polish-English); Graham Thomson (text Llorenç Bonet), Spanish-English); Leo Reijnen (parts text Pascal Gielen, Dutch-English)

Copy Editing
All texts: Leo Reijnen, Els Brinkman
Text Igor Stokfiszewski: Anna Zaranko

Proofreading
Els Brinkman

Index
Elke Stevens

Design
Metahaven

Paper Inside
Munken Print 100 gr 1.5

Paper Cover
Bioset 240 gr

Printing and Binding
Ten Brink, Meppel

Publisher
Valiz, Amsterdam, 2017
www.valiz.nl

ISBN 978-94-92095-39-8

This publication was made possible through the generous support of

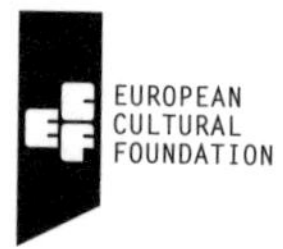

European Cultural Foundation, Amsterdam

Distribution:
USA/Canada/Latin America: D.A.P., www.artbook.com
GB/IE: Anagram Books, www.anagrambooks.com
NL/BE/LU: Coen Sligting, www.coensligtingbookimport.nl
Europe/Asia: Idea Books, www.ideabooks.nl
Australia: Perimeter Books, www.perimeterdistribution.com

ISBN 978-94-92095-39-8

Printed and bound in the Netherlands

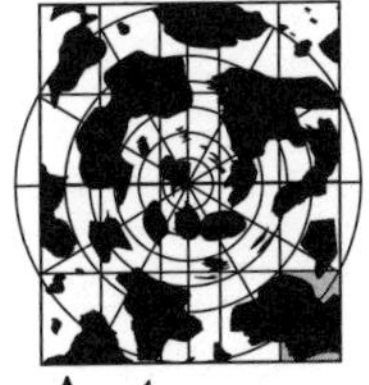

Antennae Series

Antennae N° 1
The Fall of the Studio
Artists at Work
edited by Wouter Davidts & Kim Paice
Amsterdam: Valiz, 2009 (2nd ed.: 2010),
ISBN 978-90-78088-29-5

Antennae N° 2
Take Place
Photography and Place from Multiple Perspectives
edited by Helen Westgeest
Amsterdam: Valiz, 2009,
ISBN 978-90-78088-35-6

Antennae N° 3
The Murmuring of the Artistic Multitude
Global Art, Memory and Post-Fordism
Pascal Gielen (author)
Arts *in* Society
Amsterdam: Valiz, 2009 (2nd ed.: 2011),
ISBN 978-90-78088-34-9

Antennae N° 4
Locating the Producers
Durational Approaches to Public Art
edited by Paul O'Neill & Claire Doherty
Amsterdam: Valiz, 2011, ISBN 978-90-78088-51-6

Antennae N° 5
Community Art
The Politics of Trespassing
edited by Paul De Bruyne & Pascal Gielen
Arts *in* Society
Amsterdam: Valiz, 2011 (2nd ed.: 2013),
ISBN 978-90-78088-50-9

Antennae N° 6
See it Again, Say it Again
The Artist as Researcher
edited by Janneke Wesseling
Amsterdam: Valiz, 2011, ISBN 978-90-78088-53-0

Antennae N° 7
Teaching Art in the Neoliberal Realm
Realism versus Cynicism
edited by Pascal Gielen & Paul De Bruyne
Arts *in* Society
Amsterdam: Valiz, 2012 (2nd ed.: 2013),
ISBN 978-90-78088-57-8

Antennae N° 8
Institutional Attitudes
Instituting Art in a Flat World
edited by Pascal Gielen
Arts *in* Society
Amsterdam: Valiz, 2013, ISBN 978-90-78088-68-4

Antennae N° 9
Dread
The Dizziness of Freedom
edited by Juha van 't Zelfde
Amsterdam: Valiz, 2013, ISBN 978-90-78088-81-3

Antennae N° 10
Participation Is Risky
Approaches to Joint Creative Processes
edited by Liesbeth Huybrechts
Amsterdam: Valiz, 2014, ISBN 978-90-78088-77-6

Antennae N° 11
The Ethics of Art
Ecological Turns in the Performing Arts
edited by Guy Cools & Pascal Gielen
Arts *in* Society
Amsterdam: Valiz, 2014, ISBN 978-90-78088-87-5

Antennae N° 12
Alternative Mainstream
Making Choices in Pop Music
Gert Keunen (author)
Arts *in* Society
Amsterdam: Valiz, 2014,
ISBN 978-90-78088-95-0

Antennae N° 13
The Murmuring of the Artistic
Global Art, Politics and Post-Fordism
Pascal Gielen (author)
Completely revised and enlarged edition of Antennae N° 3
Arts *in* Society
Amsterdam: Valiz, 2015,
ISBN 978-94-92095-04-6

Antennae N° 14
Aesthetic Justice
Intersecting Artistic and Moral Perspectives
edited by Pascal Gielen & Niels Van Tomme
Arts *in* Society
Amsterdam: Valiz, 2015,
ISBN 978-90-78088-86-8

Antennae N° 15
No Culture, No Europe
On the Foundation of Politics
edited by Pascal Gielen
Arts *in* Society
Amsterdam: Valiz, 2015,
ISBN 978-94-92095-03-9

Antennae N° 16
Arts Education Beyond Art
Teaching Art in Times of Change
edited by Barend van Heusden & Pascal Gielen
Arts *in* Society
Amsterdam: Valiz, 2015,
ISBN 978-90-78088-85-1

Antennae N° 17
Mobile Autonomy
Exercises in Artists' Self-Organization
edited by Nico Dockx & Pascal Gielen
Arts *in* Society
Amsterdam: Valiz, 2015,
ISBN 978-94-92095-10-7

Antennae N° 18
Moving Together
Theorizing and Making Contemporary Dance
Rudi Laermans (author)
Arts *in* Society
Amsterdam: Valiz, 2015,
ISBN 978-90-78088-52-3

Antennae N° 19
Spaces for Criticism
Shifts in Contemporary Art Discourses
edited by Thijs Lijster, Suzana Milevska, Pascal Gielen, Ruth Sonderegger
Arts *in* Society
Amsterdam: Valiz, 2015,
ISBN 978-90-78088-75-2

Antennae N° 20
Interrupting the City
Artistic Constitutions of the Public Sphere
edited by Sander Bax, Pascal Gielen & Bram Ieven
Arts *in* Society
Amsterdam: Valiz, 2015,
ISBN 978-94-92095-02-2

Antennae N° 21
In-between Dance Cultures
On the Migratory Artistic Identity of Sidi Larbi Cherkaoui and Akram Khan
Guy Cools (author)
Arts *in* Society
Amsterdam: Valiz, 2015,
ISBN 978-94-92095-11-4

Antennae N° 22
Imaginative Bodies
Dialogues in Performance Practices
Guy Cools (author)
Arts *in* Society
Amsterdam: Valiz, 2016,
ISBN 978-94-92095-20-6

Antennae N° 23
The Practice of Dramaturgy
Working on Actions in Performance
edited by Konstantina Georgelou, Efrosini Protopapa, Danae Theodoridou
Arts *in* Society
Amsterdam: Valiz, 2017,
ISBN: 978-94-92095-18-3